MALAYA
Scale: approx: 100 miles to an inch
THAILAND
COCHIN CHINA
SOUTH CHINA SEA
STRAITS OF MALACCA
SUMATRA
KOTA BHARU
ALOR STAR
PENANG
PARIT BUNTAR
KUALA KRAU
PORT WELD
TAIPING
KUALA KANGSAR
IPOH
SITIAWAN
PANGKOR IS:
LUMUT
CAMERON HIGHLANDS
SEMBILAN ISLANDS
BELAWAN-DELI
MEDAN
BRASTAGI
INASOENG
HARANGOL
TOBA MEER
FRASER'S HILL
TANJONG MALIM
KUALA LUMPUR
PORT SWETTENHAM
SEREMBAN
MALACCA
MUAR
BATU PAHAT
JOHORE BAHRU
SINGAPORE
KUALA TRENGANNU
KUANTAN
ENDAU
EQUATOR
BANKA STS:
MALAY STATES
Federated
I PERAK
II SELANGOR
III NEGRI SEMBILAN
IV PAHANG
Unfederated
V PERLIS
VI KEDAH
VII KELANTAN
VIII TRENGANNU
IX JOHORE
Straits Settlements
A PENANG IS: AND PROV: WELLESLEY
B MALACCA
C SINGAPORE IS:

MALAYAN LANDSCAPE

By the same author:

NON-FICTION

These I Have Loved

Flowers of the Sun

Costumes of Malaya

Journey Out of Asia

Desert Traveller — the Life of Jean Louis Burckhardt

FICTION

Malacca Boy: A Novel of Malay Life

The Moon at My Feet

Black Rice: A Story of Opium Smuggling

The Jungle Ends Here

Sunrise in the Dindings River

KATHARINE SIM

MALAYAN LANDSCAPE

With an introduction by
SIR RICHARD WINSTEDT
K.B.E., C.M.G.
Formerly of the Malayan Civil Service

"*Bukan mudah bercherai kaseh,*
Laksana wau menanti angin.

Hard the divorce of love and lingering,
Like a kite that waits the wind."
Malay *pantun*

Donald Moore for

ASIA PACIFIC PRESS
Singapore

First published in 1946
by Michael Joseph Ltd, London
Reprinted 1956

This edition published in 1969
by Donald Moore
for Asia Pacific Press Pte Ltd

Printed by Tien Wah Press Ltd, Singapore.

FOR STUART—WITH ALL MY LOVE

And with much affectionate gratitude to Beannie and Tommie, for keeping so carefully all the notes and letters and photographs I sent them from Malaya, 1938 to 1942.

AUTHOR'S NOTE

I am greatly indebted to Sir Richard Windstedt for his constructive criticism and his most patient replies to numerous questions, and for the quotations and translations of Malay poems which appear in this book. I am also very grateful to Miss Viola Garvin for her help and advice.

AUTHOR'S FOREWORD TO THIS EDITION

Many years ago, as P. and O. ships passed each other in the Bitter Lakes of the Suez Canal people on westward-bound ones would shout tauntingly to outward-bound passengers: "You're going the wrong way!"

It did not take me very long to realize that the reverse was nearer to the truth. And reading through *Malayan Landscape* now, twenty-three years after its first appearance in 1946, has renewed my home-sickness for a land which I shall always love with undying warmth; one to which I am deeply indebted for some of the happiest, gayest, most colourful years of my life—and most productive years too, since there I could always work in peace and quiet. Malaya has much to inspire both brush and pen.

But *Malayan Landscape* was my first book and I was young when I wrote it, young not only in age but in my knowledge of Malaya. I had lived there for just a little over three years when the Japanese invaded; I had only so-called "kitchen Malay". But, scanty though my understanding of Malayan peoples may have been, the country appealed to me enormously, so great was its fascination that I could think of few other places when I was sent home by sea two weeks before the fall of Singapore. Then, as now, the desire to return was ardent.

My husband survived the rigours of two Japanese P.O.W. camps in Sumatra and two torpedoings, and we eventually returned to Malaya as a family in 1947. Then I began in earnest to learn about the country I loved so well; previously in my three youthful, glib years, my knowledge had been superficial, although my impressions had run deep indeed.

In Penang, after the war, I studied things Hindu and, under the patient guidance of my old and dear friend C. S. Wong, of Chinese affairs—things Chinese. Later, in the truly Malay state of Negri Sembilan, I began to learn Malay seriously for the first time and with the tuition of Munshi K-R. Ja'amat of Malacca, I took and passed the Government examinations standards I and

II, and so naturally acquired a better understanding of Malay customs and the Malay way of life. All of which knowledge has made me aware now, on glancing through this book after so long a time, that there are nuances in it which, unfortunately, it has not been possible to edit out—things and expressions that I would not have dreamt of uttering in the richer light of my later much fuller, more adult understanding and love of Malaya's people—which was further developed during our last five years in Kuala Lumpur before and after Merdeka until "Malayanized" in 1960, when we retired prematurely. During this time in Kuala Lumpur, I wrote as "Nuraini" a considerable number of *Profiles and Personalities* for the *Malay Mail;* a series of articles which brought me into direct contact with a wide cross-section of the public from diplomats to dancing girls, priests and teachers to East Coast fishermen and silversmiths, whose co-operation opened up for me an endless vista of ideas and fresh fields of thought.

I would hate to give offence to any such Malaysians, among whom I am lucky to count still some dear friends, by casual or unthinking words in this book, or by any discordant note that is struck. There is perhaps no word in English that quite expresses what I mean about certain phrases or words that are *changgong* in our ears. For instance, we all now prefer Asian to "Asiatic", just as an Englishman prefers that name to "Englander", or *orang Europa* to "*orang puteh*", and the word "coolie" has now an almost insolent ring about it. So please forgive me: *jikalau adapun ayat-ayat terchanggong di-dalam isi-nya buku-ini saya minta ampun dan ma'af daripada orang-orang Melaysia yang membacha-nya.*

Malaysian life has changed and it progresses: some things in this book—such as cooks in topis, rickshas, and hill-chairs seem now almost archaic! And my ridiculous attitude to frozen food seems to me very funny; however, it was a long time before we could persuade Ah Lim ("Kuki") that we wanted to eat simple local fare almost all the time, and later both at sea and in the kampongs I never ate anything but whatever rice and curry was going, and I grew even to appreciate turtles' eggs.

Also, I must have been wrong about the enjoyment of poetry:

since my husband came back from the Far East with an ability, acquired in prison camp, to quote poetry for two hours on end. In addition, I had not yet discovered the charm and romance, the passion and beauty of the *pantun*, the Malay quatrain, which was later to fascinate me so much that I wrote a small book on the subject.*

Of course, in those pre-war days *Jawi* was much more widely used, which did not help to promote among the unversed a ready knowledge of Malay in the reading of newspapers, sign-posts and so on.

Recently, too, art has developed enormously, and there now seems every reason to hope that one day Malaya will produce a great painter.

The general attitude to lepers is also, thank goodness, very different now since the advent of sulphone, and the broader knowledge of the disease that has been brought to the notice of the public in general. I have a very good friend in Malaya who is an ex-leper.

I once made a lot of fuss about sitting correctly on the floor at a Malay wedding; this I later learned to do although never with the natural grace and suppleness of a Malay woman.

I also discovered that the friendliness of the Malay, whether in kampong or istana, has about it something of an almost Hellenic democracy, a natural equality, an acceptance of one as one is. There is pride but rarely arrogance; there is conviviality and mutual respect.

In thinking of Malaya there are some people who spring directly to mind; some of these, who feature in this book, I would like to mention in gratitude and friendship: most of all Ah Chi who became, and remains, one of the people most dear in all the world to me, and from whom we had reluctantly to part in 1960; her daughter, Ah Sah, now the charming mother of three beautiful children; "Kuki", retired and living in Kuala Lumpur who, supported by the inimitable care and thoughtfulness of Ah Chi, helped to look after us and our sons for the best part of twenty-two years; Mat and Sareh, paddy-planting in Krian, and many others; Ah Seng, who vanished in Sumatra and

* *Flowers of the Sun*, Eastern Universities Press Ltd., Singapore

was never heard of again; Yahya, who unfortunately died of T.B. during the Japanese occupation.

This book is mostly about Lumut: it was one of the last places my husband and I visited before we had finally to leave Malaya. We shipped then from Penang to Calcutta, and travelled overland* to England; so to stretch the silver cord, not break it: *biar rentang jangan putus*. I do not think that it can ever be quite broken for me. *Jauh dari mata, di-dalam hati selalu.*

Katharine Sim
In a meadow by the River Thames,
1969

* *Journey Out of Asia,* Robert Hale, London

INTRODUCTION

A TAMIL EXAMINEE, confronted with a question on the meaning of "Virtue is its own reward," hazarded the reply that the saying could refer only to remunerative employment. His pragmatic solution of an old psychological conundrum flashed into my mind, a reproach to my altruism, the moment I had dropped my letter beyond recall into the scarlet letter-box. What reward could I expect for my offer to read the manuscript of a book on Malaya by a new author I had never even met? An examinate picture of Malayan forests that teem with life? A stagnant impression of tropic seas whose glitter I can yet see under the bows of my yacht? Was I not doomed to share once more Marianne Dashwood's boredom at being told that "in the East Indies the climate is hot and the mosquitoes are troublesome"? The arrival of the typescript that was the chrysalis of these coloured chapters affected me like the inexorability of a Monday morning. And then after reading a few pages I perked up. Virtue for once was to be its own reward.

It was an accident, of course, but here were the very bays where my launch had often dropped anchor thirty years back. Here, as it happened, was the coast where a Perak Sultan went for a picnic two centuries ago, accompanied by a Malay poet ("dependent as a bat" on his royal patron), who has left posterity his old-world impression of the places visited:

> Antara laut Pantai Remis
> Pasir-nya bagai santan di-ramas;
> Gelombang dan bakat habis-lah kemas,
> Sa-buah pun tidak mara dan chemas.
>
> Tempat-nya ĕndah terlalu ĕlok,
> Sungai-nya banyak di-dalam telok;
> Gunong berator, batu berkalok,
> Aneka rupa sampan dan balok.

"The sands on Cockle-Shell Beach are as white as milk squeezed from a coconut. Breakers and flotsam are all tidily packed in the narrows, and no boat runs risk of harm.

The spot is remarkably beautiful. Streams there are in many

in the bay. There are mountain-ranges and encircling rocks. And there is every kind of boat and dug-out."

Apart from rapidly silting estuaries, the passage of time brings little change to these sequestered places, once familiar to a few of us as Piccadilly is now: the boulder-strewn sands of the Dindings, Gunong Bubu (or Fish-trap Mountain) touched by rosy-footed dawn, the tentacled clutch of innumerable mangrove roots like giant spiders caught in quaking mud. No detail, no scent, no murmur from the Malayan scene escapes the author of this book, but artist by instinct and training she gives us no dull transcript, she transmutes her material to the purposes of a vivid impression. To the visual scene where the Malayan swallow-tails perform their "yellow flutterings" and sunset flushes the white underwing of the tern, she adds dimension by recording the stridulous telegraphy of crickets, noting "the heavy wafts of the pigeon orchid" and shrinking a little from "the acrid bitter-sweet muskiness of the Malay." Malaya has captured her, and her pulses race untired and exploring through quiet hours terribly apt to dispirit Europeans of less spiritual enterprise. What is more, she can get this personality of hers across the page, which is the whole duty of artist and biographer.

"Oh for a life of sensations rather than thoughts!" exclaimed the youthful Keats misled by the dichotomy of a philosophy now outworn. For sensations defined are ideas, and here is an ideal Malaya, beyond the clutch of Japanese war-lords and rubber-kings and the officialdom of a day, the real Malaya shy and reserved to all but her lovers. It is the Malaya which a new generation will have to "experience on its pulses" in order to heal its wounds and win confidence again.

For, as fate willed it, not the least absorbing pages in this book are those describing the grim trek down the Peninsula before the Japanese invader, the abandonment of household gods and faithful servants, the numb incredulity of the Malay at the broken departure of people he had thought pre-eminent in wisdom and power.

RICHARD WINSTEDT

CONTENTS

LIST OF ILLUSTRATIONS

★

Photographs by Stuart Sim

I

STINKS AND COLOURS IN KRIAN

IT WAS HOT, so hot that the cabin became unbearable: we lay wide-eyed, listening to the purring fan as it churned but did not cool the humid air. The Indian Ocean was in one of its stickiest and most depressing moods. About two o'clock in the morning we staggered up to the boat deck, armed with cushions and pillows, and sank wearily into long chairs.

That was the beginning of the day on which the ship was due in Penang. I was new to the country: if this was a sample of the climate of Malaya then I was not looking forward to the next three years. . . .

We must have slept through the washing of the deck, because when we woke up it was wet and scrubbed around our chairs. Everything was damp and shining, even the air had freshened and seemed less sticky.

The ship was moving slowly into the lovely straits between Penang Island and the mainland. The sun was rising in a superb flame of colour over the dark blue mountains of Malaya; Penang Island, like a milky opal, swam in silver mists. The cool dawn and great beauty were encouraging: so, I thought, perhaps Malaya is going to be quite pleasant after all. . . .

As soon as the sun cleared the mountain tops and pierced the mists we could feel its burning heat. We collected our damp pillows and bedraggled dressing-gowns and went below.

Penang was a place that never failed to delight. I often wondered that it was not more famous for its loveliness. However you approached it—from the mainland across green paddy fields, or rounding its rocky northern coast, or from among the island clusters in the south—it was enchanting, friendly and yet variable. After you had lived on the mainland and were sick of the sight of endless acres of dark rubber trees, or of tall palms that hem a garden round, it gave a lift to the spirit to come out into the paddy lands of Province Wellesley and to see ahead, across that flat expanse, the hills of Penang, and the mountains of Kedah in the north.

We went ashore at eight o'clock and drove to the Runnymede, one of the most attractive hotels in Malaya in those pre-war days; it was open to the sea sounds and scents, cool too and bright with flowers: banks of hydrangeas and hollyhocks, and, on every table, sweet-scented, old-fashioned red roses. The rooms were constantly filled with the gentle sough of the waves and the whispering of the casuarina trees which grew along by the low sea wall. There was a ferry across to Butterworth on the mainland where we caught a train for Parit Buntar. It had been a bitter disappointment to hear we were to be stationed at Parit Buntar, for we had rather foolishly set our hearts on Lumut, a village on the rocky Dindings coast. Parit Buntar, in the mosquito-ridden paddy lands of Krian, was one of the least popular of Government appointments. But being on the state boundary, between Province Wellesley in the Straits Settlements and Perak in the Federated Malay States, it was quite a busy customs post.

During the short hot journey we looked out gloomily at every stop, and felt considerably chastened. For each station seemed rather more scrubby than the last. However, Parit Buntar was, after all, gay with red and gold cannas, and Mac of the Customs was on the platform to meet us. He wore an impressively large wide-awake felt hat. He and Mrs. Mac were exceedingly kind to us in the first rather uncomfortable days.

An avenue of mossy angsena trees led to the small town now sizzling in the white noon-day sun. As we drove along, Mac explained that the man who was in the Government house allotted to us had flatly refused to turn out, so there was nothing for it but to make the best of the Rest House, which we had to do for three long weeks instead of the customary two days. While all we possessed—wedding presents, books, pictures—remained at the station in cases, and we itched to unpack and arrange everything in the house. I had heard lurid stories of the ravages of white ants and silver-fish and imagined our belongings would be rapidly crumbling into dust and decay.

The young man who refused to make way was about to leave the country, and by rights should have turned out as had been arranged; several friends had offered to put him up. But he would not hear of it. Then three weeks later while we were still at the Rest House and very tired of being cooped up there, he called to apologize; as he was leaving the country the following day, this fell a little flat. To our inward amusement he became more and more involved in lame excuses. "You see," he explained at last, "it was a matter of departmental dignity." (He belonged to one Government department and Stuart to another.) This remark was too much for me and I almost laughed outright. Stuart, however, made no comment, and managed what must have been an exasperatingly straight face. When the young man finally showed signs of wilting we relented, and gently but firmly got rid of him.

The house was ours the next day. But that was after several weeks had passed, and in the meantime we lived in the "Federal Wing" of the Rest House. This sounded palatial, but was in reality only one rather dark room encircled by a very public verandah, across which was a stone bathroom. This bathroom was a revelation to me with its big "Shanghai jar" full of cold water; the earthenware kept the water deliciously cool; and there was a tin wash tub in which the hot water was poured by the Boy who quickly appeared bearing the inevitable kerosene tin when one called for a bath. (The uses of the kerosene tin in Malaya were varied and ingenious; it could be slung on a yoke for carrying water; cut in half diagonally to act as a dust-pan; hammered flat for sheeting. If the cook-boy finds there is no oven in his new kitchen he will not be perturbed but will calmly roast a perfectly good joint in a kerosene tin thrust among the blazing logs of the fire.) The method of bathing was to ladle the hot and cold water over one's body from a tin dipper, and then finish with a cool shower. The result was a glorious flood in the bathroom; but it was built for it, the water ran away down a hole in the wall, out into the garden. English bathrooms seem rather restricted after this very wet and delightfully abandoned way of bathing.

The sanitary arrangements were definitely not modern. There were *jambans* which were attended to twice a day by a *jamban* man, a rather furtive-looking, long-haired Tamil who padded up the outside stairs with a pail and a large black umbrella. There was only one "push and pull" in the town, and that was at the club.

Our luggage had been brought round from the station by ten little Tamil coolies, and we started to take possession of this Federal Wing.

The Government houses and the club built round the green *padang*[1] were painted black and white. I liked the boldly striped bamboo blinds, known as chicks, which sheltered the verandahs. From our own verandah I had a grand-stand view of the village: the police station was opposite, and once I watched a ridiculously small Malay boy marched off handcuffed between two armed guards. And when the children came out of school the road rang to the pitter-patter of their wooden shoes. Chinese women looking spotless in neat simple clothes and smooth hair pattered by click-clack in their wooden sandals, while the dark rickshaw men loped along pulling their gay red and gold rickshaws, clip-clop, flip-flop. There would be harsh Chinese voices calling, and the wailing voices of the Tamils, who sound as if in perpetual disagreement even when they are merely enjoying a friendly chat; there would be someone spitting with guttural thoroughness in the kitchen quarters; and there would be the shrill twitter of sparrows, the clatter of food sellers' castanets and the thud of distant temple gongs.

One never felt lonely. In fact it was, as I have said, a rather public spot: Stuart had to shave on the verandah, as the light was too poor inside, and the buzz of his electric shaver in the early morning attracted the wondering stares of many passers-by who stopped to gape at yet another unaccountable Englishman.

The mosquitoes were a pest. When one opened a cupboard door a cloud of them flew out in one's face. At night in the Rest House we sat in a very small "meat-safe" room downstairs. It was extremely depressing and damp; but a refuge at least from the mosquitoes. If ever we sat outside after tennis, sarongs were served round with the drinks as a matter of course, and with feet and legs encased in cotton people looked like competitors in a sack race. And even then enterprising mosquitoes would contrive to bite one's posterior through an openwork cane chair.

I was quite bewildered the first time I went out to meet the local Europeans. Some people in Malaya had a habit of talking

[1] Open field for games.

of places and departments only by initials, and what is more their conversation was freely interspersed with Malay words. This was disconcerting until one got used to it. A typical sentence would run something like this: "Oh yes, old so and so, he's living in the P.W.D. bungalow at T.A. His *Mem* has been rather *sakit* lately," or "The D.O., from K.K., came in for *pahits* before tiffin yesterday," or "My *amah* is quite *gila*; she sent my black dress to the *dhobi*," or "You should always put *ayer busok* (Jeyes Fluid) in the *jamban*. . . ."

After my first evening of this I had a splitting headache and felt very depressed. People were extremely kind; but had not the slightest idea how odd this kind of talk sounded to newcomers. I soon learnt it all; although, on principle, we ourselves tried to avoid using much Malay mixed up with English. It sounded worst among the children; some could hardly understand English at all, and called every European woman "Auntie." Most parents had become so nauseated with this habit that "Auntie" was a forbidden word for the amah to use.

A girl fresh from England, hot and tired by a long drive from the port, was greeted with what was practically gibberish to her: "Will you have your *mandi* now and a *pahit* after?" asked her hostess. The poor girl was puzzled, and no wonder. Why not say bath and a drink. How odd it all was at first! Especially the incredible smells. For the first few weeks your nostrils are so sensitive to the overwhelming pungency you wonder if it is going to be bearable. There are the smells of mud, of rotting fish and of ozone; of ripe fruit; of the deep water drains, full of rich black mud and open to the sky along every road. There is the coconut-oil smell of the Tamils, the dry smoky smell of Chinese houses, the acrid bitter-sweet muskiness of the Malays' and the sickliness of the Sikhs' ghee. Then there is the milky-warm stench of cattle and all the minor smells such as that of old rattan, of bat guano and rotting wood, and the peppery dankness of jungle undergrowth. And outsmelling everything is the unspeakable smell of the durian. Those are the bad smells. Mingled with these were heady wafts of pigeon orchid; the sweet cloying scent of the frangipanni flowers; the spicy smoke of joss sticks and smudges; the delicious tang of wood fires and the fragrant, hungry smell of curry cooking.

At first all these odours get up and smite you in an indistinguishable mass, as bewildering as the Anglo-Malay conversation; but in time it was possible to sort them out. And after a few weeks your nose objects only to the really potent ones such as rotting fish entrails on an ebb tide at noon; or a lorry load of durians in the season; or a junk full of copra. . . .

One of the first things Stuart did was to put up my easel for me and I tried to paint; but with all these distractions it was difficult. A new country needs some time to be digested: it was all too exciting and disturbing.

We got out some books. The Boy brought a vase of flaming scarlet hibiscus and golden cannas, and at once our little suite took on a less dreary air.

Then Ah Seng arrived. He had been Stuart's Boy before, and he was a good House-Boy; he had a small round baby face and a very wide smile; when he laughed his eyes disappeared entirely in good-humoured creases. He was a cheerful little creature in those days; the shadow of Japan was not so menacing then; although his wife and child were still in bombed Hainan Island he had not given up hope of getting them out to Malaya. He spoke a rather odd Malay, the Malay argot of the Chinese, also scraps of Tamil which came in conveniently at times. In fact he was a very useful person with some most unexpected accomplishments: he could box, dive and was even something of an actor. Meanwhile he was an efficient Boy who looked after us excellently. He had two words of English, and when he first brought the early morning tea he startled me by saying: "Good morning, *Tuan*. Good morning, Madam." Throughout the day he addressed me as "*Mem*," but "Madam" was reserved for the early mornings. Why I do not know.

The mornings were cool and delicious with the mist rolling off the hills and the welcome sunlight golden on the palm fronds. The squirrels cavorted gaily in the big angsena tree that almost touched the verandah; and the clatter of wooden shoes and sing-song voices began again along the road.

We were glad to disentangle ourselves from the mosquito-nets and go out on to the verandah to drink tea and eat the fruit Ah Seng had brought—papayas with lime juice and sugar. Everything felt damp to the touch in the early mornings; one's shoes grew green with mildew overnight.

The sun was almost intolerable at times, and one cursed it at white noon when all the colour was drained out of the land by the intensity of the light; but it was sweet and cleansing at dawn when it seared away the mildews of the night with its first great rays of warmth.

One afternoon we were having tea on the verandah listening to the thunder rolling in the hills and watching the darkening sky when Mac sent his car round with a chit: would we like to use it for a drive and incidentally inspect two toddy shops? Toddy (the sale of which came under the supervision of the Customs and Excise Department) is a drink very popular with Tamils. It is obtained by tapping the spathe of the coconut palm and collecting the juice which exudes from the cut spathe. The tappers, dusky little men, usually sturdy specimens, climb the tall trees with startling agility; they wear a kind of uniform consisting only of a dark, scarlet loin cloth, and a heavy leather belt supporting a gourd which is sometimes elaborately decorated and in which they keep the tapping knife. Fresh toddy is a healthy drink with a fairly low alcoholic content, but if kept for a day or two it becomes stronger and unwholesome. It was to prevent the sale of stale or adulterated toddy that the inspections were carried out.

The Malays themselves once drank toddy before the restrictions of Islam fell upon them, and one of their poets wrote an attractive *pantun* to placate the seven souls of the tree:

Queens of shorn and dripping locks,
Dwellers in dip and wave of the palm-sheath,
Palm-sheaths 'tired like tresses,
Seven queens of a virgin sheath,
Greetings be unto you!
Hither my little ones!
Hither my dainty ones!
I bend back the necks of you
Roll up the folds of the locks of you.
Behold! an ivory blade for your cleansing,
An ivory blade to shorten your tresses.
Lo! here is an ivory beaker I hold for you,
Ivory bath awaiting beneath you.
Clap hands and laugh in your ivory bath,
Bath of princesses changing their raiment.

We enjoyed that drive. It was good to get away from the enclosed feeling of the town and we were longing to see something of the country round. The Krian district was mainly paddy and was very lovely with a mass of intersecting dykes and canals for irrigating and draining the rice fields. The Malay houses, some almost in the water, were gay with hibiscus hedges and untidy red and yellow crotons. Sometimes only a single pole served as a bridge from the road across the drains or canals, the only access to the little dwellings. The water was strident with ducks. In it the people washed their babies, their clothes and themselves, cleaned their teeth and likewise filled their cooking pots. A cheerful, happy-go-lucky-looking crowd. Malays and Chinese and Tamils. The children were sweet, many without a stitch on; one small boy we saw wore nothing but an enormous Chinese cartwheel coolie hat as big as himself. Many of the babies' heads were shaved and their faces daubed with a liquid white powder for coolness. I felt drunk with the colour. The magenta pinks, the golds, the dark blues and peacock greens of the Tamils' cottons were startlingly vivid; deep rich colours suited to the antiquity of that ancient, tragic-eyed south Indian race. The Malay colours were softer and gayer as befitted a more light-hearted people: violets and pinks, purples and crimsons, light checks and pretty floral patterns. The Chinese, more austere in taste, were dressed in black or blue and pastel pinks and mauves or spotless white. Great pink lotus flowers bloomed in the canals between the tender green of the rice fields, and beyond were glimpses of blue mountains.

We drove to Kuala Krau, a fishing village, the home of a particularly tough crowd of Chinese. They lived almost in the river in tumbledown shacks on bamboo quays, among the boats and nets and mud, surrounded by myriads of ducks. On our way home the sun shone under the rain clouds that had been threatening since tea-time and lit the palms and teak trees with an unreal, golden brilliance. Suddenly the whole sky was transformed with vivid colour, vast blue and pink cumulus clouds towering prodigiously in an angry grey-rose sky.

When we got back to the Rest House Ah Seng dashed out to greet us with a huge tin bath in his arms. It had come from Penang. Why? We hadn't ordered it. Then we realized, as it was sent by Messrs. P—— & Co. of Penang, it must be due to a generous misreading of the "bath eau de Cologne and the talc powder" that had been ordered! A strange substitute but the sort of thing that happened, I was to discover, fairly frequently, often with very comic results—if one was feeling philosophical. We seemed to have a run of bad luck over bath tubs in those first few weeks. When we eventually got into our house we discovered the tin tub provided was green with moss. Stuart applied for another; but all that happened was that a coolie arrived to daub the old tub with white paint instead of enamel. With hot water in it the paint of course immediately came off. . . . In desperation we designed a bath and had the local tinsmith make it for us. It was rather like a sarcophagus, but a definite improvement on moss and sticky paint.

When we went into Penang to buy a car, Mac lent us his Javanese syce, Man, so Stuart asked him if he knew of a syce who wanted a job. Oh yes, he had a Malay friend named Mat (short for Mahomed), and it had all been arranged six months ago when he heard a new *tuan* was coming. We were amused to see how it had been planned for us long ago, while we were on leave and knew nothing about it. Man hovered around anxiously, while we bought the car, "to see we were not cheated." We got a secondhand Hillman 20 h.p. with a sun-top roof which was a joy in the evenings. Some Chinese merchant in Penang had gone broke and was willing to sell cheap. We got very fond of that big comfortable old car, though it was an expense before we had done with it.

Mat appeared the next day grinning from ear to ear. He was a grand little Malay; not five feet high, with crisp curly hair (suggestive of a possible Negrito strain), bright brown eyes and a large humorous mouth. He was so small he drove the big car looking through the steering wheel, only his eyes and his black *kopiah*[1] visible from the road.

Ah Seng had had a field-day while we were buying the car: the whole of the Rest House garden and two verandahs were filled with clothes put out to air after the voyage. Neither of us realized how many things we had until we saw that alarming disarray. Of my underclothes Ah Seng complained to Stuart: "*Mem* has three hundred pieces—all the same!" This was hyperbole, but I suppose they looked alike to him. Soon after that he wisely brought his sister, Ah Chi, and her husband, Ah Lam, to be amah and cook.

[1] Velvet pork-pie cap.

One evening the sharp banging of Chinese crackers was very loud—so much crackling would surely have the desired effect of driving off all the evil spirits—the sound came from the Chinese temple just along the road. There had already been much activity on that corner; we had seen the Chinese putting up a theatre and stalls in front of the temple, so after dinner we walked along to look. There were garish lights and a variety of noises, colours and smells. Rhythmic gongs, cymbals and drums, harsh chanting and the sound of shrill pipes and flutes came endlessly from the theatre. The costumes of the players, in the tradition of old China, were brilliant but tawdry with reds and gold. The strangely harsh, monotonous voices fascinated me: people say Chinese voices have an ugly sound; perhaps they have by our standards; but there was something about that chanting that was stirring in the same way as the Penillion singing of the Welsh. The audience appeared to take no notice of the play. They sat and jabbered at each other, ate their food, fed their children and even turned their backs on the stage. The play went on half the day and apparently all night. The little temple with its jade green walls and springing, pantiled roof, red streamers and joss sticks was the quiet background to all this noise and glare. The temple is always the hub of the social, educational and religious life of the Chinese.

Stuart passed that temple every day to and from his work, and he wrote a bit of verse about it. I have some of it here:

In the Chinese Temple as I pass
I see the lanterns hanging from the roof,
Silken banners, pots of shining brass;
Candles flicker in the dim recess
As though a light were lit to give me proof
That all this gaudiness was not excess. . . .

He finished it—though the rest is lost—and the Tamil clerk at the office who typed it out for him called it "The Chinese Lanterns." That clerk with two other brothers was supporting a fourth brother at an English university. All three men worked without envy for the good of the fourth. A splendid bit of family co-operation. The fourth brother was struggling doggedly through the course, though he complained that he found Latin *very* hard and was often lonely in England. One cannot help but admire the price in patience, money and time a family like that will pay for the education of one of its sons.

We grew to love Penang. Work over, we often drove up to Butterworth, only twenty-eight miles north of Parit Buntar, to the ferry. It was refreshing to see the hilly island across the water with great soft clouds towering over it in the red evening sky. The two flat-bottomed unwieldy ferry boats, which later had such perilous voyages, chugged and waltzed round each other in the strait. Sometimes the P. & O. mail boat was in, or a Blue Funnel liner; there was always shipping to watch, and fleets of sampans and junks. It was a delight to feel the sea breeze and to fill one's lungs with ozone and one's eyes with beauty and movement after a hot airless day among the trees in Parit Buntar. The high light of the evening was to revel in a real long bath at the Runnymede and to walk by the sea wall under the casuarina trees, unplagued by mosquitoes. Sometimes we went to swim in the salt-water pool, twenty feet or so above the sea, where, from a terrace full of scarlet salvias, balsams and gay zinnias the view across the Straits to Kedah Peak was enough to melt the stubbornest heart—to annihilate thought to a coloured ecstasy. We stayed in the warm water for hours. When the sun had set the Peak glowed gold and, as the light swiftly vanished, it melted in the brief tropic twilight to a delicate blue line, a pale mountain of the moon, like a Chinese drawing on silk. And then on a little island among the grey rocks and mangrove trees a tiny lighthouse began to wink through the dusk.

Sometimes we went into the town by ourselves and danced. One mad evening we tried out all the dance places in Penang. From the E. & O. Hotel, which had professional dancers or "taxi-girls" in those days, to the big white Chinese dance hall, the Elysée, where I've seen some bloodstained rough and tumbles amongst the Chinese; and it was popular with our Scottish regiments later on. Once in 1940, when we were sitting at a table there, a young Highlander, with flushed face and ruffled corn-coloured hair (his sporran worn most comically astern for dancing), staggered up to Stuart and clasping him round the neck breathed hoarsely in his ear: "Tell the girls—tell *all* the girls, I'm *not* as drunk as they think. . . ." The

Chinese "taxi-girls" were very attractive with their long black hair curled high in front, falling loosely at the back to their slender straight shoulders. Some wore European dresses; but the Shanghai frocks were the most effective, shimmering white, or gold satin with high collars, and pencil-slim skirts split to the knee. In these clinging sheathes the girls' figures had an almost reptilian sinuousness. When we were too broke to take the car across on the ferry we used to hire rickshaws and go careering through streets bright with the garish electric lights of Chinese shops and food stalls and noisy with people of numerous nationalities gossiping and strolling about, eating melons and fried food and *mahmee* at the food stalls: all shouting and talking at once.

The rickshaw coolie rarely understood Malay, so it would be a roundabout journey unless one yelled and pointed the right way at the crucial moment. It's a somewhat barbaric method of transport, and I never really cured myself of the dislike of a human beast of burden. I used to try and sit up "lightly" which probably only made the balance worse for the sweating puller. If we could, we usually picked out strong-looking men, trying to avoid the rheumy eye of poor opium-wasted old scarecrows. It was almost alarming to the uninitiated when six or seven rickshaw men penned one into a circle backed by their red and gold vehicles, each man clamouring for hire with shrill voice and violently importunate gestures.

We spent Christmas evening at the Runnymede as our house was not yet ready. We drank champagne cocktails sitting peacefully under the lisping casuarina trees with our feet on the low sea wall: the waves lapped below, while Kedah Peak faded blue into the night, and little crabs scuttled along the sea wall.

The hotel was run by a Swiss who later went across to the mainland, to the Cameron Highlands, when the Runnymede had to close in 1939 owing to the loss of the tourist traffic. He had a way with the food and flowers. At the end of the ballroom between two pillars there was always a great bank of flowers, a rich wall of colour, flood-lit from below with the night sky as a background.

Ah Seng and Mat we had let loose on the town; which they "did" on the few dollars each we had given them as a Christmas present. Altogether it was a good evening.

II

MODELS AND MOSQUITOES

WHEN EVENTUALLY the difficult young man decided to leave the house empty for us we went along and had a look at it.

It gave us rather a shock at first. It was filthy. All the black-painted Government furniture was crammed into one room, the mosquito-proof room or meat safe, as it was called. We laughed at the sight of a particularly hideous long-legged fern-stand which, as the finishing touch, was planked in the very middle of the room under the fan. Ah Seng simply fell on the house and with a bevy of coolies he cleaned away the first layer of dirt and we started to move in.

The hall and dining-room were attractive, flagged with black and white tiles; and downstairs there was a big room suitable for a studio. The sitting-room and two large bedrooms with bathrooms and dressing-rooms each were on the first floor.

My oak bureau had arrived safely from home, and when it was unpacked two small Tamil coolies tottered up the stairs with it; we could not think why they staggered so agonizingly, until we discovered later that the entire dinner service of fifty-six pieces had been packed in the three drawers. . . .

We had to get in stores, and Ah Seng and Kuki wanted new things for the kitchen. So we went shopping in the town, which consisted of three short streets of semi-Chinese style two storeyed houses, washed azure, viridian green and cream. The shops below were just open rooms or tunnels under the dark arches of the five-foot way: Japanese photographers, Chinese carpenters, a tinsmith and a rattan basket-maker, several Indian silk and cotton stores, goldsmiths and a pawnbroker, and a Japanese hairdresser, Chinese and Indian food shops and petrol stores and Malay coffee shops. There was an open market near the river with food stalls and portable kitchens. Fruit vendors squatted at every corner and spat red betel-nut juice all over the road, so that you had to watch your step.

They sold brilliant scarlet, prickly rambutans, golden coconuts, purple mangosteens, yellow pummeloes, slices of pink water-melon and sweet corn on the cob, and above all the great brown stinking durian which is believed by Malays to be an aphrodisiac.

We ordered all we needed at a sort of general store and four half-naked Chinese carried the cases out, Mat and Ah Seng with a few odds and ends bringing up the rear. We bought curtain material for the incredible sum of 4¼d. a yard. Then the carpenter came and made some quite good bookcases and tables from pictures in Heal's catalogues.

In the house we started a battle with coconut spiders, cock-roaches and fruit bats. The battle of the "poochies," as the insects are nicknamed collectively, was a never-ending one in Malaya. The wire net of the "meat safe" was only enough to keep out the bigger insects and the mosquitoes. The tiny things came through in their clouds at times, in spite of the fragrant smudge sticks burning under the chairs, and became entangled in one's hair. It was not always as bad as it sounds for Malaya is a strange country of variable moods. It is a point in its favour that however unbearable life might seem there occasionally, the gloomy prospect will almost certainly alter within a few hours. Its worst moods work their damnedest with oppressive heat, clouds of infuriating insects, rank smells and discomforts; but as swiftly as the insects descend so the mood lifts. The rain will fall, the air is cooled, the insects disappear, the moon comes out to silver the palm trees and shine on the wet flowers, and once more orchids perfume the air.

There was one particular amphibious bug which, if it fell into water, seemed to be just as happy swimming about as flying in the air or rolling on its back on dry land. So one did not feel safe even in the bath. After six in the evening, when the mosquitoes started, life was a little difficult out of the "meat safe." That was one of the reasons why Penang afforded a respite; there appeared to be no mosquitoes there. They were so bad in the Parit Buntar evenings that it was necessary to wear a long sarong to protect the feet while one was dressing; and even then one's arms and shoulders were defenceless and were soon covered in large red bites. We had a vast mosquito net; it was like a room within the room, and glowed white and soft when the bedside lamp was lit. There is a comfortable feeling of security—at least from swooping bats and zooming insects—inside a mosquito net, and it is good in the dark to watch a stray fire-fly fluttering against its folds. But the net must be big enough and hang well to the floor; you stifle in the tent sort and the ones that tuck under the mattress are infuriating, as you become entangled in them when you want to get up in the morning.

But a mosquito net only gives you a feeling of security when the light is on. One dark night there was a sinister padding of bare feet apparently in the room. I could not help but think of all the stories I had ever heard of Malays running amok, and then Stuart said in a sepulchral voice: "Don't move, I think there's someone in the room!" I lay sweating with fear expecting to be stabbed in the back at any moment, till Stuart found the switch and the light flooded on. There was nothing there! We searched everywhere, the entire house. But we never found out what it was. People said it was a civet-cat in the roof; but it was uncanny all the same.

Fruit bats were another pest but they were something we could cope with. One Sunday morning after breakfast Ah Seng started chasing them with a mop tied to a pole. Stuart joined in and finally eight bats were flying madly about the house; hastily I shut myself in the "meat safe," and so the landing formed a cul-de-sac. Ah Seng drove a parade of bats upstairs, while Stuart stood on the landing and swiped each one as it arrived. They killed ten between them. During a lull Stuart went to have a cool shower; but Ah Seng with the lust of battle still in him yelled: *Tuan! Tuan!* and Stuart rushed out dripping from the bath armed with the racquet, to see Ah Seng solemnly marching upstairs with his tall pole and one solitary bat flying ahead in the high roof. This went on at intervals throughout the morning. . . . Later I boasted to a local planter how many we had killed, which amounted to fifteen or so by then, but he said: "Oh, that's nothing. I got fifty in my bungalow last week." Ah Seng had thoroughly enjoyed his morning; his hair stood on end and his crinkly smile was triumphant. Usually he was solemn and immaculate in spotless white with smooth black hair, except as now when, as he said, his "heart beat fast." Dishevelled he looked most human.

Soon after we settled in, Anthony, Stuart's cat, was sent up from Kuala Lumpur where "Taffy," a good friend of Stuart, had been looking after him during leave. With him came Caesar, his son. Caesar was a perfect little seal point Siamese kitten aged six weeks. Anthony was jet black with yellow eyes, although he was three-quarters Siamese and had the Siamese voice and characteristics. Caesar's mother was a pure-bred Siamese named Minnie who later came to stay with us when in turn her master went on leave. This kitten captivated the household. His creamy coat was soft and fragrant, his innocent blue eyes large and sooty-rimmed; as yet only his nose, tail, ears and paws were beginning to show the Siamese seal-coloured points which are more pronounced later. He never put his claws out when handled and yet would enter with gusto into the maddest games. He would let one hold him like a baby in arms; he always answered when spoken to; he had an extensive vocabulary too; and, what is more, a strong sense of humour.

When we had got the studio ready it looked most inviting. It was a big, stone-floored room with a verandah and large doors. The sparrows flew in and out all day long. The lighting was a little difficult; but I managed that with hangings. The stone floor was an asset, as it didn't matter how much paint one splashed about. On the first morning which was free from arranging the house, I came into the studio to work and found that Stuart had laid out my palette and brushes and charcoal ready for me. That was a good start to those wonderfully long, free mornings—no war and no worries. One of my first models was Mat. He posed well and I used him many times. The first time he wore a black cap, violet jacket, and petunia sarong. It sounds lurid in the cool silver light of England, but out there it was just one note in the brilliant harmony. The Malays were good to paint. The men have that little-boy look which is so attractive, and the women bashfully droop their heads, shy and demure. I could not offend the modesty of Moslem Malay women by asking them to pose in the nude; but it was a disappointment not to be able to do any studies of Malay nudes. A dancing girl might possibly have obliged but it was very unlikely and numerous complications would have arisen, as both the Chinese and Malay communities, from whom no activities are hidden, would have been scandalized. Normally Malay women were so encased in stiffly folded sarongs that the wide-hipped, narrow-waisted, sloping-shouldered beauty of their very feminine figures was heavily shrouded. In the roadside bathing places they bathed in sarongs tied tightly beneath the arms and hanging in modest folds in front. But once I saw a girl, the beauty of whose body was accidentally revealed. She was walking home through the paddy fields and her garments were soaked from head to foot; she must have fallen into a dyke while working the rice. The thin cotton of her jacket was moulded to her lovely full breasts and clung about her tiny waist and rounded hips: she walked gracefully, like a sleek cat.

The Malays are a peaceful, childlike people; and their apparent indolence contrasts sharply with the ceaseless industry of the Chinese. Whether it is due to the three thousand five hundred years during which Chinese peasants have struggled to win food from the land, or whether it is due in part to the background of their ancient civilization, the Chinese make the most tireless workers on earth; they are stoical and philosophical, ingenious, cheerful and smiling. The very quietness of the Malay makes him appear aloof from the bustling world; he is happy-go-lucky, smiling, kindly. Malaria and tropical heat have undoubtedly sapped the energy of the race; but the Medical and Health Departments were already remedying disease.

Sareh, Mat's wife, was a beautiful woman. She posed for me often, afterwards; but I still remember the first time and how excited I was. She wore a blue jacket. Her eyes were downcast and lips demure, the golden brown oval of her face was framed by a sea-green sarong over her dark head.

Then one day I found a little Tamil girl called Meri to pose. She came shyly to the verandah door and walked stiffly to the dais as I directed her. She was dressed in her best. A great crimson and blue sari swathed her small body and her hair was piled in an enormous bun which projected about six inches from the back of her head; her slender neck looked hardly strong enough to hold such a weight of hair. She had strict injunctions given through Mat to wear the same dress when she came again; but she evidently did not understand because she appeared the next day looking seven or eight years younger with her hair in a heavy plait down her back and wearing a gay check sari of green and red and orange over an apple-green bodice, so I started a fresh picture. She was one of the best models who ever sat for me. One of the worst was a fisherman friend of Mat's named Pin—short for 'Arifin. We went to his *kampong*[1] with Mat to inspect him; he looked a good type, tall with a square jaw and a long, muscular throat, huge black eyes and a comic, pursed-up mouth. Stuart asked him to come in old things, as I wanted to paint him as a fisherman, and not smartened up in his mosque-going clothes. When he arrived the next day in the studio he proceeded to peel off his outer garments, and I wondered what was going to happen. Then in sarong and singlet, he seized his old pink silk jacket and tore it wildly, slashing off the sleeves before he put it on. He had evidently thought it was not sufficiently battered; he was a realist. He wore a hat made of dried palm leaves, the huge conical limpet-shaped hat[2] which the men wear in the paddy fields and fishing in the dykes, and grasped his circular net firmly in one hand. He was grand for the first half-hour, but after that he was overcome by the worst fidgets with which I have seen anyone inflicted. His long neck became painfully stiff and he kept rubbing it ruefully and asking for rests every fifteen minutes. Those sittings were a struggle.

This district, the Krian, was Mat's home and his *kampong* was in the trees beside a rather smelly drain not very far from our house. So he knew everyone and was useful getting models.

Sometimes in the lovely hour before sunset we went out sketching. Stuart drove the car along grassy dyke roads and we explored the lie of the land. The Malay houses were half-hidden by hibiscus and bamboo hedges; but when we stopped a crowd of people appeared as from nowhere and gaped at us. Occasionally one saw absolutely tiny, *atap*[3] houses, on stilts, no bigger than large hen coops. These were used, so I was told, by Malay boys who, on reaching puberty, according to the Mohammedan religion, have to learn long passages of the Koran by heart.

I remember on one of these drives stopping as we often did to sketch a Chinese shack: pots and pans and washing made a

[1] Hamlet, or settlement—hardly a village.
[2] The *tĕrĕndak*.
[3] Dried palm leaf for thatching and walls.

gay tatterdemalion scene of it, all reflected in the muddy dyke with leaning palms and scarlet flowers and a lotus here and there. Twenty-two children, several babies and adults crowded round. Stuart sat on the roof of the car and I in front. The owner of the house stood at my elbow and breathed heavily down my neck. The atmosphere was tense with excitement and oppressively hot. Some of these excursions were through the Customs boundary gate and into Province Wellesley. We used to enjoy feeling we were actually on British soil again after being in a protected Malay State.

I made some studies too of Ah Chi, the amah, a shy little thing with her small round yellow face and little red blobby mouth and downcast anxious eyes. She wore her best jacket and trousers of hyacinth blue with a white pin stripe. I painted Ah Seng too. He sat perfectly still for a good hour at a time, but when he had his rests he used to dash out of the room and I would hear an ensuing jabber from the kitchen and gales of laughter. Being painted seemed to amuse him very much. This picture later won an absurd bronze medal at a show in Kuala Lumpur and a card, like those farmers get for prize bulls, which amused us very much and was kept pinned up in the studio. . . .

The servants loved *kuching*[1] Caesar, and were very sweet to him. Whenever any of them brought in either of the cats they always carried him held out on both hands like a burnt offering. This was because once, when Anthony was a kitten, Ah Seng had carried him by one ear, mistaking it for the correct way. To make sure this never happened again Stuart had instituted the burnt offering method. While Caesar was a tiny kitten his sand-box was brought upstairs each evening when Ah Seng came to say good-night. If Caesar happened to be downstairs at the time he was carried up sitting on the sand, in the box balanced like a waiter's tray. From the mosquito room we watched this ritual with delight: the tiny pale-coloured cat, sitting up very straight, his eyes very blue in his seal-dark face, being borne aloft above Seng's imperturbable head. Once inside the mosquito room Caesar would climb the wire netting hand over hand, his small creamy body spread-eagled against the dark night. When we rolled up the carpet to dance he

[1] Cat.

would toboggan purposefully across the slippery floor to end in a perfect somersault against the roll. I believe only Siamese cats can somersault. One dreadful morning he fell backwards from the top of the stairs to the bottom. I heard Stuart groan, and rushed out to help. We were quite silly over that kitten, but he rewarded us with his affection like a dog. He always slept at the foot of our beds, and was an excellent hot water bottle on chilly nights. But he developed a dreadful habit in the early mornings of going berserk round the mosquito net and on the bedside table. He invariably threw the alarm clock on the floor. This happened so often we thought it must be deliberate and we never had an alarm clock that would go for this reason. He appeared to smile all the time; his bright blue eyes were sometimes very earnest and solemn and sometimes quite saintly—when he was most devilish.

We worked and painted, gardened and played tennis, and life was good and new. One of the many new things was a *sati* party to which we were invited. *Sati* is hot chicken or meat dipped in spicy sauces and roasted on long cane skewers over a naked flame. The Malay *sati* man sat outside our hosts' bungalow, among the ferns and flowers on the verandah, with his glowing brazier and all the sticks and dishes of sauce and lumps of chicken. It was a most delicious meal.

We had some picnics too and walks. One evening we drove to Bukit Panchor, a big reservoir in Straits Settlements' territory. We walked all round the lake and never met a soul. It was my first close-up of the jungle, but it was secondary jungle and looked comparatively neat. However, I was very much impressed by that silent wall of giant trees and tangled creepers which towered above the lake path. An iguana scuttled away before us, and monkeys played in the trees; mad games they had throwing themselves about lightheartedly and swinging on the long ropes of the lianas, the aerial roots and creepers. Seeing them like this, so gay and crazy, I lost my old dislike of monkeys—whom I had seen before with all too human faces, only behind the bars of cages.

One of the best picnics was near Bukit Merah, "Red Hill," by a large lake nine miles off the Taiping road. We went with our new friends, Jean and Jo, who were to hunt butterflies in

From an oil painting by the author

Sareh—Mat's wife, Perak Malay

Malay Houses—Lumut Estuary

the jungle while we tried to sketch. We chugged across the lake in a launch to a landing-stage above which was a steep green hillock with a Rest House, perched like a dilapidated châlet on the top and surrounded by stunted palms and purple bougainvillaea. Jean and Jo went off into the jungle and we had a look round. There were two concrete reinforced outlets to the reservoir which was used for irrigating the paddy fields. The trees were magnificent; blue mountains framed the big expanse of water. We found a comparatively cool spot under a wall of rock which seemed popular with the martins. Two old Malay women were fishing there; but the moment I started to sketch them they got up, giggling, and went off, explaining self-consciously that the fish were not biting any more. After a hot morning we picnicked at the *atap* Rest House, and watched men on the other side of the lake cutting off chunks of the shore which they ferried across the water like floating islands, punting them with large poles. As they reached the narrow culvert snakes wriggled out of the grasses. The floating islands were a tangled mass of roots, broken trees, bamboos and *lalang*.[1] Down the coast we often saw them still moving in the river mouth or even right out at sea.

The Rest House Boy climbed a palm and picked a couple of coconuts, from which we drank. It was good to hold them in your hands like great goblets. The milk was pleasant and very fresh, but warm, of course. We all marvelled at the way the green outer husk is made to allow the fruit to float and be washed about by the sea to rocks and islands and so take root on new shores. Jo said: "Well, I would never have thought of that, if I had been making the world."

Stuart was on preventive work at Parit Buntar and sometimes I was alone in the evenings while he was on an opium or distillery raid or watching for lorries full of contraband or intercepting porters known to have been hired to smuggle across the boundary. Being alone in the mosquito room felt like sitting in a lighted wire cage hung up in the palm trees. One couldn't see out, but felt that everyone else could see in, and there was only the hum of insects and occasionally the sound of a temple gong. I was glad of Caesar's company, although he sometimes wanted

[1] Long coarse grass.

to go out and chase the cicadas, which screamed with fury when he caught them. They were armoured so he could not harm them much, but like the little Malay boys who carry them in their pockets, he enjoyed hearing the shrill noise.

Sometimes Stuart was busy downstairs interviewing informers, for what seemed like hours on end to me, and then he would have to go out on a raid. His men came on bicycles. Malay and Chinese Out Door Officers (O.D.O.'s) were always punctual to the minute and they would all crowd into the car and go off. Sometimes he had stories to tell me when he returned. He saw some lovely, and some unclean, depressing things. One black midnight in a fishing village, walking across narrow, rotten planks over unseen water and mud to raid some opium smoker's hovel, he saw a mangrove bush lit with fireflies like candles on a Christmas tree. I once saw that sight for myself; it is never to be forgotten. He told me of a sixty-five-year-old Chinese fisherman who, caught red-handed smoking without a licence, tried to swallow the pill of prepared opium. To stop him one of Stuart's men seized him by the throat; so unable to swallow the old fellow threw the tell-tale pill out of the window. It was retrieved from the garden and shown to him, tangible evidence of his guilt, but he shook his head: "I am *very* old, *Tuan*—I can *not see* it." And he persistently denied every charge!

That was down at Kuala Krau. Stuart used to take me there in the evenings, when he went on patrols in the river mouth to search the junks. All the crews, to my unaccustomed eye, appeared to be the most bloodthirsty pirates. But Stuart could usually make them laugh, which he did intentionally, because he could tell by their teeth if they were opium smokers, and more than likely unlicensed ones. Once or twice he found part of the smoker's outfit, the lamp perhaps, and would stay to search the junk until he found the rest. If the smoker was unlicensed he would be arrested.

We saw a large family of sea otters playing in the mangrove roots in the estuary, and elegant white egrets pecked fastidiously on the mud beaches. Overhead a solitary sea hawk swooped and called harshly. Out at sea the breeze was fresh and good. Penang lay to the north and Pangkor away in the south, and behind us the great range of blue mountains that runs all down the spine of the country. One *tongkang* Stuart boarded was twenty-eight hours out from Penang. Such measured progress in these days is hard to believe. It only took an hour by road. The Indian boats with dark sails, ketch rig, looked like old slavers, black against the western sky. At sunset everything turned to gold and the water was a sheet of limpid flame. As we came back up the estuary after dark our wake was a pale luminous green. Stars were everywhere, shining in the sky; dancing in the phosphorescent water; gliding even in the trees as myriads of fire-flies flittered in and out among the leaves.

There was a small cinema in Parit Buntar patronized by the very mixed populace. It was what is commonly known as a real "bug-house." I wanted to try it out, but Stuart was afraid I would not approve of the "rattan bugs" which live in the arms of the greasy old cane chairs. Forty cents (about a shilling) was the highest price one could pay for a seat; but the rattan bugs apparently disregarded prices. So for our first visit Stuart, not taking any chances, insisted on my wearing a long-sleeved jacket and white gloves. We set off armed with long sarongs sewn up at the bottom in which to put our legs as a protection against the mosquitoes, also smudges, and I had a heavily-perfumed handkerchief. I was glad of the perfume, as the smells were of a type better not described though they were only too identifiable. The rattan bugs didn't bite through our protective layers (I have seen a girl's arm red from wrist to elbow with these bites), and we quite enjoyed the film. It was an old Gordon Harker one, I remember, followed by a Wild West thriller. The latter was accompanied by the delighted yells and shrieks of the audience; but I found it rather bewildering, because vital parts of every shooting scene had been cut out by the censor. It was not considered healthy for the people to see a gun fired, though they were allowed to see it aimed, then the actual "bang" was eliminated and miraculously the victim lay dead, while the villain, or hero, as it might be, lowered his smoking gun. It did not seem to worry the audience in the least and they all talked and cheered the whole time. Small Chinese boys carried round trays of sliced pineapple and bags of nuts. Malay and Tamil boys sat in the five cents seats, a few Chinese girls, shop-keepers' daughters, and Malay, Tamil and

Chinese clerks and merchants in the better seats. The only other form of entertainment locally was dining among the small circle of Europeans. But the Cold Storage called only twice a week and I soon discovered one was always asked to dine on "Cold Storage days." It became a race to get your invitation in first so as to be sure you had fresh food to offer your guests. It was very difficult to vary the food as everyone had to deal with the same firm. There was also the question of flowers. Our predecessor evidently had no love of flowers, for the big garden was a barren wilderness. We had a Javanese gardener, Kassim. Whenever I asked him for flowers he would always bring bunches of scarlet hibiscus, orange ixora, flaming cannas and all sorts of glorious flowers still unfamiliar to me. I supposed in my ignorance that he got them from his *kampong* and it was something of a shock to discover that they all came from Jean's garden. We hardly knew her then, but she was very nice about it when I realized my mistake. She was a great gardener and seemed to have a way with the difficult soil. A good many of the other Europeans did in fact send their gardeners to beg flowers from her; but I didn't know this and the joke was definitely on me when she came to dinner, and saw her own flowers all over our house.

Our first dinner party, which was for the Macs, was quite an event for our new household. Stuart and I came down to inspect the table and I found that Ah Seng in his zeal had made every napkin into a different shape: rabbit's ears, water lilies, boats and spires and cylinders; but when this was tactfully altered and only his demure water lilies reposed uniformly at each place we stood back to admire. Even the heavy black Government table looked pretty with smoky glass, lace mats, flowers in the fingerbowls and tall red temple candles in glass candlesticks and a few big double hibiscus floating in a black glass bowl. That was a mistake, because by the time we came down to dine, those flowers had calmly closed up and died, a habit of theirs at sunset, unknown to me then. All that remained were three or four rather bruised-looking twisted petals.

III

A SULTAN'S BALL AND A CHINESE MERCHANT'S BUNGALOW

EARLY IN FEBRUARY that year, 1939, we went to Kuala Kangsar to call on the Sultan. This was only a matter of signing our names in the big book at the gates of his strawberry-coloured Palace. Kuala Kangsar was a town of real character. Heavy lichen-grown trees lined its roads; the palaces and the mosque were perched on a hill overlooking the wide reaches of the Perak river and the mountains beyond. The great curve of the river added grace to the charming little town, but the waters were muddy and constantly flooding. Soon after we "called" we received an invitation to a ball which was being given on March 4th to celebrate the Sultan's installation.

Feeling rather festive on the night of the ball, we broached a bottle of champagne for dinner before starting out on the long drive. We ate by candlelight with alamanders and frangipanni flowers and purple balsam petals in a bowl on the table. A full moon was rising behind the clouds and shadowy palms. It was an aesthetic prelude to an entertaining ball.

When we reached Kuala Kangsar the route to the Palace was gay with bunting, and lit by the naked flames of wicks burning in coconut oil, and giving out a pungent smell. Crowds of gaping and rather weary-looking Malays stood around, strings of colourful Tamils trooped along the road. The Mosque was floodlit, its great bulbous dome and minarets a deep emerald green. It seemed to float like one of Dulac's faery palaces; lit as if by a yellow fire below and luminous above, almost phosphorescent, with the emerald light. After this the little lights and bunting looked very poor and draggled. The cars crawled in at the gates of the *Istana*, which were guarded by a khaki-clad policeman. The pinkish building was lit with a yellow light; the highest dome glowed a lurid red inside.

Flowers were banked lavishly in the hall; bowls of sumptuous salmon pink gladioli, great masses of blue hydrangea and pink bougainvillaea. I was surprised at the chromium-plated modernity of the cloak-rooms.

People were drifting up the long staircase, into the ballroom. We started to dance to a languid air. Some of the Europeans sported F.M.S.V.R. dress uniforms, the Malays in their dress clothes were very decorative; most of them wore a black silk jacket and trousers with a stiff gold or silver embroidered sarong and an upstanding head-dress of the same material, which was very striking. There were a few very smart Chinese merchants in black silk with their ladies in heavily embroidered satin Shanghai gowns. The Indian women, instead of wearing their own graceful saris, came in dreadful semi-Europeanized frocks of candy pink and turquoise embroidered with beads and silver thread.

The Malays sat in rows round the ballroom looking rather bored: as their own women do not appear in public, they were pleased to dance with Europeans. At one end of the long room on a dais was the great throne, draped in dark silks embroidered with gold thread, looking—as immemorial tradition requires it—exactly like a large four-poster. A few ancient, wrinkled Malay women sat sedately in high-backed chairs near it; the young women, not supposed to be seen, were crowding over each other in a balcony above. Fluttering their veils, giggling, hiding behind each other while they peeped down at the dancers, their eyes round and heavy with kohl.

We wandered about the terraces and verandahs and discovered a circular room with windows open to the sky on three sides, full of ferns and flowers. There was a bar there and we tried to get cold, soft drinks but were served with martinis by a too generous barman. He then tried to open some other drink for us, he had lost his bottle-opener, but was quite undaunted and with dreadful grinding noises he used the iron window-frame instead.

At last we ventured up an iron spiral staircase which led through a series of bare stone rooms to the topmost dome, filled with the hot red light we had seen from below. When we spoke our voices rang and echoed round about. Curving ourselves to the walls we looked out of the windows down the hill to the river banks where numerous Malay and Chinese theatres and a cinema glittered in the night. There were flaring lights and voices, chanting and gongs. In the *wayang* we could see the Malay scenery being rolled up, one backcloth after another.

Later on Stuart took me to meet the Sultan when he was disengaged for a second. His Highness looked rather thin and pale, in black silk, over which he wore a beautifully woven black and silver sarong. Stuart had not been sure the Sultan would remember him, but he had the proverbial royal memory for he referred at once to the games of tennis they had played together. He was a very keen player. We sat down on the high-backed velvet chairs. The Sultan spoke perfect English and was charming with an easy manner. He must have been very tired after the lengthy business of the installation celebrations, which had already lasted several days. From the terrace we could see the floodlit outdoor throne, on which he had been sitting all that day.

The next day was a delightful contrast. For a long time we had been irked by the fact that, although we were almost within sound of the sea, there was nowhere where it was possible to bathe. The whole coast was mazy with mangrove swamps, deep in black mud and tangled roots. But Mat came to hear of a place further north where he believed people bathed, and one Sunday, before the ball, we had set off with him to look for it. We crossed the boundary into British territory and drove north. There was a river to cross at a picturesque village which was quite old, as tangible antiquity goes in this country, and had Dutch fortifications along the hillside. Waiting for the ferry under a stone-tiled shelter by the water front we suddenly discovered we hadn't a cent between us; but to our delight there was nothing to pay. This seemed to typify the whole place; there was something unworldly and generous in all that happened to us that day. The very name of the place appears to mean Friend's stone—Batu Kawan.

Tamil coolies rowed us across in the car ferry with giant sweeps like banana leaves. The road on the other side was only a rough track through rubber and mangrove. Very soon we came upon a *kampong*, which proved to be Batu Kawan, beside a small tidal creek. We left the car in the shade of a great tree near an old Chinese house. Through the dark front room could be seen an open courtyard with a well, and we caught a glimpse of the family shrine in an inner room. We left the little village sleeping in the hot sun, with its miniature temple in the shade of a banyan tree, and set out along a sandy track through the coarse *lalang* grass at the foot of a steep hill. Mat came with us carrying a stick as big as himself. I personally was glad of his company in case we encountered a *kerbau*, the huge black water buffalo, which has an innate aversion to Europeans and is liable to charge them at the first sniff! Buffaloes have no objection to Asiatics, and a small child will often be left to guard a herd. The sun was almost overhead by then, baking the red earth of the hill, casting deep pools of shadow under the fruit trees. It was very hot; but beautiful enough to make one disregard the sweat dripping into one's eyes. Suddenly we smelt the sea and as suddenly a few seconds later we came out on to rocks at the river mouth. The sea at last! To the right after a short walk along a shore, made grotesque and uninviting by the mangroves' spidery roots, we came to a tiny headland where flat rocks enclosed a miniature sandy bay, and steps led up to a small house with a stone verandah under leafy shade trees.

A half-Malay, half-Indian woman, her Malay husband and their mixed brood of children lived in a shack beyond. They all came out to greet us, smiling:

"*Tabek, Tuan! Tabek, Mem!*"

We felt as if we had come a long way into a younger world and were being greeted as old friends. They showed us round the bungalow which, to our amazement, we learned was owned by a philanthropic Chinese merchant, who lent it to anyone who wished to use it because he thought "it would do them good to feel the sea breeze and because it is such a beautiful spot." The peasants brought out cane chairs for us and long glasses of delicious black coffee. We were amazed at so much unexpected kindness, combined with the peace and idyllic beauty of the tiny place. We lay back in our chairs and breathed in the "sea breezes" that the kindly Chinese gentleman thought were so good for us. He was quite right. A jungle-covered island lay to the north-west, and beyond it there was a glimpse of Penang and the shipping in the Straits.

We seemed to have forgotten everything that day, for we had come without bathing dresses as well as without money; perhaps we had never really hoped to get a bathe. But the woman lent us clean sarongs. Mat bathed hurriedly before we did, "to see if it was safe," he said. The peasants gave us old lifebelts and we floated lazily in the warm deep water for a long time. It was a dreamlike place: the miniature shore, the jetty-like rock, the little house under the trees and the view across the sparkling water to the islands. When we were dressed again the woman offered us eggs and more coffee. We were terribly upset that we had no money and said we would come again; but it was apparently all part of the hospitality of the unknown merchant. We read the "Visitors' Book," in which everyone like ourselves were overcome with gratitude. We had to go at last, loath to leave, because rarely is such an atmosphere recaptured. Two of the children showed us a short cut back over the hill through a coffee plantation. The name of the place was Batu Musang (civet-cat's Stone). It had been a pleasance for Chinese merchants in the old days. We passed several ruined bungalows on the way home. Mere heaps of stone, now shrouded in creeper and long *lalang* grass. It had been what the Malays call a place to *makan angin*. I love that expression. It literally means "eating the wind," as we might say a picnic, a joy-ride, or a stroll in the country to get a breath of air.

When we went again, on the Sunday after the ball, we did not quite recapture the first feeling, partly because we had thought it our duty to call on the Chinese gentleman before using his bungalow again, and this led to complications. He lived, we discovered, in the old Chinese house we had noticed in Batu Kawan under the banyan tree, and we had arranged to call. We were entertained by a young relative in the courtyard room with tea and sweet wafer cakes. There were joss sticks stuck between the bricks of the well and a blue fragrant smoke drifted up from the courtyard. A large iron bowl stood in the middle of it, in which, we were told, the family were going to burn paper in honour of their grandfather and grandmother whom they were reverencing that morning as it was the Fifteenth day of the Chinese month, the Feast of the Lanterns. The big table in front of the family shrine in the room beyond was decorated with a red and gold embroidered cloth, joss sticks and two red temple candles in big brass candlesticks.

After a little while he took us out to the creek and we all, including Mat and a boatman got into the long slim *kolek* (Malay canoe) that was waiting for us. We had half hoped we might go alone, and assured the young relative we should be all right, but he evidently felt it was his duty to escort us and he impressed upon us several times that he had given up a big show in Penang to do so. "Sorry my Boy not come," he said, "he has typhoid fever." I thought of the well in the courtyard! The Malay stood up to row and we slipped quickly through the greasy, green water between the twisted mangrove trees, whose roots were like giant spiders in the mud. Brilliant kingfishers flashed across the streams, which branched and curved in and out the swamp until I quite lost my bearings. Very soon we were at the mouth of the river, where we had walked before. The mangrove trees were deep in water and dark against its brilliance; a *kolek* was tied up among them; it was a vivid picture and, oddly enough, made me think of a punt in a flooded old apple orchard. The islands lay to the north shimmering in the heat.

"You can shoot wild pig there," said our guide, pointing to the jungle-covered hills of the island opposite Batu Musang, "but you must have plenty dogs."

The coffee plantation on the hill he told us was run by Chettiars (a southern Indian caste of money-lenders), and each tree cost five dollars. All his interests seemed to centre in money, so we entered into the game. He saw a book of Smythe's *The Valley of Flowers*, among our belongings.

"How many shillings this cost?"

"Eighteen—about."

"At home I have a book cost five dollars"—and so on.

When I put my bathing cap on he asked: "Where did you buy that hat you're wearing? Is your bathing dress a Janzen?"

And then: "You dlink whisky? I have a friend in Peenang, he all round, he dlink whisky."

"No, we *don't like* whisky." (In those light-hearted days our tastes were more flippant.)

"Oh yes, *all* Europeans like whisky. O.K.! I dlink gin sling in Peenang—after a little the head it turns very fast—heah! . . . Have you see the Marcus show—velly nice—they take off evelly thing—velly nice—velly nice."

Conversation was *not* easy. No one would have expected that evidently appreciative and philanthropic Chinese merchant to have quite such a relative. We could not help wishing the young man had not so nobly given up the "big show in Peenang" in order to accompany us. We landed at the steps in front of the bungalow, and Stuart and I bathed at once and spent the rest of the morning drifting about in the eddies. The Malay children sat with Mat and our guide under the trees languidly, while the great white galleon clouds piled on the horizon above the green islands.

When we were dressed, Mat brought a mother and baby king crab to show us, extraordinary primeval-looking creatures. The baby sat on its mother's back. Only the eggs which are in the head are edible. The Malays told us how to cook them and gave us several crabs to take back; but that evening Ah Seng refused to let us eat them, and he was so insistent that we had to comply. He said that if any of the other parts break and touch the eggs in getting them out of the shell they become deadly poisonous. So Mat had them all; at dinner time he sent some in especially for us, cooked in the correct way, but Ah Seng still implored us not to eat them.

After we had bathed, our Chinese friend sat and talked of how good the king-crab's eggs were and of red-fish boiled with egg sauce, and of the excellence of roast boar's head, while Stuart and I got more and more hungry. We had brought a picnic basket, but didn't like to produce it, thinking probably a curry was already being cooked by the Malay woman. So at last, partly in order to find out and partly from interest, I asked to see the Malay house as I had never been inside one. The smiling woman showed us round. Up the two steps into a small dark room—the husband was curled up asleep on the table and a jumble of clothes and rags, sarongs and children was heaped up behind him. A baby swung most comfortably in a cane moses basket slung from the roof, and near by was an open stove with a huge cauldron bubbling merrily. We dashed to it hopefully. "Vegetables!" said the woman brightly. Three wooden steps led up to a higher level, a small platform which was the family bed; only a strip of matting and a little row of pillows.

It was a blow about the curry, but we thought we might now produce our picnic basket without seeming rude. Our guide would only eat a very little.

"I never eat, afraid of getting fat—no rice—no butter!" Perhaps the kindly old relative was very fat. The children were delighted with the sardine tin and handled it as if it were a wonderful new toy. Our guide said: "Ah! Cold Storage, heah!" and smacked his lips noisily over the MacVita asking what kind of bread it was. When I asked him if he ever thought of going to England, he answered: "No; but I *have* travelled: I have been to Singapore and Kuala Lumpur."

There was something pathetic about this young Chinese. I think he was trying to break away from the old traditions and was obviously getting very muddled ideas of European standards. I would have liked to have met his generous old relative.

On the way home I noticed the first *kramat* or holy spot that I had seen; I saw many later further down the Perak coast. It was only a cluster of rocks, a tiny islet with a small white flag stuck in the silver sand. Stuart told me it was a kind of religious spot, a holy place where spirits live. I hoped our Chinese friend would be able to explain; but he would only say a lot of big Chinese people came from Penang to pray there and he did not seem at all interested. A jungle tree of exceptional beauty and size is often chosen as a *kramat*. In the solitary splendour of such trees it is not difficult to see an almost holy loveliness, made grander by the small, rather pathetic signs of human worship—a paper flag and a handful of charred red joss sticks at the feet of the giant.

It was while we were at Parit Buntar that we first caught the gardening craze. Our people sent us seeds from home and from South Africa, Jean gave us plants and advice. We learned that all the earth had to be sterilized before seeds could be planted in boxes. This was because the soil was poor, and full of weeds and germs that attacked plants. It had to be "cooked" on big tin sheets stood on bricks over a fire in the garden, then sifted, put in boxes and watered ready for the sowing. The lazy Javanese gardener after a quiet time under our predecessor now had to bestir himself. The soil was nothing but mud; in fact the whole of Parit Buntar, built on a swamp, was only eighteen inches above water. Waiting at the level crossing, as a train passed, you could feel the car rising gently up and down, as if on a raft at sea in a swell. Houses a hundred and fifty yards from the line would shake and rattle whenever a train went by.

After rain the sun came out and baked the mud into solid lumps pitted with craters and cracks. Only tough plants like cannas, and shrubs could stand up to this. All the delicate seeds had to be planted in the specially prepared earth, and eventually potted out and put to flower in the shade of the verandah-porch.

With great pride we nursed our seedlings, the sun-flowers and zinnias and hollyhocks: some were the special ones sent from home as an experiment and some Australian brands from Ipoh. The time came to plant them out. At the Chinese New Year holiday Stuart erected a rather leggy-looking stand for the pots and we put it under the porch. Sweating with fervour and covered in black mud, we spent a whole evening potting out the seedlings. Then, imbued with the self-righteous joy of new-born gardeners we stood back to admire the rows and rows of pots on the stand.

We had bathed and were having a well-earned drink in the mosquito room above the porch, when a wind got up whispering in the palms; thunder boomed around the hills and soon there was half a gale blowing. Above the noise we heard a faint crash: we looked at each other in horror. Our new seedlings! We rushed out in the dark and the rain, and there lay the stand upside down, and nearly all the pots were broken. We were miserable; but working feverishly, disregarding the gale, we rescued all except two small sunflowers. Such was our fervour in those early days; but it did not last at such a pitch. The struggle against the poor soil in Malaya is a trying one and eventually we achieved less ambitious, but quite effective results with hardier plants. The next day when the garden was half-flooded and full of peacock-blue kingfishers after the rain, we bought dozens more new pots, from an Indian pottery along the south road, and started all over again. Mat entered into our gardening craze with so much sympathy and interest that he was rather embarrassing at times. Whenever we went out to dinner anywhere he would prowl round our hosts' garden, uprooting plants and taking cuttings and seed-pods of anything we had not got in our garden. And when we came out to the car accompanied by our host and hostess, he would appear grinning from ear to ear with his arms full of plants, looking so pleased with himself that we had no heart to scold him. We were constantly apologizing for him; so after a while he developed a less obvious technique. We had always heard "stolen" flowers did well, but actually it was not at all necessary to steal as people were most generous with cuttings and roots. Our garden was too big for us—it had so much grass, it needed three men. We had two Tamil grass cutters always at it, with their dancing scything movements, and the Javanese. We designed vast flower-beds and laboured at them almost daily. Caesar always accompanied us, trotting round with tail erect and digging busily beside us in the new beds.

The old padre came from Taiping to call. He was an ardent gardener himself and told us the names of many trees and flowers. The beautiful mauve flowering tree which dripped blossom on our lawn by the bamboo hedge was a jacquaranda, and the shrub with the glorious bell-shaped yellow flowers was an alamander. He gave us, and continued to give us, all the time we lived in Malaya, much practical help and advice on gardening. He had to drive out thirty miles from Taiping to take services at Parit Buntar. The church there was tiny and smelt of damp and wood rot. It would have been interesting to know what the Tamil coolie, who stood outside to pull the *punkah*, thought of our rather reedy hymn-droning—sometimes with no organ to accompany us—compared with his garish noisy ceremonies. That is, if he thought about it at all. Taiping church, where we went occasionally, was a stone building under the hill; gay with cannas, all open to the light and air and full of birds which swooped and twittered cheerfully during the services. A young Indian priest acted as assistant. There was something of the Early Christian about him; so much devoutness and singleness of purpose in his expression. His dark face was radiant with an inner beauty and simplicity. His powerful figure was neat and austere in long white robes gathered in at the waist by a heavy leather belt.

Unfortunately, the church was near the barracks and at times the service was drowned in the early mornings by military noises: a persistent blast of bagpipes and bellowing brass. The poor old padre's protests always went unanswered. The Dogras were stationed there in those days.

Taiping lay cool and delicious under the hill, at dawn. Its name in Chinese means Great Peace and it was a peaceful little town, in spite of the bands. The Hill (Maxwell Hill) dominated the place. The soft mists that rolled off the jungle-covered slopes in the mornings, and the cold water plashing down from the heights seemed to keep the town cool longer than most places. Sometimes there was a rainbow mist over the waterfalls, and the long avenues of old angsena trees and flame-of-the-forest were still bathed in shadow as the sun rose high over the hill.

Once we went crocodile-shooting, in the mangrove swamps near Taiping at Port Weld. The moonlight shone on the mud in the creeks and through the long black roots of the trees. One or two junks loomed darkly in the silver expanses, and the distant mountains were blue and misty under the moon. It was very beautiful; but we did not get a single croc. I remember the drive out from Taiping, along an avenue of stunted trees. Nightjars or toc-tocs, with flashing red eyes got up, disconcertingly huge, in front of the car. These toc-toc or brain-fever birds are terribly aggravating. They have a monotonous call which gives them their name. They croak several low notes, then one a shade higher followed by a final one in the original key. You are forced to listen to them, unless you are very strong-minded. The Malays actually play a game in which they make bets on how many tocs will occur before the high note. At Port Weld the soupy water was full of little snakes and, from the wooden jetty, by the light of our torches, we watched them fishing.

The bathing pool at Taiping was one of the loveliest of places. Rough steps led to it up a jungle path at the foot of Maxwell Hill; it was surrounded by a riot of vines and flowers. There were *atap* thatched houses for dressing rooms and an open bar beside the pools. The water plunged down from the jungle-grown cliffs towering above. Part of this cascade was diverted to feed the three pools and made a water chute into the topmost one, the second was shallow for the children and the third deep, clear and very cold. Taiping had a very heavy rainfall, and it was there we heard what had happened recently at a ladies' hockey match in a rainstorm. In the wet season the rain almost inevitably comes about five o'clock, just when games are starting in the two precious hours of comparative coolness before dark. The Penang Ladies, in blue, were playing the Ipoh Ladies, in white. It had started to rain; but both teams, having come so far to play, were anxious to carry on and decided to disregard the downpour. It was very heavy and the European spectators all fled indoors. No one was left round the field but lines of Sikh soldiers—a Sikh regiment was garrisoned in Taiping then—in ten minutes the poor wretched Ipoh Ladies, being in white, were completely transparent, soaked through. They went on playing valiantly, but the crowd of soldiers grew so vast and the linesman was blushing so furiously that they had to give up at last and retire to the club-house. . . .

On March 1st at midday Stuart rushed home, with great armfuls of fragrant pigeon orchids one of the Customs men had given him, to tell me some exciting news. We were to go on transfer on the 17th of the month to Lumut. *Lumut!* The place we had always longed for; it was magic; it was almost too good to be true. We had wanted it so much.

After that we were very busy every evening, taking cuttings of the scorpion and Vanda Joachim orchids, the camelias and the alamanders, and tending the seedlings, for we were going to take all the pot plants to Lumut as part of our household belongings.

One evening in the midst of all this our Chinese guide from Batu Musang came to call. He was full of admiration for the house and shouted with delight, exclaiming so loudly over everything that we found ourselves shouting back. He kept on rolling his eyes up to heaven and sighing. We were very sorry not to be able to go to Batu Musang again or to meet its Chinese squire.

We did, however, go to Penang once more. We were determined to have one long last day there and to drive right round the island as we had so often planned to do. We toyed with the idea of going up Penang Hill again, but it was impossible to fit in everything and as we had done this once before, we decided on the drive round the island. It was the only real reason we were sorry to leave Parit Buntar—that we should be too far to go to Penang often; Lumut being over a hundred miles from Penang down the Perak coast. Apart from that we were delighted to be getting away from the mosquitoes and the stuffiness to the sea. Sometimes the afternoons in Parit Buntar were so stifling one could only lie sweating under an electric fan longing for the evening to come.

We had been lucky the day we went up Penang Hill, for the clouds kept off and the views were magnificent. It was not long after we had settled in at Parit Buntar and the sight of all the English flowers made me quite homesick; it was cold too, almost as cold as an English June or so it seemed. We went in the little mountain railway straight up over two thousand feet. The track ran between elephantine rocks grown with moss, giant ferns and creepers brushed the train. At the top we walked along a narrow twisting path to the Crag Hotel which in those days belonged to the Runnymede. It was very quiet. The rock rose sheer on our left and fell away to the tree-tops on our right. Suddenly, three tricycle rickshaws hurtled round a bend, swift and silent on rubber tyres; startled we leapt out of the way and flattened ourselves against the rock. In each ridiculous vehicle, poker-faced under the hood, sat a European woman. They looked so quaintly solemn and were propelled at such a furious speed by three sprightly young Chinese, that when they had gone flying past we were seized with childish laughter.

We sat in a sort of turret overlooking the Straits and had our tea among fat clusters of purple bougainvillaea, over which trailed a scarlet and yellow gloriosa superba and a sweet honeysuckle. Kedah Peak and the pale, silvery paddy lands of Province Wellesley lay across the Straits; out to sea the sun shone through the clouds on some fishing boats and before us, vivid against the dark, misty blue of distant mountains, were the great scarlet-gold cups of a tulip tree. At dusk, going down in the train, we watched the lights coming out in the town beneath and the moon rising above the clouds. I had never heard the jungle noises so loud; cicadas screamed and whirred, like

Chinese food clappers and electric bells, while all the tree frogs boomed. Penang was so beautiful; every Malayan felt the loss of it as a personal tragedy.

But there was no shadow hanging over it then and our last day there was a success, every minute of it.

It was the Saturday afternoon of the week-end before we went on transfer. We took the car across on the ferry for the last time. As usual it was full of a motley crowd. Predominant were the Straits' born Chinese women. They wore dainty long-waisted white jackets, and floral sarongs of gay charming colours, their faces were heavily powdered and their hair, done high on their heads, was elaborate with gold combs and beads.[1] They bore themselves stiffly and with pride. We inhaled deep breaths of the salty air; watching the busy crowd of sampans and junks under the lee of the island with a faint regret, trying to imprint on our minds the long sweeping lines of its curved back so that we should have it always with us in our visual memories. I can see it now with the typical ochre-pale clouds piled high on the silver horizon.

Starting from George Town, we drove right round the island. Past beaches of white sand with black hump-backed "elephant" rocks and bending palms, little cliffs and Chinese temples, sampans and fishing stakes and *kramat* places. Towards the northern end of the island the road turned inland into the hills, in a seven-mile long pass. At the top of this pass we stopped for a picnic tea, looking down over the floor of the island where areca palms and paddy grew to the open sea—the Indian Ocean—with nothing between us and Africa. We were wildly happy that day.

The road twisted down the pass beyond in a crazy manner. We did not meet any cars, but several little yellow "mosquito" buses which came flying along at a fearful pace, swinging all over the road. They seemed to hunt in couples, which amused us in our cheerful mood. We were trying to find the two famous temples that all the tourists are taken to see in Penang—the Ayer Hitam and the Snake Temple, but we failed to discover them and when it began to get dark we faint-heartedly gave up

[1] The Babas, as they call themselves, are Chinese who have been domiciled in the Crown Colony for several generations—many having quite lost touch with China. They no longer speak Chinese, but their own kind of Malay.

the search, as neither of us relished the idea of meeting the snakes by candle light. So we went to the Runnymede and had a bath in a long home-side bath. I liked the tub and dipper method, but a real wallowing bath was a great treat. The room we had was close to the sea and the waves were breaking almost under the windows. The homeward-bound P. & O. mail-boat, brilliant with lights, was steaming slowly out of the Straits; she looked very beautiful in the tropic dusk and the sight of her subdued us for a short while, but not for long for we were loathe to dramatize ourselves as exiles. There were homely red roses on our table again at dinner, we danced afterwards, and caught the last ferry across to the mainland. I slept most of the way home, but woke up in time to see a string of elephants walking through the night from Parit Buntar fair to Penang. When we got home Caesar was shouting to us in his Siamese voice to hurry up; he held his head on one side like a well-bred terrier and complained how dreadfully late we were.

Before we left, the Macs went on long leave. So the Customs staff gave a *Ronggeng* (Malay dancing show) and dinner in their honour to which we were invited. The dinner was in the Customs Clerks' Club down by the river; the room was elaborately decorated with coloured streamers and baubles—the Malays are childishly fond of gaudy paper flowers. Through the window we could see the lights across the road shining in the black water. I sat between Mac and a young Malay clerk. We each had heaped plates of rice before us. Little dishes of curried chicken, liver and goat, cucumber and pineapple were massed in the middle of the long table. Everyone was expected to dip repeatedly into the communal dishes but we helped ourselves to what we wanted straight away; which must have appeared greedy I realized afterwards, though it was rather more hygienic.

Afterwards everyone made speeches, some in English and some in Malay. One very fat Out Door Officer read a poem and was most amusing and expressive, although I could not understand much of what he said. When Mac had made a speech, we all went down the narrow wooden stairs and ceremoniously drove the hundred yards to an open space by the river front where an *atap* roof had been erected over a sanded floor. The place was decorated with bamboo leaves and hedged round with solid phalanxes of Malays, men only; Tamils, Sikhs and Chinese of both sexes. The four dancing girls, their full lips scarlet, their faces pale powdered masks and their eyes enormous with kohl were already doing the first slow steps of the dance. They each wore long heavy silk jackets fitting to the waist and outlining the hips, over flowered sarongs; gold necklaces over their high stiff collars and gold anklets round their bare ankles. Their black hair was done in a large knot at the back of the head, encircled with heavily scented white flowers, while each wore a single pink flower tucked coquettishly behind one ear. The colours of their clothes were apple green, magenta pink and orange. The scene was like a Gauguin come to life, warm and glowing and Oriental—with the lights and the colour surrounded by green leaves and a sea of faces against the black night.

After a little while some of the Malays got up bashfully to dance in front of the girls. The girls must not be touched, the men can only follow their steps while the monotonous music gets faster and faster working up to a terrific crescendo. Curiously, in spite of the mounting speed there was nothing abandoned about it. Most of the girls danced with a pretence of aloofness and boredom. They were, of course, all professional dancers, hired for the evening as one would hire a cabaret show, and of a low class. Moslem women are naturally very modest and self-effacing and no "respectable" girl would dream of appearing in public in such a way.

One of the girls was a wicked-looking little thing. She never moved a muscle of her cynical powdered face in spite of the increasingly furious tempo of the dance. Another was like a painted doll; the third really seemed to enjoy herself and was so careless of etiquette that she could not resist laughing and giggling behind her fan. The fourth was plump and rather stolid, obviously new to it. Some of the Malays who got up to dance looked splendid. One wore a brown silk jacket and trousers and *kopiah* to match and a beautiful dark red sarong; others were in deep blue with silver thread sarongs or black and pale blue, and one was outstanding in dark green with a rich-coloured plaid sarong. When they wear their best clothes, silk jackets tucked into short sarongs which are wrapped tightly over their slim hips, the Malays are extremely elegant. There is something of the Latin about them; but they often look effeminate and incredibly slight to our Western eyes. It is difficult to believe that the slouching men you see on work days, with loose jackets hanging outside long sarongs over grubby bare legs, are the same as the dashing, self-conscious young bloods of *Ronggeng* and feast days.

The steps of the *Ronggeng* dance are little more than a rhythmic shuffle which becomes more difficult and intricate as the music grows faster. There is some system of "cutting out" the men which gives an appearance of the girls' line weaving through the men's line, each always taking great care not to touch the other. I sketched all I could as we watched and it seemed that hundreds of people peered over my shoulder. In the middle of the noise and dancing two men came to our little group of Europeans with baskets of flowers, garlands of sweet-scented frangipanni, tasselled with great golden daisies and sparkling with tiny artificial flowers of ruby red, emerald, gold and silver. Stuart had known this was going to happen, but had not told me, so that it should come as a rather lovely surprise. They put a garland round my neck and handed me a sweet smelling posy on a silver stick, even the handle of which was decorated with one tiny fragrant temple-flower. I had thought this sort of ceremony took place only in the South Sea Islands, and was the more charmed. All the guests of honour were garlanded.

After this pleasing ceremony some of the Europeans were persuaded to dance. It was amusing to see them, so large and long-legged beside the dapper little Malays. Most of them found it very difficult and floundered about; though Stuart did not do too badly.

We spotted a little girl in the audience, a Bengali child with a small, wistful, brown face and delicate pointed features. We managed to get hold of Mat in the crowd and pointed her out to him so that he could speak to her parents to ask if I could paint her portrait. He did so but after several days of prevaricating the father of the child said "No—he could not allow it," I was most disappointed as she was particularly lovely. This sort of thing was depressing, for so often a forbidding father or an anxious husband stepped in and forbade a sitting, when negotiations seemed to be going well.

In some ways as it had been our first house we were sorry to leave No. 4, Maxwell Road. (The fourth house in the town, not in the road!) The last week was a chaos of packing cases, straw, Chinese workmen and distracted cats; but Ah Seng was splendid, and throughout it all served us appetizing little meals in the half-stripped house. For the last night we retired again to the Rest House, which, after three months in the country, now seemed quite a friendly little place and not nearly so trying as at first.

With the servants' luggage, we discovered we had a hundred and nineteen cases and boxes. The plants looked like a young nursery garden and occupied two railway lorries; we went down to look at them when they were loaded on to a truck at the station, and helped Kassim to water the sunflower plants and precious seedlings there. We left the rest to Ah Seng and Mat who superintended the loading of the boxes on the truck at the station to see that they were not "thrown about." Ah Seng, in a singlet and black shorts, was quite a different person from the quiet white-clad Boy. His fierce, concentrating expression was due to the zeal with which he watched the handling of each article in his care. A good Chinese servant shows a constant and loyal responsibility for his master's property. His "heart must have been beating fast," because his hair stood on end and his shoulder muscles rippled, as he heaved cases and shouted hoarse orders to the coolies. Most Chinese, when they don't smoke opium, have a good physique and he had particularly; he was an anatomical delight. I have seen rickshaw coolies with insteps as high and arched as a ballet dancer's; but some of these coolies are a dreadful spectacle, with wizened sunken chests, their bodies wasted with smoking, their faces prematurely ancient. It's difficult to blame them; the life of a rickshaw coolie is not a fit life for any human being; the strain in that heat is such that they can only work for three weeks out of four and then they lie about for that one week relaxing. I believe I am right in saying that not a single rickshaw coolie missed paying his regular ten cents to the China Relief Fund, however poor he might be.

We went round to the house again on that last evening, to

put Caesar to bed, and found Ah Seng just catching him in the drive. There was a Sikh watchman there to guard the empty house and he met us at the door with a lantern. It was an absurd procession to put a small cat to bed. Stuart and I went first, I carrying Caesar, then came Ah Seng followed by the tall bearded watchman with his lamp. The kitten's sand-box was ready for him in the mosquito room and while the Sikh held the light up for Caesar I poured him into his box and we both solemnly said "good-night" to him. Ah Seng, hardly able to repress his giggles, was wreathed in broad smiles.

"So Caesar and the night-watchman are to sleep in the same room, are they?" I asked Stuart, doubtfully.

"I suppose so. I *do* hope Caesar won't mind the smell," he answered, trying not to laugh.

IV

THE HOUSE ON THE HILL BETWEEN THE JUNGLE AND THE SEA

THE EVENING before we left for Lumut we heard the news of the German occupation of Czechoslovakia. The misery of the shadow of war was a terrible contrast to the sunlight and peace of Malaya, where there was always an atmosphere of cheerful friendliness. So many nationalities, seventeen I believe, lived amicably together. The people were well cared for; there were no destitute, no tramps or beggars; even the very poor had their gay clothes; the sick were encouraged to go to hospitals, the coolie children given free milk each day on the estates. It was a model country. Everyone was learning and being encouraged to learn simple rules for better health. Hospitals, education, agriculture and industry proceeded along carefully organized lines. It was a prosperous, happy place. Right up to December 1941, we felt badly about the war; we felt we were so safe, protected (as we were led to believe) and shut away. We felt we were out of it all while the whole of Europe was in agony, an agony we could only share in our minds and hearts. But our turn was to come.

The cats were put into boxes padded with kapok for the journey; Mat was driving them down in the car with Sareh, Ah Chi and their respective children, Ah Ham and Little Mat. Ah Lam and Ah Seng had already gone by train. We were given a good send off at Parit Buntar station on the mail train. It was the first time I had travelled in an air-conditioned carriage, the "ice-box" as everyone called it. It was delicious after the steamy heat outside. One's skin felt light, dry and cool; everything one touched was cold. It was incongruous to look out in cool comfort on the tropical scenery through the double windows of smoked-glass. It was a change too to be able to stare at the people at every little station instead of being stared at by them because, of course, they could not see in past the smoked glass. It was amusing to see them look through us with unseeing eyes, instead of meeting their usual inquisitive gaze. It was only sixty miles to Ipoh; but it took over two hours even in the mail train. When we alighted from the ice-box the outside atmosphere was suffocating and for the first five minutes we felt as if we were completely swathed in warm damp cotton wool; but it became bearable again surprisingly soon.

Ipoh lies in a great semi-circle of limestone cliffs and was a big tin-mining centre. At the Station Hotel where we lunched, Stuart was greeted with beaming smiles from the Tamil porters and one or two elderly Chinese Boys who remembered him when he had been stationed there for a short while some years before. This sort of thing was always happening; people never forgot him. Once, almost on the top of a mountain a Chinese Boy appeared from a tea plantation and hailed him, grinning amicably, claiming to have waited on him at dinner in some *Tuan's* house in Kuala Lumpur several years ago.

We drove out from Ipoh in a hired car. The sixty-five miles of road seemed very long and hot that first time, through acres of Forest Reserve and dank-smelling jungle, in which, not long after, the chief Game Warden, Shebbeare of Himalayan fame, captured some wild elephant. The country was far from self-supporting, but an effort was being made to encourage the cultivation of rice on a bigger scale and elephants were needed for clearing the densely forested, swampy land. In this particular neighbourhood, near Bruas, a rogue male was wandering and it was necessary to rid the jungle of him before the herd could be dealt with. So a tame female elephant was tethered near the Ipoh Road, and—apparently her charms had the desired effect—the rogue was caught.

There were a few small towns and acre after acre of rubber trees. Two roads led into Lumut village. Exactly half-a-mile from it the road branched, one arm leading round under a rubber estate on a hill by the river and the other, the older road, went through the jungle over a miniature pass, Dickson's Pass. Stuart was most anxious I should see Lumut[1] for the first time from this entrance. So we came into the village, down

[1] Which means moss, and is pronounced Lōōmŏot.

a green valley past the new shining white mosque and a Chinese temple, to the broad estuary, our car dodging ambling ducks and agile turkeys. The sea and Pangkor Island lay out to the west beyond the wide-flung arms of the hills; to the east the land stretched faintly away beyond the spreading waters of the river to distant hills veiled in heat. Opposite the little town, across the water, was the long hump-backed line of a jungle-covered hill, blue in the velvet shadows, gold and green in sunlight, soft like moss under its cloak of dense trees. Against this background stood the big white building of the Customs office and godown with one old cassia tree spreading its shady branches beside it and the little jetty. In front there was a triangular *padang* or playing-field, with the Post Office at one end, where the professional letter-writer sat waiting for business. Chinese with portable kitchens carried on a roaring trade and men with barrows sold sliced fruit, pineapple and pink water melon, and bright virulent-looking drinks. During the day the buses sheltered from the heat of the sun under the great trees beside the building, while the drivers drowsed inside their vehicles, waiting for the time to leave for Ipoh. This was the very heart and centre of the town. Beside the *padang*, opposite the Customs office was a short street of shops, Chinese, Indian and Malay. Beyond the office was a row of very tall, elegant casuarina trees, beneath which lay the short grass sward of the river bank; tiny waves lapped the stony foreshore; the placid waters led the eye away to the west and the far horizon of the open sea beyond. It was very beautiful.

We went first to the Rest House, beyond the casuarina trees. It was a long low black and white bungalow, with a sandy garden full of flowers and a lawn leading down to the water, which was planted with temple trees and pink oleanders always in flower. The scent was delicious like almonds and honey, heady and sweet. Behind the village the hills rose in soft, tree-covered peaks; two of the lower spurs had been cleared of jungle, and houses for the four Government officials built there, high up, with fine views of the estuary. On one was the District Officer's house, an old wooden building which years before had been transported bodily from Pangkor Island, where the Government Offices had originally been situated. The second hill was "ours." The Customs officer's house was the top one, with the Policeman's just below and beyond his, the Engineer's. Our hill was two feet higher than the District Officer's hill, therefore Oriental ideas of "departmental dignity" required our house to be built *just* below the crest. It was a pity: our view would have been even more superb a few feet higher. This siting must have dated from the days when the Dindings had belonged to the Straits Settlements; only a few years ago the Dindings had been handed back to Perak and one of the things done to commemorate this was the building of a very modern Customs office and godown of white ferro-concrete. Here was Stuart's new job and he was in sole charge. The District Officer was a Malay, and the Forest Officer who lived by the estuary was an Eurasian; the police officer and the Engineer were Europeans; both were unmarried, so I was the only European woman in Lumut.

We stayed in the Rest House for two nights while the people from whom we were taking over moved out. They were very loath to leave, having fallen in love with the place, just as Stuart had done when he had been stationed there for a few months some years before. We certainly had the most amazing luck in getting the very appointment we wanted so much.

On the first evening we walked up to the house which was to be ours, the house on the hill between the jungle and the sea. It was some three hundred feet above the town and as we approached it we looked up to the terrace of the garden above. It was a blaze of bougainvillaea and frangipanni. Behind the mass of flowering shrubs the house stood four-square. It was cream-washed, with wide eaves, red tiles and black and white *chicks*[1] in the verandahs. It had a charmingly compact and pleasant aspect, set as it was on its little terrace cut from the jungly hillside. The majestic trees dwarfed it, but did not oppress or hem it in. It was a lovable house. Far more solid than the one at Parit Buntar, as it was built entirely of stone to withstand the gales from the west, the "Sumatras," blowing off the sea from across the Straits.

The plants had arrived safely and our predecessors' gardener, a Tamil boy, Kandasami by name, had watered them all. We had been most anxiously asked to take over the gardener with the house. He certainly was an attractive lad and I noted him

[1] Blinds made of slatted bamboo.

at once as a paintable subject; but we were warned that he had a weakness for toddy, and this we discovered for ourselves soon enough. Some of the English sunflowers had all but burst into flower in the train; there seemed to be no damage and even the tender carnation shoots had survived the journey. The cats were let out and raced about gleefully. They were thrilled at having real sand from the sea-shore for their scratch-pans. The servants were all smiles and everyone seemed delighted with the change, except our poor predecessors who were thoroughly miserable at leaving, and I was commissioned to do a sketch of the view from the verandah-room upstairs. It certainly was magnificent, looking out over the tops of gold Pride of Barbadoes, white temple flower trees and great clumps of bougainvillaea to the shimmering turquoise of the estuary, to the distant blue hills beyond and to the mountains far inland. I did that sketch very badly: the scene was too splendidly vast. Not until I had absorbed something of its beauty, which became a never-failing source of delight in our everyday life, could I even attempt one of its transient moods.

The house was small and rather like a cottage. Its short twisting staircase, with the round window half way up, where I always had a bowl of flowers, led directly into the verandah-room which had fourteen large windows round three sides. Two bedrooms with swinging half-doors led off this room, each with its little bathroom at the back, and there was a miniature verandah between them. From our bedroom windows we could see the jungle rising straight up behind the house to the 1,000-foot hill-top, golden in the glorious sunlight. From the edge of our small semi-circular garden, the hill fell steeply away and we looked down on the tops of rubber trees in the valley hiding a *kampong* three hundred feet below, where sometimes at night fires of coconut husks glowed under the trees. Occasionally blood-curdling shrieks rose up from the Tamils who lived there, as they quarrelled harmlessly in their cups. Generally all was peaceful with nothing more than the sound of quacking ducks, a barking dog or two and perhaps the distant thud of festal drums or the crackle of Chinese fire-crackers.

Sareh, with Little Mat and the solemn child Ah Ham, wandered down to the shore at once. Mat was delighted to be near the sea again; he had once been a fisherman in his chequered career, before becoming a 'bus driver and eventually a syce or chauffeur. He seemed so pleased with Lumut that for days his mouth was never shut, he grinned continuously with a flash of white teeth in his brown face. Ah Seng, too, was wreathed in smiles; he had hated Parit Buntar. Even poor old Kuki (Ah Lam) never stopped grinning, with his gold tooth to the fore, and quiet little Ah Chi too seemed to come to life. She looked less timid and smiled a good deal more. Like me, she was learning Malay. When she first came she spoke only Chinese and everything had to be told through Ah Seng as interpreter, but she soon knew enough Malay and became very efficient and was most amazingly hard-working.

As we were in the midst of sorting our things and trying to see that our predecessors' boxes, which were waiting to be taken away, were not carried up by mistake for ours, Ah Seng came in to say anxiously: "*Kuching*-Anthony is breaking up all the china in the Ohceepeedee's house, *Tuan*! The Boy has just come up to complain!" (O.C.P.D. stood for Officer in Charge of the Police District, invariably spoken of thus as if all one word I think it beat all the other initials in this country of initials.) Apparently "Cat-Anthony" had gone down to visit the policeman's cat immediately after arrival and was dashing about in the pantry smashing the best china. Ah Seng was sent down to retrieve Anthony; but it was a bad start and the servants of the two houses never really became friendly in consequence!

There was a tea-party given by the Customs men in the godown, as a send-off to our predecessors and to welcome us. There we met the District Officer, a genial Malay, who was a distant relation of the Sultan, and the Government doctor, a quiet, charming Indian, named Menun, whom we grew to like very much, although we never got to know him well because of his intense shyness and reserve: he shared our passion for Siamese cats. His hospital, on a hill to the west of the town, high up above the estuary, was like a small garden village; but he was always zealously hankering after more and more improvements. He was very modern, very keen on his work and an excellent doctor.

After the tea-party we escaped to the house, but it seemed a long time before we had it all to ourselves and could explore it in peace and arrange our belongings. All the books had to be re-varnished as the cockroaches were particularly rampant. Downstairs there was only one big long room, paved with little red tiles. This was dining-room and hall combined; the problem was what to do for a studio. We eventually solved this by screening off the west end of the room. We were thrilled to discover one of the windows had glass in it like an English house. Most windows only had shutters. This window, set at an angle to the front door, looked out on to an oblong tiled space and wide steps leading down to the drive. Here we put the special flowers that needed coddling. The verandah-room above, supported by four pillars—like a big porch—straddled the width of the drive, affording protection from both sun and lashing rain. The cool sea-born breeze at noon each day was delicious. Caesar would go delirious with joy when it got up. He pranced, capered and turned innumerable somersaults for sheer delight. It was much better than any electric fan. We could not have used a fan had we had one as the power was only on, we understood, from six o'clock in the evening until six-thirty in the morning. This was hard on Stuart, with his passion for his electric shaver, as it meant he had to leap out of bed very early each morning to get shaved in time. This went on until one day we overslept, and, coming out on to the verandah-room for our orange juice we looked down the hill and saw a lamp glowing palely in the sunlight. The power was still on! Apparently it was not after all turned off till seven a.m., which was a relief for Stuart.

The sun rose out of the jungle behind the D.O.'s house; between our houses lay a wild little golf course in the valley. The early mornings were superb. The sun gilded the trees and gradually the whole shoulder of the hill was bathed in gold. Some sea hawks had a great nest in one distant jungle giant and their wings were white in the morning sunlight.

The night we moved in there was a storm. Everything was soaked in the sitting-room, even the sofa (a real one and a relic from Straits Settlements days). The rain lashed in through the slats above the windows and through every crack in the shutters; but it was worth it for when we woke up the next morning, the atmosphere was washed clean and we beheld peak after peak of clear blue mountains which we had never seen before, now made visible, up the river to the east. They were the Taiping and Ipoh mountains, fifty miles away; exquisite shapes in the fresh gold light of dawn, shapes which every day became more perfect as one's eyes grew accustomed to their beauty and learned to look for the changes of light and colour that the weather and passing hours brought to their contours. Each morning those mountains were a joy to look upon—the refreshing first event of each day.

Everything had to go out in the hot sun to dry after the rain, including the unique sofa. I had already heard a lot about this sofa; it was a part of the furniture supplied by Government, but unlike most Government sofas, it was not of cane; but the real thing, with springs, of a sort; it was soft and much envied! It was, however, very old and on its last legs, but we could not have had it repaired for that was beyond the powers that be, and we should only have received an unmercifully hard cane one in exchange. Government supplied heavy furniture: beds, tables, wardrobes, chairs, and so on. This lot was particularly nice, having once belonged to the Straits Settlements which on the whole supplied better furniture than the Federated Malay States. We had to get our own mattresses, cushions, easy chairs, carpets, bookcases and all that sort of thing. We had brought a little furniture out from home, and Stuart had some nice things already there.

After the rain the Tiauk birds or rain-birds were calling their strange cry, a throaty "Talk! Talk! Tiauk!" which became so familiar. They were big black birds rather like crows.

The garden seemed full of birds and the house too; not sparrows here as in Parit Buntar; but martins. There were always three nests above the verandah in which were constant relays of babies—and the six parent birds swooped shrieking under the porch to encourage the young to fly. Sometimes, if one were standing on the verandah, it was quite alarming as they dived towards the nests just above one's head. There was always a great deal of chattering and excitement but we were very fond of them. Occasionally Caesar would suck an egg that had fallen from the nest, but neither he nor Anthony caught any of the birds; although they adored chasing the little house lizard, the *chichak* as the Malays call him from his shrill cry.

Sometimes if one of these fell with a plop off the ceiling Caesar tore after it, causing it to shed its tail in its fright, then the tail would jump about intriguingly on the floor, throwing Caesar into ecstasies of excitement. The *chichak* readily grows a new tail and I have seen a freak one with three tails: what a thrill for a cat!

In the garden a Straits robin sang in the oleander bushes, a dapper black and white bird with a voice rather like an English robin—hence his name. Vivid green and yellow birds flashed in and out of the jungle across the strip of grass between the garden and that wall of foliage; streaks of prismatic colour against the dense green background.

After a few days we noticed a little restlessness among the servants and Ah Seng complained he had heard in the town that the house was haunted: "A *tuan* who lived here a *long* time ago saw people no one else could see. He used to throw glasses at these people. A lot of glasses were broken, but no one ever saw what it was he hit. What was it, *Tuan*?"

Stuart calmed him down and tried to explain as best he could in Malay—without maligning anyone's reputation. Anyhow Ah Seng seemed satisfied that the house was not really haunted, but I don't know if he understood about such things as D.T.s. . . . The next trouble was they all began to be afraid of the jungle. At six-thirty every night the sound of the cicadas opened up like a barrage at zero hour and the jungle, which had drowsed in sunlight all day, came to life with the shrill din of myriads of insects. And not only that; it made itself felt as a dark looming mass over the house. I knew exactly what the servants meant when they said they were afraid. I had felt it myself; the jungle was so near. But it was worse for them, for their quarters were separated from the house by a covered way and lay even nearer to it. It rose almost directly behind their rooms. As Ah Seng said: "Beside the noises it is so high you cannot see it all at once." Stuart explained: "The noises are only little beasts rubbing their legs together." The nearest he could get in Malay to describing how cicadas make their ceaseless whirring. Ah Seng was half amused about their fears and I do not think they minded very much; anyhow they soon got over it.

Caesar was scared of the jungle too. Whenever we went on a

From an oil painting by the author

Yahya—Selangor Malay

A brand new Chinese junk off Pangkor Island

tour of inspection round the garden and came near to it, his tail fluffed out like a flue-brush and every hair on his spine stood up on end. He gazed in an awestruck way and sniffed the air. Perhaps he smelt monkeys; the trees were alive with them at times, or perhaps he smelt tiger.

At first we were all a little conscious of the proximity of the jungle. I know I was, for I dreamed of it. In my dream the dense wall of trees had stepped closer to the house. Tiger, rhino and other alarming big game loomed at the verandah edge. The nightmare quality was terrifying and I woke in a sweat. When I plucked up the courage to look out, the jungle wall had, of course, receded and looked peaceful enough in the moonlight. At the threshold of the jungle stood a particularly graceful giant tree. Rough wooden steps were nailed at wide intervals on its pale, slim trunk. These were used by men who climbed up to get the green paroquets said to nest there.

One week-end the Sunday morning peace was rudely disturbed by six Tamils rushing through the garden chattering excitedly, taking a short cut, unasked, to the paroquet tree. One of them, wearing only a loin cloth, climbed that jungle monster with the agility of a monkey: he did not get any paraquets and we never saw any ourselves; but huge sea hawks and occasionally hornbills as big as turkeys perched there.

We became even keener on gardening at Lumut. The garden was small and much more manageable. We worked in it nearly every evening and planted out our cuttings from Parit Buntar. The sunflowers grew four inches each day. Such was the speed of growth in that intense humidity that one despaired if seeds did not come up within three days of sowing. It was very different from the slow, sure processes of English gardening. The garden was full of frangipanni trees (the temple flowers), great bushes of bougainvillaea, oleander and alamander and all kinds of flowering trees, including the sweet flat blossoms of the camelia and the scarlet-leaved poinsettia.

One of the Customs men presented us with blue hydrangeas in pots and some diminutive dwarf red roses. There were already pompom roses, and we grew old-fashioned red and white and yellow roses from cuttings in big tubs, with surprising success.

One evening we watched some white lilies opening. I do not know their correct name, but people called them spider lilies from their rather thin leggy appearance, I suppose, though they were much too lovely to bear such a name. There were nine separate flowers on each calyx, the long pointed blooms opened as we watched, just before sunset. As soon as the golden, pollen-laden stamens swung free of the white petals, numerous minute bees came to hang on every hinged stamen. In five minutes the glory of the flower was gone, but its unfolding and consummation were an exquisite sight. Curiously enough, those same miniature bees were very fond of oil paint and often came to sit on my pictures when they were wet, especially on yellow and white pigments, and occasionally I had to rig up a mosquito netting protection over the easel as their minute footmarks ruined the surface of the paint.

At dusk, sometimes a humming-bird moth hovered over the flowers under the porch, feeding on their honey with its long uncurled proboscis, incredibly delicate among the chalk-blue clouds of fragile plumbago blossoms.

Kandasami was very willing and leapt about at one's call, like a dusky, long-legged sprite, bringing water for the newly-planted flowers. He was extremely handsome with great dark eyes, full of the age-old suffering and mysterious tragedy of his race. Even young Dravidian eyes look old: Kandasami was only seventeen. I painted him a great many times, although he smelt rank of coconut oil and other things; but he sat so well, never seeming to tire, that he was worth his drawbacks. Malaria was in his blood and he was constantly ill. He indulged in violent drinking bouts on which he used up all his money and was consequently always in debt. We used to pay his wages in small sums at a time to circumvent this, but he was rather a hopeless case.

After gardening we often went down to the estuary, sometimes having a shandy at the little club on the way. Those Lumut sunsets were never to be forgotten and they flame now in my memory, framed as they were in the "golden gates" of the two western headlands. There was a white seat under a cassia tree on the bank and I remember the first time we sat there while the colours rioted madly, changing every second in breath-taking glory, from rose to blood, to gold and bronze and copper-green. . . . We could not speak, it was far too beautiful. When the sun had gone and the colour died away, the water lay, a sheet of translucent green, at our feet, the silhouettes of *koleks* slid by as they came in silently from the day's fishing, and the pink shred of a new moon hung over the estuary. Tired and happy we trudged home up the hill. There was a honey-fragrant breeze blowing off the jungle. Scorpio sprawled across the heavens above the house and the Southern Cross hung low over the hill.

That night we were awakened by strange sounds, Caesar was having a rough and tumble with some unknown creature in the folds of the mosquito net. A bit nervous still from my recent nightmare I hoped it was not a snake. We could not see it properly, but presently it began to make a most odd noise, which can only be described as "Mugwump! Mugwump!" It went round and round our room and out on to the verandah, Caesar following nose to tail, with Stuart after them both. The procession finally disappeared into the bathroom where the small "mugwump" vanished completely, presumably down the water-runaway. From what we could see of it, it had a long tail and small ears laid back; we concluded it was a baby civet cat, as on the previous occasion when our sleep had been disturbed by weird noises. Caesar was wildly excited and took some time to settle down.

He slept in the most abandoned attitudes during the heat of the day, on his back with his legs flung out and the tip of his tiny pink tongue protruding from his lips. Occasionally he would open one blue eye and gaze at us, and Stuart swore he grinned. I expect he did. He spent a lot of his time hunting cockroaches and often pulled the books out of the bookcases to get at the unpleasant creatures. This was very helpful as they ruined the bindings. Once, when he was quite small, I found him behind the books fast asleep, exhausted evidently by the ardour of the chase.

A travelling salesman, a vendor of silks, embroidery and china, came one day; a cheerful rogue of a fellow from Sumatra. Stuart had met him before and he knew several of our friends. He hadn't anything we wanted, but promised to try and get some special green bowls. He came into the house to undo his great linen-wrapped packages and was full of admiration when he saw some Lalique bowls we had. He looked at my canvases and we were amused at his remarks: "*Mem* will make a great deal of money, and so *Tuan* will be rich too!" He gazed a long time at the pictures. . . . "*Mem* does not remain silent," he said. This was his original way of saying that I tried to express myself in paint. . . .

V

THE LOTUS EATERS OF LUMUT

STUART'S OFFICE was a large white oblong building with two stepped-up tiers of flat roof which projected at the ends like great eaves as a protection from the fierce sun. Below was the godown and upstairs were the offices of the Asiatic clerks, mainly Chinese, and Stuart's own room which had french windows opening out on to the flat roof close to the spreading branches of the old cassia tree by the wharf.

All day long the water taxis chugged to and fro, nosing in to shore on the white sand below the office. The sound of their outboard motors was in my ears all the morning as I worked up in the house on the hill a quarter of a mile away. Stuart in his office and I from my windows could see them crossing the estuary with arrowy ripples fanning out astern in the glassy blue water beneath the hill. At sunset we could hear the voice of the muezzin from the mosque turret calling the faithful to prayer.

Twice a week the Straits steamship from Penang put in and tied up at the jetty. A comic tub of a launch also called regularly, on its way north from Telok Anson, and there was an up-river boat; incredibly ramshackle, always piled with bicycles and bundles; which acted as a water 'bus for people living in the *ulu* (up-river lands). There were often junks anchored out in the stream; they brought charcoal and wood from Penang and shipped copra. Big sampans too from estates in the *ulu* brought down cases and bales of rubber to be loaded into the Straits steamship. From Pangkor came the ice early every morning and the previous night's catch of fish which was unloaded in big baskets on the sand and carried to waiting lorries which took them up to Ipoh to be put on board the midday mail train. The Pangkor fishery was a big local industry.

The Government launches were moored a little way upstream. The Police launch with pleasing lines, the District Officer's, rather a tub, the two Customs launches, the *Rimau* (or Tiger) and the *Kerita* (or Octopus). The *Rimau* was a sixty-foot boat with a crew of six Malays. She was for sea-going patrols. The *Kerita* was a small, rather decrepit launch only used for local work, or when the *Rimau* had to go south for refitting at Port Swettenham.

The Out-Door-Officers (O.D.O.'s—one cannot escape the initial habit) were mainly Malays with a few Chinese. One was on duty day and night in the charge room next to the godown. The rest of their time was spent overseeing the unloading of ships and on preventive work.

There was a good deal of this preventive work. Lumut had a hot spot which lay in the triangle formed by the sea road and Dickson's Road. As its incongruous apex it had the local Chinese temple. And, forming a facade to the river, was the schoolhouse with its brilliant cannas. Between this schoolhouse and a row of shops and billiard saloons, which formed the other arm of the triangle, lay a rabble of wooden shacks and hovels in loose, dirty grey sand under the palm trees. The most notorious of these houses was not only a brothel, but the favourite haunt of unlicensed opium smokers. When raided, its habitués retreated upstairs and sometimes succeeded, if not too far gone, in escaping precipitously through a hatch, aided, of course, by the little Chinese harlots.

In this area among the scum of the town there lived a perfectly delightful soul, the Chinese carpenter. One waded through loose sand to reach his shack, where, on a miniature verandah, surrounded by numerous offspring, he miraculously made almost anything you could ask for in the carpentry line. I say miraculously because he had no bench, and no elbow room either, but from a small sketch in a catalogue, he could make intricate bits of furniture by "looking slowly" at the picture. He made me among other things an elaborate folding drawing table, and for Stuart a large carpenter's bench. This filled his entire verandah and it was impossible to imagine how he worked. He was always smiling and cheerful, a thick-set, nut-brown person in blue coolie clothes; for in spite of his skilled craftsmanship he spent most of his time unloading the ships. We hated seeing him do this; it seemed a waste of his talents, for he was undoubtedly an artist at his job. His sturdy legs were laced with the worst varicose veins I have ever seen, knotted and blue-black, but he never seemed to complain. His tough brown face was wreathed in smiles and he was exquisitely polite. When he came up to the house to bring his finished work, picture frames or whatever he had been making, he put on his best clothes, short black silk trousers and a white jacket, stiff and spotlessly clean. I saw him once striding up the hill carrying our new tea-table on his head. I remember him measuring my frames one day when an enormous hairy coco-nut spider appeared from behind a picture. I had become fairly brave about the numerous insects by then; but I never over-came my loathing of spiders and I let out a small yell. The old carpenter responded gallantly; one neat flick of forefinger against thumb and the spider was no more.

Stuart was busy clearing up this area; and as well as that there were *samsu* raids on Pangkor and up river, and all the usual cases. He came back from Pangkor covered in black mud one day having climbed up into the hills through the jungle to find an illicit still, a big one cunningly hidden in a cave. *Samsu* is made by the Chinese of fermented rice mash, and it was illegal to distil it privately. Stuart was generally busy before the big festivals and Chinese holidays when all the hidden stills would get to work. When he went out on raids at night he in-sisted that I kept a large elephant bell within reach, so that I could make the servants hear if I was scared or needed them. There were no electric bells in the house and normally when we wanted the servants we had to shout; a very uncivilized method, and one which might not be effective when they were asleep. But that elephant bell would have awakened the dead, and I must say I liked to feel I had it by me. Caesar slept at my feet for company.

The district was fairly big, which sometimes entailed driving a hundred miles to get to a case across the river; because, if the car was likely to be needed on the other side, it was useless to cross by boat and there was no car ferry. So Stuart had to make a wide détour, and having carried out the raid or inspection, he would leave Mat to drive back and come home himself by boat across the river. We often marvelled at Mat. He never grumbled at the long hours, and, after driving more than half the night, he would be up early and smiling next morning. The car was always bright and clean when he brought it to the door and he himself neat in white jacket and trousers with his black velvet *kopiah* set jauntily on one side of his curly head.

When the raids were in the day time, up in the *ulu* or on Pangkor Island, I used to go too, and of course remained well out of the way on board the *Rimau.* Just before we reached the place to be raided the launch would stop; Stuart and some of his men went ashore in the dinghy, as quietly as possible, and climbed up the bank among the bushes. Then they had to run. It was difficult to surprise a *kampong*; news of their approach went swiftly: small boys careered before them on bicycles, and very often the guilty people shot off into the jungle. Sometimes the offenders managed to lose themselves, but more often they were caught before they reached the trees or else they floundered in the swamps and were brought to bay. However, if they were not surprised they frequently had time to destroy the evidence, the *chandu* (prepared opium), the marked dollar note, or the illicit still.

The first trip into the *ulu* was to me an interesting occasion. It took two hours to sail up the great estuary. At every bend were fresh views of the rocky, jungle-covered hillsides on one hand and miles of mangrove swamps on the other; beyond lay range after range of cobalt blue hills. The stream grew narrower and on the sandy banks were infrequent and extremely primitive dwellings; or an occasional charcoal burner's dump with cone-shaped kilns. Some little time after Stuart and the men had gone ashore the *Rimau* weighed anchor and proceeded to the village, a forlorn dead-end sort of place built on a reclaimed swamp. A few ancient steamboats were moored there, their latrines, mere iron rings, projecting astern. Crowds of children came out to gape and I was, as usual, the lonely cynosure of many bright black eyes; mainly young and belonging to little Chinese girls. There was generally not much to choose between the tireless inquisitiveness of the small girls or the small boys: all would stare fixedly for an hour or more.

The water was evil-smelling and green; the mangrove trees, spidery on their strange roots, were a livid yellow against the angry, steel-blue sky of an oncoming storm. Thunder grumbled around, and in the still sunny sky lightning flashed. The water was thick with jelly-fish: not at all a savoury spot. After a little time Stuart came on board with the O.D.O.'s and a Chinese woman they had arrested, followed by a grinning crowd of Malay and Chinese youths. The woman carried her things for the night done up in a newspaper parcel and had kept the men waiting while she insisted on changing into her best clothes and titivating for her visit to the Lumut jail. She had unlawfully concealed sixty tubes of *chandu* (prepared opium) in her house; but had been warned of the raid and had thrown them all away; just by luck, however, Stuart had found one or two.

The woman became very excited; everyone talked at once in three different languages. She proceeded to invent an impossible story at which Stuart laughed, so then she attempted another one, saying she *herself* needed all the sixty tubes of *chandu*—and became hopelessly involved. She was reputed to be the richest woman between Lumut and Taiping. She had gold-capped teeth and gold bangles on her wrists and wore a white suit edged with black, the trim high-necked jacket fastened with pink embroidered flowers.

In one house Stuart raided in the *ulu* he found a Chinese woodcutter and his wife, her lover and swarms of children all living amicably together. Apparently the lover worked for the husband as a labourer and the wife was thrown in as part of his salary—a strange arrangement, but economical. . . .

While Stuart was out working I was busy at home painting Kandasami and Sareh, writing, and playing with Caesar who loved to help me write by sitting firmly on my papers, and watching and sometimes grabbing my moving pen. The mornings were long and full. It was a deliciously peaceful life. . . .

The food came from the Cold Storage in Sitiawan seven miles away; and almost everything else as well, from lipstick to writing materials. But after a while Ah Seng found a Chinese shop in the village, run by a family of delightful smiling people, Eng Wah. With an eye to business—for he probably picked up a little commission on the deal—Ah Seng said that Eng Wah would order any tinned food we wanted much cheaper than the Cold Storage. This proved true; they stocked everything we ordered and it was odd to see bottles of Barsac, champagne and whisky, tins of MacVita, Cadbury's drinking chocolate,

Heinz' soups and English canned vegetables looking bright and new among the rather dubious Chinese foods, the dried delicacies, the roots, the fish and fungus, the cakes of sticky figs, and baskets of old eggs and ground-nuts, tinned lichees, cheap brandy, tooth-paste and ear-cleaners, in the musky, dusty odour typical of a Chinese village shop. Our English foods became quite popular and Eng Wah did a roaring trade. It was great fun shopping there, just helping oneself to all one wanted, being trusted implicitly while we kept our own account in a large ledger, and one of the smiling brothers occasionally added up the amount, if he felt so disposed, on his black wooden calculating machine, the *abacus*.

About three weeks after we were settled, Stuart had to go back to Parit Buntar to give evidence in a court case. So we called to see the man now in our old house. He was out; but we saw the garden. It was sad. The zinnias we had planted were struggling valiantly in beds already choked with weeds, and a new bed Stuart had dug with much vigour was ruined by the large tyre mark of a carelessly turned car. We felt depressed. Chaos comes so soon to a neglected garden in a country like Malaya, where weeds and coarse grass grow at a pace that is utterly overwhelming.

When we got back, we worked harder than ever in the new garden to forget the chaos of the old one. The pink double balsams, planted on arrival, were already weighed down with blossom; small buttony flowers like fat rose-buds. Occasionally white ants attacked flower roots; we often laboured to save the flowers by transplanting and then tried to eradicate the hateful, sluggish ants. It was necessary to find the queen first, a relatively enormous creature, considered a delicacy, I believe, by Tamils and Chinese. At regular intervals the Government White Ant Man would appear in the garden with pot and brush to smear all wooden steps and posts with ant poison. He was a comic little old Malay with a dilapidated *kopiah* and a friendly mien.

The Customs was barely half-a-mile away. So I never felt lonely. Occasionally Stuart would come back to the house to fetch something he needed—a coat and tie perhaps if he had to prosecute in a court case—he never wore more than white shirt and shorts at the office. Or sometimes Mat would come with the mail. When he brought my letters into the house he would leave his shoes at the door, Malay fashion, and tiptoe shyly into the hall as if he was polluting the very tiles he walked on. But this air of self-effacement was only for inside the house, outside in his own domain he was buoyant and natural. Sometimes we took him fishing in the estuary. There we would tie up to one of the sea-plane buoys often with a strong ebb running. It was beautiful there in the cool of the day. Great galleon clouds shadowed the mountains in the east and the water was burnished gold. But we never caught much, except talking-fish which shrieked their protests in no uncertain accents and blew out their chests like tennis balls—revolting fish which we threw back hastily before they exploded; Mat sat up in the bows chuckling. The *koleks* came in from the sea as the sun flamed in the west and the cicadas in the hillside started to sing. We went back to the jetty then; at that hour most of the Chinese, freshly bathed and in clean light clothes, were out playing with their babies on the *padang*, while their older sons were busy flying kites; the Indians lounged under the casuarina trees by the water looking at the changing colours in the west; the Malays had already returned to their *kampongs* under the palms and were lighting little oil lamps inside the fragile *atap* shells of their houses on stilts.

VI

DREAM OF A SOUTH SEA ISLAND

THIS PARADISE was disturbed for us at last by outside influences —callers. Actually we were very glad to get to know a few people: the callers were planters who lived from seven to fifteen miles away along the Ipoh road. There were not many Europeans in the district and they were widely scattered.

We also had disturbances in the household. Ah Seng suddenly became very unhappy about the Japanese war. His home land, Hainan Island, had been invaded and he was convinced his wife and child must be dead or starving. He wanted to learn to drive a car so as to be able to help against the Japs in China or to drive a lorry on the Burma Road. We, of course, told him he was free to do whatever he liked. But he hung around for some time getting more and more restless. It was rare now that his eyes disappeared in the creases of his crinkly smiles; instead his brow grew blacker and he became sunk in gloom.

The news from Europe too was depressing; the great clouds of war seemed to be gathering and spreading fast. I suppose no earthly paradise can last for ever, but we still had glorious days in wild unspoilt places where it was impossible to feel oppressed for long.

One of these places was a long sandy shore called Telok Muroh on the coast opposite Pangkor Island. Built on an elephantine rock among tall palms was a small Chinese temple. The first time we walked there from Lumut across a narrow isthmus, but it was quicker by car along a rough track; the tide was flooding over the white beaches of Telok Muroh and lapping the great rock. We climbed the twisting steps and stood on the terrace before the temple. Green and red dragons sprawled on big lanterns hung in the doorway, and the dark interior of the temple seemed entirely filled with a large shrine that glittered with greens and reds and the gold of brass; coloured streamers with Chinese lucky sayings hung thickly from the ceiling; the rest was lost in shadows. The old priest came out of an inner room to greet us. He was very small and wizened; but smiling. Iron-grey hair grew sparsely from the crown of his head; he wore dark green trousers and a thick serge jacket of grey with wide sleeves. He was very polite, fetched stools for us to sit on and offered us cigarettes, and, on one occasion, even insisted on giving us some very sticky moon cakes.

"I have lived here thirty years, *Tuan*," he said as we admired the view looking westward over the Strait to Pangkor, "and before that I was seventeen years in Penang. I am a *very* old man—I am seventy-nine!"

Later we went to paint there very often. It was a gloomy, mysterious place at sundown, with the fires licking round the thick roots of the coconut palms, casting weird shadows on the sands; the grey priest would come silent-footed out of his dark temple, and miserable thin cats prowled about looking for grains of rice. Once I turned from my sketch to see below the rock two fat Tamil women on the white sand, with their smooth chocolate-brown backs bare, and flowing magenta saris in swathes about their ample lines, their loose black hair was jet against the white sand: another perfect Gauguin. I longed to try and paint them as they were, but the light was fading fast and we had to get back along the tortuous sandy track. When we brought the car there it was sometimes a matter of digging it out of the sand and putting palm leaves under the tyres, and I shall never forget the crazily unsteady bridges at the bottom of each dip, the tyres slipping on the sand and the awkward right-angled approaches.

It had been one of those stifling hot days: so hot that we had taken turns to sit in the Shanghai jar to cool off in the deliciously cold water. Feeling restless and suffocated we went down to the estuary in search of a breath of air. The sky was almost purple and the water a deep viridian. Suddenly a tearing wind sprang up, whirling the dust on the dry road into mad spirals like small tornadoes. In a few seconds the water was whipped into white waves. We got out of the car to look and were nearly blinded by the dust. Stuart tore off to get the Customs keys from the charge room and we went up to his office to shelter and watch the storm. A very battered old junk lay at anchor in midstream. She had come in that afternoon from China, with refugees on board, thirty-eight men, women and children escaping from the Japanese. They had braved the changing of the monsoons and the buffeting of the China seas and reached Pangkor that day with no food or water left. They had no passports. So according to the law they had to be arrested and fined, which seemed only too miserable a welcome after all they had been through. Eventually, however, the Protector of Chinese cancelled the fine and they were allowed to take their junk down to Singapore to settle there.

As we watched, some of the men were being brought ashore in the police launch, a pathetic procession of filthy, ragged people. What a reception!

The wind was blowing madly from the west. Five or six of the clumsy river taxis tied up to the right of the godown broke their moorings and came rocking and crashing towards the jetty where the waves were now breaking to the top. One by one they drifted by; it was only about a hundred yards or less; in each was a Chinese boatman trying desperately to start his outboard engine single-handed before the boats piled up on each other against the jetty. It was chaos. The men took it cheerfully and some succeeded in getting back and tying up once more, but their ropes parted each time under the strain. They repeated this performance over and over again with Chinese persistence. Then the rain came in a great cloudburst; the water was wild, the whole scene a dark green-grey and the waves thick with tossing boats and little brown men up to their armpits in water struggling to hold their boats off the quay, as men might struggle with frantic horses. It was a grand primitive sight: men battling with the wind and the sea, leaning back against the waves, arms raised out of the water, great brown rippling deltoids, and forearms knotted like trees. They stayed in the water like that for a long time valiantly; they performed all sorts of marvellous feats, optimistically hurling the anchors ashore and then racing, half swimming, through the water and up the steps to catch them before they slipped back into the greedy waves. No one went to help, although there was a chattering crowd of Indians and Malays sheltering under the godown eaves. But the Chinese seemed quite philosophical and were laughing and shouting all the time, yelling to each other in their terse click-clacking syllables. One elderly man had just got out of the river to grab his rope when his trousers, which were absolutely water-logged, began to descend. There were roars of laughter from the crowd and another boatman went to his assistance.

Suddenly the lightning seemed to run right through the office; I thought the whole building was coming down on top of us and ducked my head; but it was only a tremendous clap of thunder. The rain abated a little and we went outside. The car was soaking. Everybody had obviously left their jobs and run. Road-sweepers' boxes, and huge baskets and loads were left lying about everywhere in the deserted roads. The drains were tearing rivers.

There was a small Customs station on Pangkor Island and a toddy shop, both of which had to be inspected regularly, so with raids and inspections to be done Stuart quite frequently went across there. When he had finished his work I used sometimes to join him ashore and we walked or bathed.

The island is about five miles long and not much more than a mile broad, lying a little to the south of the river mouth and just under an hour out from Lumut in the *Rimau*, roughly four miles. There were always junks from Singapore and Penang anchored in the narrow straits between the island and Telok Muroh where the little Chinese temple was. The village of Pangkor consisted mainly of Chinese huts built half on the shore and half on stakes and rickety wooden quays, where the fish were dried; extremely picturesque, but most unsound. Perched airily above the water at the end of each crazy jetty were little *jamban* houses, like Heath Robinson drawings. The great nets of madder brown, rusty red and black were hoisted up to dry on masts erected on the quays. The dye used for these nets, made from the reddish bark of the mangrove, faded to the most delicious colours, indescribably rich. Even the black freshly-dyed ones seemed to glow with a ruddy warmth in their voluminous folds. Hoisted at different heights in the sun against the white clouds and blue sky they made a picture of graceful flowing lines that lives in the imagination. It was a noisy, busy place, reeking in the hot sun. The Chinese fishermen prepared for the night's fishing, or perhaps for two or three days at sea, with raucous sing-song chants as they hauled sampans up across the bows of the motor boats. These sampans were very heavy and clumsy and it looked an almost impossible feat to put them where they had to be. Each motor boat had a crew of about fourteen men and boys. Their hoarse cries had a desperate ring as they struggled to get the heavy sampans on board with nothing more than a rope round the stern on which to haul, while one man pushed from a dinghy in the water. Muscle and will power achieved what always looked impossible. Every sampan had a great eye painted on the bows to keep a good look-out for the crew. It was typical of the Chinese that they did the bulk of the fishing; they had quite a fleet of motor boats at Pangkor; while the Malays pottered about in their graceful *koleks*. It was an example really of the power of capital; the Malays apart from being less industrious were not financially subsidized, whereas the Chinese had, as well as their natural energy, a backing of rich Chinese merchants who each owned several boats. On the other side of the island was a settlement of Indians who fished exclusively in the seaward bays with giant seines. They never came across except to shop.

Three or four old junks were beached at Sungai Pangkor Kechil, a village a little to the north of Pangkor "town" itself. Chinese families lived in them, making roofs of *atap* and little rooms. The old hulks encrusted with age and worn with sun and rain had become as much part of the landscape as were the palms on the shore. The tilted decks swarmed with children and cats and were gay with multi-coloured washing.

Near this village was a small cemetery at the foot of a bare, red hill where some English sailors had been buried, murdered long ago by the Malays. The shallow bay of Pangkor village was guarded by a miniature lighthouse. One or two cream-painted Government buildings, the Customs and the police station faced the shore. Under a great shade tree the men of the village, mostly the Malays (the Chinese were too busy) sat and gossiped in the only car on the island, a twenty-four-year-old Bean owned by a thin, cheerful Malay, Abdullah bin Hamid. Drawn up on the sand were two or three of the splendid Malay boats from Trengannu on the east coast. These boats had high carved prows and gaily painted gunwales. Unluckily,

I never saw the east coast; but I was told the Malays there were a more vigorous people, an unspoilt, hardy, sea-going race. Very occasionally they came round in these great boats, like war canoes, to the west.

The first time I went ashore at Pangkor, Stuart wanted me to see the old Dutch Fort. Places of historical interest are rare in Malaya; it is, I think, one of the things most lacking, the beauty of antiquity in buildings, the atmosphere of tradition and solidity. We walked through the main street, the only street, of the village. It was a sandy track between the fishermen's houses and a few shops where for twelve cents each, less than threepence halfpenny, you could buy the biggest and most luscious pineapples I have ever tasted.

The street was only a few yards long. Some of the very old Chinese women here still had bound "lily" feet; their tottering walk was pathetic and horrible; what a burden to bear all one's life! A naked foot that has been bound is a lamentably hideous sight. Beyond the main street the track wound past sandy beaches between "elephant" rocks covered in lichen under the palms. Men were twisting hemp for ropes on primitive machines, working small forges, building boats and making nets; industries as old as the hills. On the outskirts of the village were a few tumble-down Malay houses. The ducks and baby chickens got under your feet. In places the path was so narrow a fat man could not have squeezed between the great rocks, at others it widened out under impoverished rubber trees. The ruin of the Dutch Fort, well hidden from the sea, was close to the shores of a bay facing south-east: its purpose had been to control the Kinta tin route. We found it under the palm trees, still solid-looking and square and built of bricks, with all the toughness and durability of the west in its walls beside a flimsy Malay house of *atap*. It was strange to think of those Dutchmen just two hundred years ago living there in terrible discomfort, in appalling heat, with little water, no doubt ridden with fever and constantly attacked by the Malays, who are now so friendly and child-like that it is almost impossible to imagine them as a once fierce and resentful people. It is quiet and lonely there now. Every brick of those solid walls must have cost blood and sweat and tears. . . .

We went down to the shore and looked at a great stone

which had been the Dutchman's landmark; they had carved their names there and the Lion of the Netherlands with the date, 1743. . . .

In the evening, on the way home, Stuart inspected some junks at sea; the crews were having their evening meal, squatting on deck, holding their rice bowls close to their mouths, shovelling the food in with their chop-sticks as fast as they could chew. And on the island every little valley became blue with smoke as the people prepared to eat; the homely scent of the wood fires drifted out across the quiet sea.

The sky was heavy with towering citadels of cloud which changed slowly from pink to apricot in the east; the night swiftly darkening behind them. The night was already in the eastern sky almost before the sun had set in the west. Sheet lightning played in the cloud-banks throwing the lovely shapes into relief. All the lights of Lumut were glittering brilliantly under the dark hills as we crept up the estuary.

The next time I went to Pangkor with him, Stuart had to use the small launch as the *Rimau* was being overhauled; so instead of anchoring in the bay as usual we tied up alongside a fishing boat at the wooden jetty. Stuart went ashore to work and while I waited I thought I would try a sketch of the boats and billowing nets. Immediately I began all the usual things happened: boats were moved, the nets were hauled down, and a slow gentle swell got up. The launch moved in a short wallowing roll and gradually, in the white heat of the afternoon, the stench of the putrid fish became more and more unbearable. I stood it for an hour working on my sketch, then the Chinese in the fishing boat alongside began taking kerosene tin after kerosene tin, each full to the brim with blood and oil, out of the well of the boat and emptying them over the side. This was nearly too much for me; my stomach rose and I all but parted with my lunch. Fortunately, Stuart had almost finished his work and I had not much longer to wait before he came to fetch me. We scrambled over the boats, over fish drying odoriferously on the bamboo slats of the jetty, and stumbled through the houses, which were the only exit, staggering finally into Abdullah's old car which was waiting in the welcome shade of the great tree. In our dash through the wooden buildings I did manage to notice the huge vats for salting the fish and a Chinese baby sleeping in a tiny room among all the smell, slush and litter. The Chinese ate and worked and slept in these places. Picturesque as the fishing villages were they were appallingly insanitary, and the Government was endeavouring to get something done about it; new houses built and a concrete jetty. Improvements are slow, but another three or four years would have seen those changes, I suppose.

Abdullah drove us across to the seaward side of the island. We rattled along in and out of people's gardens and dodging round palm trees. Dismissing Abdullah, we dumped our belongings under a shade tree by the water's edge and fairly leapt into the sea. The tide was full and brimming up to the sandy bank under the trees like milk in a saucer, and the water was gentle and velvety to one's skin. It was cool and deep and we felt refreshed and clean again. Stuart had also had a trying afternoon measuring toddy in the very Tamilly Toddy Shop with gaping, sweaty people standing around.

There were three or four bungalows along that stretch of sandy shore which lay facing the west. This was Pasir Bogah[1] Bay; its shape was like the curved mouth of a lovely woman. Across the Bay was an island called Pangkor Laut (Sea Pangkor) where there had once been a leper colony; a clump of rocky islets white with terns' wings and beyond them the big waves of the open sea. Down in the south a series of small islands, the Sembilan Islands, led the eye away like stepping-stones to the horizon.

The bungalow at the end of the bay was run as a kind of hotel by "Teddy," a retired planter, and his wife. But they were such generous, hospitable people they could not bear to take money from their guests, so I am quite sure the place did not pay. We often had a struggle to pay for our tea or drinks when we went there; one of us would occupy "Teddy" while the other sneaked off to settle with the Head Boy on the quiet. "Teddy's" hospitality was such that it positively hurt him to see people pay for food and drinks in his house. He was always asking us over there to meals at the week-ends and after we had wallowed in the warm sea for hours, he would give us a delicious *ikan moleh* (which is a sort of curried fish with creamy sauce made of ginger and coconut milk, curry powder and

[1] Dragon Sands.

spices) and entertain us with wonderful stories. He had a way of telling them that was so vastly amusing. It did not matter whether they were exaggerated or not: one just enjoyed his raconteur's gift. He could never forgive Somerset Maugham for choosing Malaya as a background for crime and scandal.

He told us one story that concerned his own coffin. He was desperately ill with fever and had been given a whole injection of a drug by mistake instead of the correct one-sixteenth. He was expected to die at any moment, the coffin had been ordered and—although it was held up at the Customs gate, as coffins were frequently used for smuggling—it was on its way. His friends were so miserable at the thought of losing him that they opened some of his best champagne to get a little cheer. Suddenly, he felt better, and rose from his death-bed to join them in the next room, where he consumed a good deal of that champagne himself, recovered miraculously and lived to tell the tale. The District Officer kept the coffin as a memento. . . .

On that first visit he showed us his aviary and we learned the names of some of the birds I had seen in our own garden in and out of the jungle. The long-tailed green ones were bee-eaters; and the little yellow fellows I had seen hanging upside down on the ceilings of our house were called sun-birds in Malaya, but were really the local equivalent of the South American humming bird. It was lovely there by the sea, the garden was all sand, but blossomed like the desert with red and purple bougainvillaea, roses, lilies, orchids and hibiscus. There were at least six varieties of hibiscus: single-petalled, apricot-coloured with velvety dark centres, double pink, flaming scarlet and many others. Perhaps most lovely of all were the creamy white ones whose pale blooms glowed like moons in the dusk. We dragged ourselves away at last, for Abdullah was waiting. The drive back across the island had a dream-like quality; the narrow track through the dark trees was lit only by the light of one feeble bicycle lamp on the car. Near the village bonfires blazed under the palms and a few shadowy figures moved about in the glow. They were burning rubbish round the thick, dark bases of the coconut palms; this was done regularly to destroy the beetles. The village was shadowy; but as we came out from under the great shade tree on to the sandy beach, we walked into dazzling moonlight: there was a silver sea, with seven junks anchored black against the light.

Once when I was waiting on board the *Rimau* at Pangkor, I chanced to see a Malay funeral procession, a real chance, for apparently they were not often to be seen. Moslems are rather secretive about their burials. I heard a melodious chanting of men's voices coming over the water and saw a procession winding down from the headland into the village, men in sarong and *songkok* carrying a pink-draped bier. What interested me was that their Arabic chants did not sound Oriental, but like a Christian hymn. I never saw another Malay funeral, but there were plenty of Tamil ones, noisy affairs with furiously beaten drums. Kandasami used to attend all those at Lumut and generally got drunk on toddy afterwards.

The most terrible and yet most moving Tamil funeral I saw was that of a child. A brilliantly coloured procession of men and women carried aloft a little canopied throne bedecked with flowers, and on it, sitting up, staring ahead, was the body of a very small boy.

VII

IPOH AND THE BAY

WE USED to go into Ipoh two or perhaps, if we were feeling reckless, three times a month, to shop, see a film and dance. A hundred and thirty miles there and back was a long drive for that; but so far out, we sometimes felt the need for mental change and stimulus, for entertainment and the comforts and sophistications of a town. Lovely as it was at Lumut, one became restless occasionally. A film does not compensate for the lack of plays, the ballet and picture galleries, but it does give one contact with the outside world, however untrue to that world it may be. The news reels were best of all; it was an indescribable thrill to see a glimpse of London and the people at home.

As we had to leave in the worst heat of the day to get to Ipoh in time to do all we wanted, the drive was fairly exhausting, and we were generally sticking to the car seats in a state of limp dampness by the time we arrived. But there was plenty to look at to distract one's mind from the discomforts. Some of the roads, especially the Taiping one, twisted madly in sea-sick coils. This was because in the "good old days" when the roads were being made, there were not enough European supervisors to go round; the work was entrusted to contractors who were paid by the mile—therefore they made it as long a road as possible. The main north and south arterial road, Singapore to Alor Star, was continually being straightened out mile by mile.

The Lumut-Ipoh road was not as bad as some, but the journey always took just on two hours. Sometimes I used to think during those first months that it was like a pageant, so varied were the nationalities and costumes of the people by the wayside, and I never lost my delight in watching them. Young Chinese girls were gay in the bright colours they wear in their youth; the Chinese coolie women looked crisp and clean like little nuns in their neat black suits and red or white scarves, tearing along on bicycles or plodding on the grass chattering at the tops of their shrill voices. Malay women were in all colours like flowers and their men folk also; there were fishermen, whose enormous limpet hats contrasted with the small white *haji* caps of the Mecca pilgrims,[1] and smart lads in silk jackets tucked into gay sarongs, untidy urchins in grimy coats. The Tamils were in orange and green and magenta or, on special occasions, very smart in blue and pink, white and silver. There were Sikhs in white with yellow and orange turbans, blowsy Bengali women in loose white trousers and saris; tiny infants in nothing at all but silver "modesty" baubels. It was an endless procession. The Sikhs, whose religion does not allow them to cut their hair, wear it piled up under their turbans. The boys when they are too young to wear turbans bind their hair in a tight little top-knot on the crown of the head, in a wisp of yellowish cloth. I saw six or seven of these little fellows, a covey of them on bicycles passed us in a town; wild, tall, lean-faced and handsome with top-knots of different shades bobbing about like a lot of oranges and lemons and limes in the crowded street.

The villages swarmed with ducks and chickens and curly black and tan goats with frisking kids, and from the Chinese woodcutters' communal dwellings herds of little black pigs trotted out. Huge lumbering water buffalo, their furry babies nuzzling their flanks, cropped the sward by the roadside or wallowed in mud pools with nothing but pink nose and murderous horns showing above the ooze; and in every coolie line the mild, milk-scented, humped Indian cattle wandered at will. Near Ipoh the open-caste tin mines had laid the country bare. One mine by the roadside struck me as being a perfect *décor* for a rather original ballet of *chinoiserie*. Beyond a gnarled tree and a few stunted bushes stretched a dazzling white expanse of old workings across which processed a string of little black-clad figures, the coolie women wheeling their squeaking barrows. Rhythmic toil expressed in black and startling white, relieved only by the scarlet head scarves. The clicking wooden sandals and the shrieking axles of the wheelbarrows formed a

[1] Haji is the title given to Mohammedans who have made the pilgrimage to Mecca; Malay Hajis wear these white skull caps or a small turban to signify this.

weird accompaniment to the coolies' characteristic, uniformly lolloping gait.

The first time we went to Ipoh we had to find a man who would make new chairs, as we had not then discovered the Lumut carpenter. We had drawn our own designs, as so many people did in Malaya, and the chairs when we got them were really very comfortable indeed and effective. We went to an Indian silk shop and revelled in "civilization" again; though Ipoh was not very civilized and never much of a town at the best of times—poor little place later, so very battered by war. Patriarchal bearded Indians sat on their doorsteps smoking their hubble-bubble pipes. The covered five-foot way in front of the shops was full of a motley crowd: slim Moslem Indian boys in red fezes, youths in the white Gandhi caps of Congress, tall Sikhs pungent of ghee, and swaggering pot-bellied Chettiars jostled shoulders with Europeans in for a day's shopping from the country estates, neat Chinese housewives and pretty little dancing girls.

There was a Singhalese jeweller in Ipoh whom we liked, a fat amiable little man, whose shop was fragrant with sweet-smelling benjamin which his wife burnt in a flat copper vessel.

At night the martins collected on the telephone wires in their millions; they slept there shoulder to shoulder, packed literally as close as sardines. They patronized only one half of the town, the main shopping quarter, beyond which there was not a martin to be seen.

We were not then members of the club, and, failing to get a room where we could bath and change at either of the European hotels, we resorted to a rather dubious Chinese place where they let us have a bathroom and bedroom apparently belonging to someone who was away. We felt finicky over this, scrabbled through our change as quickly as possible and went down to the bar to consume gratefully unexpectedly good Million Dollar cocktails, frothy with white of egg and streaked with *crême de cacoa.*

In those days there was a little café in Ipoh, the Chez Luthy, run by a Swiss with a Dutch-Javanese wife. From the outside it was vaguely reminiscent of Soho, with plants in tubs on the five-foot way. A lame Austrian Jew played the piano with feeling and gaiety, anything you asked, from old Viennese songs and waltzes to modern syncopated stuff, without a page of music. He beamed continually through thick lenses in a curious, white, shut-away face, and occasionally, when he was worked up, he would produce his accordion and play nostalgic Alpine songs. M. Luthy himself prepared the food; it was excellent and better cooked than any other we had tasted in Malaya. And in those days it was still possible to order a delicious sole.

The insidious chit-signing habit of Malaya was the undoing of Chez Luthy; people, even one or two who lunched there regularly, failed to pay their bills and the place went bankrupt in a year. It was sad to see that pianist playing in the Chinese dance hall next door, hopelessly lost in an expressionless band. To get to Ipoh one had to cross the Blanja Toll Bridge, a long pontoon bridge, guarded by the police, over the wide, muddy Perak river. One never quite knew if the bridge was still going to be there after heavy rain when the river was swollen with floods. The long drive home at night was very tiring and occasionally Mat went to sleep at the wheel. That, he said, was what happened when he forgot to put the lime in his eyes; the juice of a lime he meant, which was apparently the only way he could keep awake. This was forbidden as it sounded too drastic, and so Stuart generally found he had to drive most of the way home himself. I selfishly developed the ability of sleeping nearly all the way, and the height of this achievement was when I once remained asleep all across the Blanja Bridge in spite of the heaving and crashing of the pontoons. Sometimes wild pig dashed out of the jungle in front of the car, no doubt with tiger giving chase; but we never had the luck to see a tiger. Snakes slipped across the roadway and occasionally we caught a glimpse of the long form and thick dark tail of a civet-cat as it flashed across to disappear into the darkness. Once or twice we were narrowly missed by coconuts falling from overhanging palms; but, on the whole, driving there was probably less dangerous than on the roads at home, though the Ipoh road was very narrow and in places bordered by deep dykes. I have seen cars hopelessly ditched to the roof in water. In one spot the surface was so bad, owing to sinking of the swamp beneath, that it was always bumpy and, if one did not go dead slow, it was only too easy to fly off the narrow crest into the gaping ditch.

These sprees in town were quite fun and made a good contrast with our extremely rural existence at Lumut. But the days by the sea there were always better than any others. There was one particular nameless bay along the coast which we called simply *The* Bay because it was outstandingly perfect in every respect. We hired a river taxi to go there from Telok Muroh; it lay about eight miles by sea from Lumut, on the mainland coast to the south. Even Batu Musang paled beside this place.

Stuart had told me a good deal about it, for he had discovered it when he was stationed in Lumut previously; but it was even more lovely than he had led me to expect. Over a miniature crescent of white sand, trees formed pools of flecked shade. Backed by the jungly hill, the shore was sheltered by rocks grey-warm in the sun and limned with deep shadows. The sea was cool and green. We used to send the man away to a bay a quarter of a mile to the north, and we camped in the shade of a big tree overhanging the white sand. The peace of a long golden day was before us, unruffled and undisturbed. Occasionally some sea otters visited us and monkeys chattered in the jungle, but The Bay was ours absolutely. We took paints and books and picnic meals. There was no need for clothes in that far away place, except for the Chinese cartwheel hats which were a good protection from the sun while bathing. They were ridiculously unwieldy as I discovered when once I laughed so much that I sank in the deep green water and my coolie hat, creating a vacuum, became clamped to the surface. That first day it was nearly sundown before we signalled for the boat and the man was frantic because he had not any lights—so like a Tamil to come unprepared. We waded to the boat hastily and climbed in; the sea was roughening and, of course, the outboard motor refused to start as the plugs were wet. The waves grew higher, and the boat tossed in the narrow bay, and the little Tamil groaned and wailed as she neared the rocks. Stuart, calming him, kept the boat fended off. I thought the Tamil was too distraught to manage the engine, but in spite of his shrill lamentations it fired at last. Then we had to cross to Pangkor to borrow some lanterns. We put in there among the dark and smelly boats and drying nets. Half-naked men were still at work among the bales and boxes on the rickety bamboo wharves; the water was black and oily, lights danced mysteriously in the immense shadows. . . .

It was at The Bay that we saw *memerang*, sea otters, closer than anywhere else. They are rather friendly animals and some Malays keep them as pets. One still afternoon a pair of them dived off the rocks and swam across The Bay watching us intently all the time with their little pointed faces turned shorewards. They evidently wanted to come and play in the waves on the beach; but as it was already occupied, they landed at the farther corner and walked, snuffling at our foot-prints, across the narrow tongue of sand and disappeared into the next bay. We waited to give them time to get away and then followed to watch them; they had swum along the shore and were playing boisterously in the waves. Their tracks on the sand were as big as those of a large dog. (The otters were about three feet long excluding the tail.)

It was quite lively at The Bay that day for, after the *memerangs'* visit the Imperial Airways mail 'plane swept low overhead on its way to Singapore. It was always cheering to see the 'plane go over, a visible if not exactly tangible link with England.

There was not usually so much going on at The Bay. It was the quintessence of peace and we were frankly very selfish about it. On one occasion when we were getting into the sampan at Telok Muroh a party of Chinese picnickers hailed us and enquired amicably where we were off to. Stuart guardedly replied: "*Jauh sa-kali!*" (*Very* far away. . . .)

On one of the numerous holidays—there were about fourteen of them during the year—we decided to spend the whole day at The Bay. Just as we were starting, the mail 'bus arrived from Ipoh and we collected our letters and read them in the boat. They were all from home.

The Bay was particularly good that day with a very high tide which pushed us closer and closer under the big tree. We decided to move to a small gap, where we could retreat comfortably into the jungle if necessary. We transported our belongings to this sandy ledge on the lip of the jungle, and in the rush of rescuing the books and food from the waves a scrap of paper appeared; it was wet and covered in sand. Stuart picked it up: "What's this? It's in your Mother's writing!" he exclaimed. I read it. It said that a short story I had written recently had just been accepted for publication in London. Naturally I was thrilled; but I could not understand at first how the note had appeared as if by magic on the sand so far from its origin. It seemed crazy but delightfully so; it was a mysterious and exciting way in which to hear of one's first publication. The note proved to be a hurried postscript to my Mother's letter; it must have fallen from the envelope when I had opened the mail in the boat and luckily for me had not blown away, but become entangled in the books, and later fallen on to the sand. The sunlight on the sea seemed to sparkle more than ever now and the reflections danced brilliantly on the under-surface of the leaves. In the shadow of the trees we hopped about gleefully in the waves. Time did not exist as such that day, but when at last the sun began to dip behind the Pangkor hills we climbed on the rocks and signalled to the boatman.

We went home across a sea of red and blue and gold to the west, and blue and silver to the east; the path of the sun on the one hand and of the moon on the other.

One morning at the end of April Stuart received sealed instructions "to be opened in the event of war." The news from Europe was bad, the storm seemed about to break; we were sunk in gloom, far away from it all and unable to help.

On May 5th, which was a Friday—the Mohammedan "Sunday"—the Sultan was to come down to open the new mosque at Lumut. It was small and rather dainty; very new and very pink and white like a sugar cake with minarets and dome. On the same day that the depressing papers arrived Stuart met one of the local Malay officials whose ribald remarks, in sharp contrast to the general trend of thought, made us laugh afterwards in spite of our gloom. The Malay had just returned from Penang where he had been arranging for a band and dancing girls (a *Ronggeng*) to celebrate on the night of May 5th. So Stuart politely asked him:

"Did you get a good *Ronggeng*?"

"Oh *yes*! *Very* good!" was the delighted answer. "One of the girls is a *virgin* . . ." A virgin *Ronggeng* girl is more expensive;

she costs $500 for three months of companionate marriage and after that she goes into circulation again. Her presence at a *Ronggeng* is therefore an additional attraction and raises the value of the company.

May 5th was one of the hottest days I ever remember. Partly, I expect, because we had to dress up in stockings and shoes, hats and ties and coats, instead of the usual brief scraps of silk and drill. Everyone went down to the Rest House lawn by the estuary to welcome the Sultan; the Resident and his wife from Taiping, the planters and their wives from the surrounding district, the Government officials of Lumut, with the Malay District Officer, resplendent in silk jacket and sarong, while the Policeman, in dress uniform, boiling and puce in the face, was controlling the traffic. The crowds of Malays, men, women and children, in the shadows under the trees, looked like beds of gorgeous flowers. No Malay but members of a royal family may wear yellow, but they wore every other colour: magenta, turquoise, peacock blue, vermilion and dark green, royal blue, rich purple, pale pink and apple-green.

The Sultan arrived with his retinue in six cars and was escorted on to the lawn under grey and saffron sunshades hung with blobby gold coins and baubels. A planter, a rather dictatorial "Old Hand," then proceeded to read out a speech, which should really have been read by the too-modest District Officer. It was a very conventional speech; it had been printed on silk and was presented to the Sultan, poor patient man, in a silver casket. The presentation was followed by a short breathing space at the Rest House. The Sultan was easy to talk to and friendly. He always seemed glad to talk about tennis—à propos of his love of it he suddenly informed us that he was fifty-two; I was surprised as he certainly did not look it. He soon left to open the mosque, and we Europeans retired from the scene until it was time to reappear again for the luncheon. Stuart and I rushed up to the house for a shower and change, for by then we were limp rags.

At luncheon I was seated next to the Raja Kechil Tengah, a son of the late Sultan—the line goes from uncle to nephew, not from father to son—a lively cheerful person whom I rather liked. The man on my right was very quiet, a little grey person in grey silk, a secretary, I believe. The Raja Kechil Tengah looked gay in an apple-green sarong and a jacket of very fine pale silk. The Raja Muda was very dashing in purple silk and tall *kopiah* worn at a rakish angle: he was obviously an *élégant.* The Sultan himself wore white and his consort, very silent and shy, was in green and gold.

The Raja Kechil talked of England and Bourne End and London's policemen. I often wonder if the Metropolitan Police are duly flattered or not by the wonderful things said about them all over the world! The Raja's point was that the English look upon their police as "kindly fathers," while here the Malays look upon theirs as enemies. (The Malay police had military training and were armed. The people, expressively, called them *Mata-mata*, meaning—eyes.)

We were served with a rather peculiar curry; when it was all over, Stuart and I went to the sports to give away prizes. We sat together on the *atap*-shaded *Ronggeng* platform in the middle of the baking hot sports-ground and all the funny little school-children swarmed round us. The Chinese girls were sweet, and as mad on sport as the boys, in fact they looked alike, for they all wore black briefs and white tops. We got quite good at picking the winners. There were egg and spoon races, with purple egg-plant fruit instead of eggs, sack races and all the usual things. Some of the Malay boys were so tiny they were able to run inside their sacks.

At first the children grabbed their prizes silently. Then one tall Chinese boy bowed deeply and the others followed suit; the Chinese boys bowing elegantly, the Tamils stiffly with a salute and a "Tank you!" and the Malays with their "*Terima Kaseh*"—when they remembered.

We sweltered in the heat. In the distance we could see boat races in full swing, a sailing race, a *kolek* race, the boats black with men, and finally a motor-boat race. The children were fascinated by my stockings and squatted down on the floor to inspect them, and perhaps the open-work pattern in my shoes puzzled them—they could not make it out at all. They pressed round, each small body giving off heat like a radiator and they had to be kept back by a strident-voiced Chinese schoolmaster. When it was all over we unglued ourselves and went to see the end of the men's swimming race from the office roof; it was really very funny, as half the competitors walked. . . . The sun sparkled on the waves; it was a brilliant blue, cloudless day and scorching hot.

Then we had to have another bath and change before the tea-party in Downing Street. Some humorist long ago had so called the lovely road that went up from the sea beyond the Rest House; a flight of stone steps led to a wide short road completely shaded by great angsena trees. Here were the police station, the court house, the District offices and the Public Works Department; hence the name as the centre of the Government services. The tea-tables were laid out in the shade of the trees; it was unusual and pretty. We met some people from over the river and made some new friends. Everyone was talking about war, which now seemed inevitable.

After tea we all went to the Club for tennis. Stuart and a Chinese, Diong Leong Dee (always known as Ding Dong) and two Malays played an exhibition match.

The Sultan asked me to sit between him and his wife, saying to my horror: "You do speak Malay, don't you?" For she did not speak a word of English, and my Malay was not up to polite conversational standards. I struggled along but broke down and completely wilted under the eye of a real *Mem* of the Old School, who was gazing at me fixedly in a devastating manner from behind the Consort's head.

The Sultan got up to play a set, looking very slim and fragile in white flannels.

The sun sank in a blaze of wild colour. Across the open grass spaces beneath the hill the mosque glowed more like an elaborate sugar cake than ever. When the last rays of the sun had gone and the cool shadows crept out, the mosque still shone lemon-coloured in the dusk and we saw that it was flood-lit. Sitting there that evening exhausted by the heat of the day we relaxed and listened to the Old Hands. Their stories, some a bit steep perhaps, were of the Dindings in the bad old days, when it was called the "White Man's Grave," and everyone else's too, because of the malaria; when bullock-carts took four days over the journey to Ipoh and when every creek was thick with alligators. . . .

It was stifling that Friday evening. We were too exhausted to go down and watch the *Ronggeng*. There was not a breath of air; the jungle noises seemed to fill the house, the whirr of the insects was shriller than ever in the stillness. It was piercing, it dinned in your brain on an unbelievably high note and to add to it the toc-toc bird called monotonously. Our heads ached with a throbbing dryness.

Even the night was hot, which was not always the way by any means up there on the hill; the next morning was only a little better with the sun blazing down from an enamelled sky.

Then at midday with alarming suddenness a Sumatra swooped on Lumut, and I appreciated the vividness of the poet's[1] imagery describing just such a bombastic storm:

> Wind searching as a sieve of brass,
> Laying all things flat before it,
> Driving clouds in pointed wisps,
> Like the trump on day of judgement;
> Wind that's palpable in form,
> Tearing up the shrub in court-yard
> From the muddy soil the plant up-rooting,
> Tumbling buffalo in meadow,
> Toppling coconuts in garden;
> Wind that strips the coral reefs
> Till they show like slabs of metal;
> Tossing mullet on the deck-house,
> Bringing shark to door of cabin.

Papers were swept off tables, photographs and vases crashed down, the cats went wild and leapt about in thrilled abandon, prancing at each other crab-wise and swinging on the long curtains. Everything whirled around deliriously; the flowers bowed their heads and the trees swayed and cried in the tremendous onslaught from the west.

Kuki and Ah Seng and Ah Chi rushed in from the back and we all hurried to close the shutters as fast as possible against the gale.

Then came the rain. Crashing, beating, lashing down as furiously as it does on the films. In a few seconds the gutters were filled and the drain-pipes cascaded frothy waterfalls. The concrete drains round the house were fierce rivers. The drive was a pond, the hill road a waterfall and the valley a lake.

All day long it poured. We sat inside the darkened house with the shutters closed and listened to the rattle of the water in the drain-pipes. A fine spray came in through the shutters

[1] An anonymous Malay poet.

From an oil painting by the author

Kandasami—young Tamil

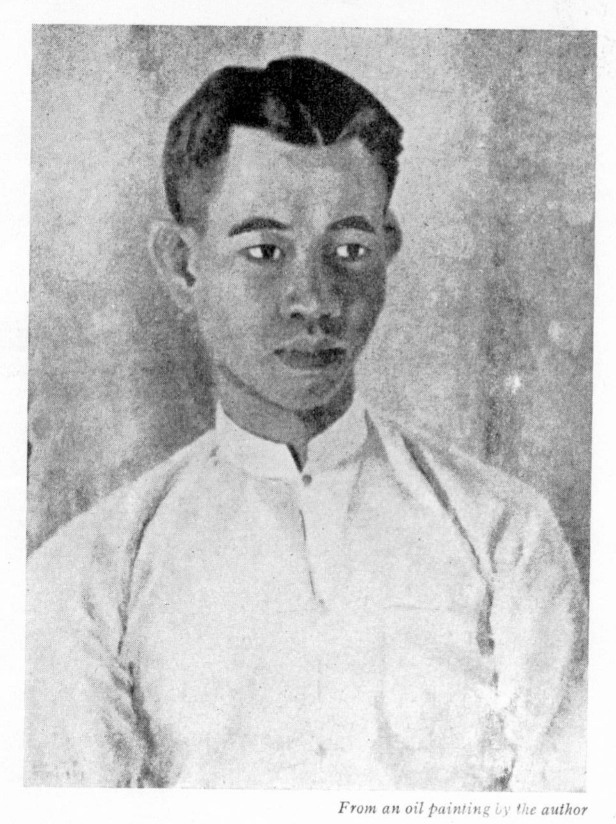

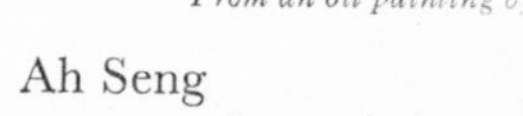

From an oil painting by the author

Ah Seng

The beach at Rumbia

and the slats above the windows, and we shivered and longed for a fire. The studio, soaked as it faced west, was like a shower-bath. Once when the violence abated slightly, we went down to the "town" in the car to shop and happened to see the new chairs from Ipoh sitting on a lorry in the deluge. Hot with rage we sought and dragged out the Tamil driver from an eating-house, where he was calmly having a prolonged meal and an argument, Tamil fashion, with the proprietor. I suppose he not unnaturally thought an hour or two more in this rain would not make much difference to the chairs already brought sixty-five miles in it.

That evening we pulled the furniture into the middle of the sitting-room as far from the spray as possible and wrapped ourselves up. It was cold and damp. It rained all night but we slept long and deep, disregarding the storm noises; the coolness was refreshing. When we woke on the Sunday the ceilings had leaked, large pools lay about everywhere. We could no longer sit in the upstairs room, the last dry spot left was the middle of the dining-room facing the one and only glass window. So there we had a little daylight, while the other rooms were gloomy with closed shutters. We camped there that evening in deck chairs—every other chair was soaked—with one rigged-up reading lamp between us, like a little island in the damp chill of the shuttered house. Suddenly out of the dark and pouring chaos appeared the young Engineer from the house down the hill: he had come to call. Like us he must have been shut up all the week-end and felt it was a good time to get his call over. It was the best thing that could have happened from our point of view as our state of dampness was clear enough to him and quite soon after this he got those leaks mended for us and in time glass was put over the open tops of the windows. It was most appropriate and fortunate that it should have been he of the P.W.D. (Public Works Dept.) who came to call at that moment.

That night we went to bed fully expecting the roof to leak over our heads, but thank God it held. All the tin baths and basins we possessed were lying around to catch the drips from the ceilings, and bath mats and towels were strewn all over the place to soak up what water they could.

Next day the rain stopped and Ah Seng and I were trying to

air some of the things in a gleam of sunshine when down it came again. It went on steadily until the Tuesday morning, which dawned sweet and brilliant with the mists rolling off the jungle. Everything then had to go out into the garden to air; the little lawn was crowded with chairs and cushions, the precious sofa, mats and almost all we possessed. Clothes, shoes and books smelt musty with damp and had to be aired too. Normally cupboard doors were left open all day while the sun was shining to dry out the dampness of the night; but after being shut up for four days during the deluge everything smelt as if it had been buried in dank vaults for years.

Once a week regularly on dry clear days every single garment one possessed was taken out and hung in the shade to air and put back fresh and sweet, beautifully folded, and pressed with her heavy charcoal-heated iron, by the neat and industrious little Ah Chi.

As time went on we grew to know Lumut and love it more. There was a path along the water front under the hospital hill by the sea wall. Sometimes, if we were worried about anything, or more than usually depressed about the situation at home, we used to go and sit on that warm sea wall before sunset, or better still walk up on the little hill beyond Dr. Menun's garden hospital to the Convent cliff. This was a quiet place in front of the old white building with its temple trees and oleanders. The local inhabitants called Lumut Tanah Merah, meaning red earth, from its laterite soil, which here was very noticeable. The red cliff fell away to the green water below. It was peaceful sitting up there watching the red ants stalking each other. One could look out across the great expanse of glassy water to the west. Beyond this were little bays, mangrove trees with amphibious fish in their branches, sparse rubber trees and queer sandy Chinese gardens by the sea, a few tiny houses, and jungle, rocky jungle leading to the narrow headland opposite Pangkor. Over the estuary to the north the coast opened out in long wild sandy beaches.

We hired a boat and went there once or twice. Red fruit shone in the dark fleshy-leaved trees above the sands. Tiny spider crabs got up on their hind legs and ran. Mat loved to chase them, trying to jump on them with the unthinking cruelty of a small boy, but he was shamefaced when he knew we had seen him. The waves from the open sea broke noisily on the white sand. It was a lovely, deserted place.

Over the river there were a few *kampongs*, dark behind the palms. One of these was besieged by ants, which came in their millions, persistently marching through the houses until at last the people were driven out.

The plague of ants got on my nerves. Ah Seng and I waged battles against them with fire and water, with treacle and poison; but nothing seemed to have much effect. There were tiny brown sugar ants, ordinary house ants, the big red *keringas* in the trees, white ants, flying ants and jungle ants. At sunset there was always a strange procession of great jungle ants. They would march from the jungle down through the garden, spaced out with a gap of about six feet between each. Caesar watched them doubtfully, but never gave chase. The worst of all were the flying ants which rose in a cloud like steam out of the ground at evening after rain. The most sensible thing to do when they appeared, was to go to bed under the protection of one's mosquito net. They invaded the house in thousands, shedding their hateful fluttery wings everywhere and crawling over the floor. Their loathsome soft bodies were soon carried off by the house ants long before they died. There was nothing left of the orgy by morning except wings, brown wings everywhere. We learned that the best thing to do if we had people to dinner—and so could not retire under our net—was to put a lamp over a basin of water and sit in semi-darkness. The ants then mostly fell into the water and were drowned. The *chichak* on the high ceilings had a field day when the flying ants came out; I loved the fussy, comic little *chichak* cleaning up the objectionable insects with gusto and precision.

Beautiful creatures as well as loathsome ones came in from the jungle at night. Glorious swallow-tailed butterflies, which had to be protected from the *chichaks* with a barrage of well-aimed cushions; green moths with gold markings, pink ones with gold and silver markings and feet like boots of white fur, and all kinds of exquisite minute creatures of vivid colouring. One night a butterfly shaped like a torn leaf with brown, gold and black markings sat on my wrist the entire evening, poised and elegant. Stuart remarked that it was the height of sophistication to wear a butterfly, like the girls of Mexico who wear them caged in gauze in their hair; but this one was uncaged. Twice we saw the rare leaf insect. The stick insect was quite common and also the rather alarming praying mantis with its suppliant "hands" and baleful expression, and there was a small beetle, as brilliant as an emerald, commonly known as the stink bug, because when touched he gives off a very rank, green odour, out of all proportion to his size. Brown cicadas as big as mice bumped against the ceiling and fell down on to one's head with painful force. Once I went into the bathroom and saw a pair of tiny red eyes gleaming. I switched on the light; a huge spider was struggling with a gay-coloured butterfly. . . .

The mosquitoes at Lumut were the striped species that carries dengue rather than malaria; the same mosquito which in other tropical countries carries yellow fever. I heard it said that if one yellow fever-infected mosquito were to be brought accidentally to the country, possibly in a 'plane, people would be wiped out in a short while because the striped species is so numerous all over Malaya. The mosquitoes were not anything like as numerous as at Parit Buntar; but the sand-flies were annoying and the little beasts were active all day as well as all night, and small enough to penetrate the finest meshed mosquito net.

Between bouts of gardening or exploration we played tennis during the two cooler hours between tea and sundown. Generally we played at Lumut club,[1] but sometimes at Sitiawan, at the Asiatic's own club, with Dr. Kong Kai, a dapper little man and his plump chuckling wife, and with the Diong Leong Dees. Diong was large, husky and cheerful. I shall never forget the first time we played tennis with his delightful little schoolmistress wife. If she was shocked at my abbreviated linen shorts, I certainly was fascinated by her outfit. She wore a dainty white jacket and trousers cut in the usual Chinese way but made of transparent voile. Beneath these, completely visible and extremely seductive, she wore an entrancing pair of diminutive, white, lace-edged knickers. Our tennis was not very serious that afternoon, but we enjoyed ourselves and laughed a lot.

Diong and Stuart were playing in a tennis match one week-

[1] Used by *both* Asiatics and Europeans.

end at Taiping. We had been rather unsociable and thought it was time we met some people again.

After the match, when we were sitting outside to cool off, watching the sunset colours die away from the hill, we met an Army couple who had recently come from India. We began to talk about Louis Blomfield's vivid book, *The Rains Came.* I asked if it gave a true impression of life in India. The Army wife replied that it was "A perfect picture of hill station life." Stuart and I dared not look at each other, for she could not possibly have read a word of the book, as it is entirely about the plains. Hastily Stuart changed the subject. The film of Whymper's ascent of the Matterhorn, *The Challenge*, happened to be on in Taiping, so he turned the talk to it: "Do you know Zermatt?" he asked. "No," answered the Officer, "I haven't been able to get around much yet. My car hasn't come from India."

We hastily buried our noses in our drinks; but I found it impossible to avoid Stuart's eye that time.

We went on to a party after that and stayed the night in Taiping with our friends, Alice and Henry, who bred Siamese cats, and they promised us a female kitten out of the next litter. We decided then to call her Cleopatra. Anthony and Caesar would be delighted. Next morning we breakfasted with the old Padre. He enquired tenderly after the garden as usual and gave us seeds and cuttings from his own.

On the way home we came upon the most colourful Malay market I had ever had the luck to see. It was just off the road in the shade of some trees. Magenta and peacock sarongs flamed on the stalls, and limpet hats painted red and orange, Reckitts blue and gold were hanging among them, all splashed with dappled leaf shadows. Men squatted beside their wares; fish of every kind, black and slippery, rainbow-coloured and enticing, blue crabs, yellow dried fish, black rubber-mouthed sharks and coral-coloured chili paste. Baby ducks and chickens chattered away at the tops of their voices in great round shallow baskets. And the curry powder! Big jars of it were presided over by a dark, cross-legged man. Each jar held a different colour: rich red-browns, Venetian red, yellowish umber and deep dark saffron. We bought some and later sent it home to my people, but not realizing its potency they used it too liberally and nearly went up in smoke. We also bought some of the painted hats for the studio. They were "food hats," called *tudong saji*, used by the Malays at weddings and feasts to cover their dishes.

VIII

THE ISLANDS AND CLEOPATRA

THE SEMBILAN ISLANDS, which from Pasir Bogah Bay had looked like stepping-stones to the horizon, lay in the sea patrol area. *Sembilan* is the Malay for nine. There are nine islands and one or two rocks as well: Pulau Nipis, Pulau Rumbia, Pulau Lalang, Pulau Buloh, and the tiny islets of Payong, Rosa, White Rock and some others that are nameless on the Admiralty chart, though the Malays have names for them all. They lie a few miles off the Perak coast, straggling down to the south-west, some fifteen miles from Lumut. The biggest of them, Pulau Rumbia, is about one mile long and half a mile wide; none of them is inhabited; but Rumbia has the only reliable fresh-water spring and Malay fishermen put in there to refill their casks.

The sea patrol was done about once every six months. The Whitsun week-end that Stuart chose for the first of these, could not have been more perfect, for the sea was glassy calm. There were flying fish skimming away from the bows and those crazy-looking sword-fish or *ikan parang* (fish shaped like curved knives) that leapt up out of the water and flicked over the surface on the tips of their tails. The *Rimau's* Malay crew consisted of the serang, four boatmen and an elderly engineer, who curiously enough had been captured in the last war by Germans and made to work for them. Two of the boatmen were so alike, short, stocky and snub-nosed, that we called them the Twins. Then there was Yahya, a good type from Selangor who became one of my best models, and lastly there was the odd job man or dog's body.

After all the junks in sight had been inspected, including a beautiful, brand new one with clean white sails and hull freshly painted in emerald, scarlet and ultramarine, we headed for the islands and the nearest convenient anchorage, to lie up for the night. We dropped anchor in the little bay under the hill at

Rumbia at six o'clock in the evening. I shall never forget that island as long as I live. With each visit we grew to love it more. The sheltering curves of the bay, like the arms of a sphinx shrouded in soft green, were stretched out to greet us, after a hot day at sea the island was cool and green and friendly. Presently, when we lay at anchor in its shadow, two martins swooped out to perch in the awning.

That first evening there was a dead calm. The green-blue water, reflecting the towering jungle on the abrupt hillside, was so magically translucent that the rocks and coral beneath were clearly visible even at eight fathoms. The pure white strip the sandy shore was backed by a fringe of palms and the leaning mass of the jungle, alive then with the sunset song of myriads upon myriads of cicadas, its corruption and decay hidden behind the dense vines and creepers and all the lovely mass of vivid vegetation. Above these giants with their towering grey-pink stems, two sea hawks circled, slowly drifting on the soft breeze with hoarse ringing calls. The green-blue sea was flooding in to the rocks of the sheltering headlands.

We went ashore in the dinghy and bathed from the beach, the water over the white sand was a pure, transparent viridian. Two little *atap* huts, fishermen's shelters, huddled under coconut palms by a fresh-water spring at the far end of the bay. A few Malays were squatting there; they had drawn their streamline *koleks* up on the sand.

Now and then a turtle fishing in the bay heaved its brown back out of the water, or stuck up a snake-like head on a long thin neck to look round. After we had bathed we took the dinghy across to the gold and black rocks of the headland where the trees and bushes grew low to the water. It was here that we saw some of the most beautiful things either of us have ever seen.

We dawdled along, Yahya gently moving one oar as we gazed down into this other world beneath us. It was magically lovely. Between the white coral, the red-brown rocks and the strange olivine and crimson rock life, the sand made patches of pure jade, and great baskets, nature's own fish traps, gaped up at us. Huddled against the ledges, mysterious and cool in the depths were the electric-blue bodies of huge jelly fish, glowing as if lit from within. Suddenly, the greatest delight of all, striped black and white sea-angels darted beneath the boat in all their grace. That was a rare moment. We had watched them and drawn them in the London Zoo Aquarium, and to see them here in their natural element was fascinating. They were followed by a shoal of blue and gold fish, slim oblongs of colour. Then down among the shadows of the sea floor a large, luminous blue fish drifted like a cloud of frozen fire. Tiny finger-length fish, brilliant points of light, and minute striped fish followed close behind us inquisitively and we could almost hold them in our hands as we hung over the stern gazing down into the emerald shadow of the boat. Caught fast between some rocks we saw what appeared to be an ancient sword. It set our imaginations wondering—how did it come there? Of course, it must have belonged to a Dutch sailor we said; in some skirmish long ago it had been cut out of his hand by a Malay pirate armed with a *kris*; in the eighteenth century it must have been, when the Dutch were fighting the Malays up and down the peninsular and in and out the islands. . . .

Bewitched, we drifted about, entranced by the emerald depths, forgetful of time until it was too dark to see any more. When we looked up there was a lambent gold cloud over the headland and the reflection of the moon on the still water.

Reluctantly we went back to the launch. Mat was excited about the sword and offered to dive for it, but it was too dark then. When we had changed out of our bathing things we sat on deck sipping our drinks, watching the darkness fall over the island while all the cicadas in the jungle rasped themselves tired in a frantic crescendo and settled down to a steady hum for the night. A feeble lamp glowed from one of the fishermen's shelters.

In the long slow swell that was getting up the tiny galley with its smelly primus was not too pleasant, but we succeeded in cooking a good supper of sausages and bacon, Stuart proving himself a stauncher cook than I. The Twins put up our camp-beds well forward on deck, we never slept below, it was much too hot and alive with cockroaches. Then, drugged with sun and colour we turned in. It was a wonderful night; in the moon-light the giants of the jungle loomed enormous on the hill top, and the sand at its foot was a dazzling white. Lulled by the gentle swell we were soon asleep, a cool breeze blowing.

In the morning, the *Rimau* had swung right round and we were facing the silvery east. I opened my eyes to see a long low line of rosy cloud above the pale horizon, and to the north the tail of Pangkor Island stood darkly against range after range of the brilliant blue mountains of the distant mainland. We lay in bed and looked at the freshness of the morning for a long time. As we watched, fishing *koleks*, with the precarious square sail of the native rig, rounded the headland and put in shore to pick up water and to dump their catch, some of which the men salted on the spot in big tubs. The boats came swiftly one by one and as quickly left again. The brown naked backs of the crews were glistening and muscular. They crouched silently on the narrow boards.

As the sun rose and the cicadas began to shrill, a man in a pink sarong came out of one of the huts and attempted to sweep the sand with a broom. Such an amazing display of energy made me feel lazier than ever as I lay comfortably in bed. The sun climbed the sky rapidly and already the rare freshness of the morning was vanishing. The serang and the engineer and Mat went ashore to bathe. Mat brought us back a cloth full of turtle's eggs. He was grinning and very pleased with himself. Then we took the boat ourselves and bathed for an hour; the water was cool and delicious. Back on board for breakfast, we decided to tackle the turtle's eggs at lunch time, as their soft skins were a little repulsive so early in the morning. Mat had caught twenty-four red-fish during the night while we had slept lazily, and he gave us some which we cooked and ate after our grape fruit. There followed coffee, brown bread and butter and marmalade. A real breakfast!

After this we lazed on deck with the canvas screens down against the growing fierceness of the sun and read until we felt like having another swim. We went ashore again and this time the sea was brimming in over the white sand and up under the shade trees in the corner. By some rocks there, we stood in the green crystal water and looked up into the mystery of the jungle; cool and dank in its dense heart, flecked and dappled on its edges. The cicadas were like thousands of electric bells whirring and throbbing. Hundreds of tiny whitebait swam about our legs and the jewelled pattern of the sunlit waves on the sand beneath the lustrous water was brilliantly gay.

We took the dinghy once more across the bay and looked for the sword, but the surface of the water was too broken to see into those depths again. We looked many times on other occasions, but we never saw the sword again, so we can retain our dramatic illusion—if it was only that. But another illusion—about turtle's eggs being a delicacy—was shattered once and for all at lunch time, on the homeward patrol. The launch was rounding the southerly end of the islands at dazzling, hot noon, in a long, slow swell. The *Rimau* was always only too liable to roll and pitch in the slightest swell and it was doing its best when we rashly tackled those fabulous eggs. They were like funny little damp ping-pong balls, perpetually indented, and they proved too much even for our hardened stomachs, the very feel and softness of them was repulsive. I ate one just to say I had done it; but all the rest went overboard, secretly so as not to offend Mat.

Rumbia was very much part of our lives in the years at Lumut; between patrols we talked of it and looked forward to seeing it again—always afraid the next would be the last trip, as we might go on transfer at any time.

About the time we discovered Rumbia, Cleopatra joined our household and, with her strong personality, became a very important member of it. She was abbreviated to "Cleo" from the start. We brought her home from Alice's house in the car. She clutched me all the time round the neck with her tiny pins, her small dark mask was puckered anxiously and she raised her Siamese voice in shrill enquiry and complaint. Caesar did not know what to make of her at first; they yittered doubtfully at each other. He spent all the next day staring at her; she seemed fairly unconcerned by him, but she positively gaped at Anthony who took no notice of her whatsoever. She was absolutely tiny with a little pointed face, very blue eyes, which squinted when she was excited, and the seal markings and large bat ears of a good Siamese cat. She was continually getting lost inside the hollow backs of the cane chairs which became a favourite place for all the later relays of kittens, for there they could escape from their elders, whose bulk prevented their entry. Cleo was very feminine, she shrieked provocatively at Caesar when he tried to play with her; he soon became her adoring slave and even gave up his hunting hours, six-thirty to eight-thirty, to playing instead of going out. When they got used to each other, they had tremendous boxing matches; he would prance up and bowl her over like a little moth; she screamed, her minute pink mouth wide open, ears flat and blue eyes snapping and squinting. They had wild games all round the rooms and under the sofa and tied knots in the mosquito net. When she got a little bigger Caesar would wash her and bite her gently; she shrieked so much one would think she was dying; but she always came back for more. While Stuart dressed they would sit in the open drawers of his dressing-table and use his hair brushes to brush themselves against. Then they used to rush into my room and dance a fandango in my shoes. They never went downstairs until I was ready. So we all came down to breakfast in a rush together, their thirty-six little claws skidding and pattering on the wood. I am sure the servants thought we were quite mad, especially as Cleo was particularly conversational; she answered each remark addressed to her in her shrill expressive voice. She was almost as affectionate as Caesar and always greeted us with a characteristic "hullooh!" When she had her families and grew a little more sedate, the wild early morning games ceased and, instead, Caesar would gravely accompany Stuart on a garden inspection before breakfast every day.

We went down the short cut below the garden to call on the new Policeman one evening. Caesar and Cleo followed under the temple trees. We stayed an hour or so and when we left, the two cats were still sitting on the Policeman's verandah waiting to go home. This was the first time we had known them to come out with us and we realized how dog-like Siamese cats can be. After that, Caesar often came down to meet the car and would dash up the short cut at the bend trying to race it to the house. It was generally a dead heat; he lay panting under the porch, his eyes very blue with excitement and his pink tongue hanging out.

One evening just as we were starting to take our baths, Cleo came in and flopped down by the door. I thought she looked a bit peculiar and when I spoke to her she got up and came rather unsteadily across to me. Then I had a shock; she was covered in red ants a quarter of an inch long. Her eyes were sore and running; the beastly creatures were at them and in her paws; burrowing in her fur and lined up in rows at her little pink stern. Her face was sopping wet and she seemed in some miraculous way to have half killed the ants. We thought she must have put her head in water to relieve the stinging; but perhaps it was wet only from her frantic licking. Stuart held her wrapped in a shirt. She was very good, but her heart was pounding. They hung on with jaws like vices and had to be tugged off, and there were two in each ear which had to be extracted with tweezers. We bathed her eyes and petted her, afraid she would be ill; but after she had slept a little she was rushing about as usual catching buzzers and beasties. She must have gone up the durian tree which was full of fierce red *keringas*.[1]

At this time Jean came from Parit Buntar to stay. She had just recovered from a bad go of malaria, contracted on a bird-watching expedition when sleeping out unprotected by a mosquito net. She had had a temperature of 105 degrees and had not been expected to live. We pictured her arriving a pale ghost of her former self and had planned quiet days, but when she appeared, she was as lively as ever and still very sunburnt. I painted her portrait while she was with us; it was my first Malayan commission. She too was a felinophile. We took her into Ipoh one day to do some shopping and to see a film. She insisted on sitting in the front of the car which was the hottest and most unpleasant place for that long drive. Nothing would budge her until Stuart and I thought of a plan. We told Mat sharply to stop the car. We leapt out and ran back. "What is the matter?" Jean asked.

"Oh!" we wailed, "we've run over a kitten; *do* come and help, Jean, quick!"

[1] Cupid must have discharged a very fiery arrow into the Malay who composed the *pantun*:

Kerengga di-dalam buloh,
Serahi berisi ayer mawar:
Sampai nasrat di-dalam tuboh,
Tuan sa-orang jadi penawar.

or as Sir Richard Winstedt has paraphrased it:

Red ants in a bamboo! the passion
That tortures my frame is like you!
But like flask of rose-water in fashion
Is the cure my dear flame can bestow.

The ruse worked, it got her out of that hot front seat, and goes to show that we were not the only cat-crazy people in Malaya. I cannot remember what Jean said on that occasion, but I expect it was an irate: "Bloody hell! Bloody what! Bloody Woozles!" (the name of her own cat) which was her particular war-cry in those lighthearted days. . . .

We were getting to know a few of the planters of the district. The homes of some were old rambling wooden bungalows, dark and gloomy; but others were attractive modern houses, built solidly of stone. The Steeles' house near the aerodrome at Sitiawan was new and light, set in a big garden backed by the rubber, but not overshadowed by it as are only too many estate bungalows. They had so many sparrows sharing their house that they had to put boxes up to prevent the fledglings falling out of the nests and to keep the floors clean. I liked the way the birds shared our houses out there. It made me think of Varè's *Gate of Happy Sparrows*. Joan and Bertie became very good friends of ours and we experienced some happy and, later, some very terrible days together.

As I saw more of life on the estates I wanted to know why the Hindu estate coolies could worship so lavish an amount of gods with apparent indiscrimination. It was all very baffling and confusing. Each estate temple possesses different gods; but the coolies, if moved from one estate to another, did not seem to object to transferring their worship—even possibly from a benevolent Vishnu to a terrifying Kali, God of Vengeance. Often one saw a ruined temple near the coolie lines, deserted because the gods had been unpropitious and the disappointed worshippers had decided to start all over again with a change of gods in a new temple.

Frequently we would meet processions of Tamils carrying a god from one temple to visit a goddess in another with the idea of encouraging human fertility: a step hardly necessary judging by the swarming population of the lines; however, the two crude statues would be placed naïvely, face to face. Once, driving through Sitiawan, I saw three gods being carried to a new temple, their eyes stared grotesquely from pale plaster faces. The women in the crowds lining the road wore their brightest clothes and, as the gods passed by, held up naked babies and kissed them on their privy parts; a hint of the phallic note so dominant in the Hindu religion.

Bertie knew I was looking for models and took me round the estate school to choose some. We arrived at eleven o'clock when every child was being given a glass of Horlicks. I chose a pretty little Tamil girl, her name was Kamanalpal. She was very solemn and clean. Her mother brought her over to Lumut and waited each day while I painted her. She wore a sari of cerulean blue threaded with gold which turned to silver in the lights. Her mother told me with pride that it had cost seventy dollars (over £8).

When I had seen the school-children, Bertie showed me the coolie lines. Inevitably smelly, with the soft-eyed Indian cattle wandering about, the goats, chickens and pariah dogs. The babies were slung up in voluminous saris hanging from beams under a shelter where one woman could look after them all while their mothers laboured on the estate. At the factory itself it was interesting to see the rubber being worked in all stages, from the liquid latex as it comes from the tree, coagulating in the acid baths, to the dried, solid sheets. That particular consignment I saw in Bertie's factory was for shipment to Hamburg of all places; but war came before it was ready.

Yahya and Sareh were always my best models. Yahya was so handsome that I thought he would probably turn out to be a hopeless sitter like the fisherman, Pin, for it seemed almost too much to expect that such good looks could be combined with the qualities of a good sitter. But like Sareh he was splendid. His features were classic, of the best Malay type; a high domed brow and slanting eyes not over large as in some Malays, an exquisitely modelled nose, proud curved nostrils which curiously enough did not give a look of arrogance, a wide bow of a mouth with deep indentations of laughter at the corners and, to save him from being too beautiful, a large firm jaw and chin, the chin rounded and slightly cleft. A little taller than most Malays, he held his head well up, the expression contented, smiling and yet not "set." From the shape of the cheekbones and the extremely long lines of the eyes it is possible he had some Siamese or Chinese blood in him. We often found that there was a foreign blend in any Malays we admired particularly. As a model Yahya was a gift from the gods.

Generally when I was painting, Cleo slept under the easel, but when Yahya came she invariably went and sat on the dais with him. She was a little minx.

Malays are fond of cats, but their religion does not permit them to touch the wet nose of a dog.

Sometimes the mornings were disturbed by people ringing up the house in mistake for the office. One man wanted to know if he had to pay duty on a barrel-organ from Penang. Sometimes enquirers even came up the hill in person. One day two rather fishy-looking Pondicherry Indians came to the verandah and solemnly asked *me* the duty on certain bales of cloth. Later on, when the war started and food prices were controlled by the Customs and some commodities occasionally vanished from the market for a few days, irritatingly thoughtless women would 'phone to enquire *why* there were no oranges that day. . . . It was anyhow not the fault of the Customs if there were none. I did leave the receiver off sometimes, but it worried Ah Seng's tidy mind to see it lying about. . . .

In August that year we went to Kuala Lumpur on a few days' leave for the Malayan Agricultural and Horticultural Exhibition, the M.A.H.A., initials really essential in this case! Driving down the arterial road south from Ipoh we passed the fantastic limestone cliffs of Kinta, riddled with Chinese temples and cave houses, some elaborate with facades and balconies, flights of steep steps and jutting, curled eaves below soaring pinnacles of stone. In front of the temples in the marshy ground at the foot of the white cliffs were lotus lily ponds. It was like something out of a dream told by a "traveller from an antique land . . ."

Not so long ago preventive work in these hills used to be a dangerous task. Distillers would ambush the Customs men and roll stones down on their heads from the crumbling limestone crags. It was in these caves that an anthropologist recently found Austro-Melanesian remains.

We were on the main Singapore-Alor Star road, which was in the process of being straightened out. The new road was literally being carved from the living jungle by gangs of Chinese and Tamil coolies, both men and women. Every little hill was cleft in two by cuttings in line, north and south. The coolies worked with *changkols*—the right-angled, all-purpose spade of the Asiatics. The earth was carried away in bamboo baskets. As the old road twisted and turned, carefully avoiding every possible obstacle, one glimpsed vistas of pleasing precision; straight lines between great shining new red walls of laterite crowned with torn jungle chaos.

Whether it was the curly road or excitement or what I do not know, but I suddenly developed the most devastating hiccups. The more we laughed, the worse they became. We stopped on the Perak State boundary at Tanjong Malim Rest House and cured my hiccups with a drink from the "wrong" side of a glass, and I managed some lunch. On again and we reached Kuala Lumpur about tea time. Stuart got very excited showing it all to me and I developed hiccups again. This was worse than appears because I was to meet two of Stuart's great friends, Derek and Tommy, for the first time and had no desire to punctuate introductions with violent and, by this time, painful hiccups. So we both went and drank a tumbler of water again from the "wrong" side of the glass at the Station Hotel, feeling conspicuously mad in the busy bar—especially as Stuart, not wanting me to feel alone in my madness, drank in a similar fashion. . . . Kuala Lumpur, always known as "K.L." to Malayans, was a town full of big creamy-white buildings with domes and minarets of Moorish or, as the ribald called it, More-or-less style; the station, like a gigantic mosque, was simply encrusted with British Byzantinism. The Mosque itself was fragile and charming.

My hiccups cured, we drove to the Selangor Club, that brown and white building known as the "Dog," to meet Derek and Tommy, and I did not disgrace myself or shame Stuart. Later we drove out to Tommy's estate where we stayed. He doctored and finally cured me with bicarbonate of soda from the estate dispensary, for the hiccups had recurred once more on the dusty drive out! We had arrived with our faces powdered with red dust from the unmetalled, laterite road to the estate.

Tommy's house was charming; set up on terraced lawns in front of the rubber trees. He had a retinue of Malay servants, very decorative in white with emerald green sarongs and black *kopiahs*. It was the first time I had stayed on an estate and although I always hated living inland in Malaya because of the enclosed feeling of the millions of trees, it was interesting. Rubber trees in the early morning are reminiscent of a beech wood and, ridiculously, one almost expected to see bluebells. We were shown the crêche for the coolies' children where Tommy had thoughtfully installed rows of wooden cots instead of the swinging sari, in which the children usually hang like bundles from the ceiling, with their heads and feet sticking out unsupported at either end. He had a big job on hand of clearing a new strip of land and terracing it for planting; each tree had to be spaced geometrically, at the exact angle and distance from the next.

After the M.A.H.A. Exhibition Derek and "Taffy" gave us a party as a welcome to Malaya. We had changed at The Dog and started off festively with champagne cocktails; when we left to dine at the Club Chambers Derek and Taffy rushed on ahead, and we wondered what they were up to. We emerged, and there they were waiting for us with a couple of rickshaws and they insisted on pulling us themselves, as this was such a special occasion. One of the rickshaw coolies was convulsed with laughter and spluttered behind his little gold paper and straw hat, the other one was rather alarmed; he thought at first he was going to lose his rickshaw, but soon realized it was only a joke and trotted along behind; so we progressed—somewhat hilariously. As the evening wore on we discovered Derek could quote reams of Keats and Rupert Brooke and some of the most sonorous passages of Shakespeare in his quiet gentle voice, his long dark face solemn and yet gay.

Crazy and cheerful in those days, parties like that with real friends are good to remember, but very far away now. There were many parties that week-end, but that one only, for its sheer atmosphere of welcome and spontaneity, has lived in my memory.

We returned laden with presents and plants and our own Christmas shopping for home: Chinese embroidered shoes, Port Dickson baskets, and Malay brocaded sarongs. When we reached it, Ipoh was curtained in rain and the mountains an angry indigo in the clouds. Stuart drove the last weary lap while Mat slept in the back half-buried under a sea of suitcases, parcels, Malay baskets, damp plants, paintings and a basket of fruit for Sareh. We were greeted at home by Cleo and Caesar, who was wearing a huge bandage round his neck. We had been worried about him when we left as he then had a lump under his chin. Both Ah Seng and Kandasami had long stories to tell. He had been seen coming out of the jungle where he had apparently operated on his lump himself. Conferring with Ah Seng, Kandasami decided Caesar must be taken to the hospital. So they carried him there at once, which must have been extremely difficult as he was big and strong; the long-suffering Dr. Menun dressed the place which was in a horrible state. The nearest vet was at Ipoh, sixty-five miles away, so Menun dressed the wound every day until we returned. He was always most patient and good-hearted about our cats, and, unlike the doctor in the story (who was called by an artist to vet his dog) he did not ask me to go and paint his gate.

It was good as always to be home again at Lumut high up on the hill with the breeze off the sea. The house was shining and spotless and Ah Seng had put up vividly bizarre vases of flowers everywhere.

IX

WAR CLOUDS.
MAT'S MATRIMONIAL ADVENTURES

THE WAR CLOUDS were gathering. At the end of August all leave was cancelled, people on the way home were turned back; the Mediterranean was closed.

Stuart had instructions to make precautionary arrangements for the food rationing of the Dindings, for about twenty-five thousand people in all. He had to distribute licences to every rice dealer. He was also asked in event of war what he wanted to do with me; this made me feel horribly depressed as separation loomed; but the food control job appeared to take precedence over a call up, though for a long time this was very vague.

Some of the Malay officials could not be roused from their general apathy which made things difficult for the European Government officials to carry out their new jobs. Sabotage was expected and a guard put on the aerodrome and petrol dump. One evening one of the local Volunteers came bringing Stuart's rifle and equipment, much to Ah Seng's glee. His eyes sparkled and he fell to putting a tremendous polish on everything. He was certain we were going to join China at last against the Japs. His newspaper insisted that Hong Kong was "shut up" by the Japs and therefore we should have to come in. He talked war with many excited gesticulations to Stuart for a solid half-hour one evening, a rare outburst from the gloom into which he was sinking.

Stuart could never leave the end of a 'phone except to go out on long rice licensing expeditions up-river, across to Pangkor and up and down the Dindings, arranging for transport lorries and ascertaining who were genuine dealers. The news was grim and yet it seemed like a nightmare from which we must awaken.

We saw a lot of the Steeles; the fear of what was going to happen at home drew us all together. While we waited tensely for the inevitable declaration, in a sudden fit of optimism, I sent a large order for more paints, brushes and canvas. But that sanity to which such things belong seemed very distant. On Saturday, September 2nd, the local Volunteers, Stuart among them, went to the hospital for a medical examination, typhoid injections and vaccinations. That night, just to add to the tension, a Malay on Pangkor ran amok in the audience at a Chinese *wayang*. He killed one woman and injured other people with his knife. Running amok, which used to be so common an occurrence among Malays, had become almost unheard of since asylums were built.

At a quarter to six in the evening of Sunday, September 3rd, we heard that England had declared war. Sadly we went down to the estuary and sat in the Rest House garden alone. We watched the sampans and *koleks* coming in against the sunset up the brilliant coloured river. It was so beautiful and peaceful it seemed impossible to believe we were at war at last. The frangipanni petals dropped to the grass one by one and lay there creamy white and pure; a dog barked in the village; tiny waves lapped the gunwale of a passing *kolek*. *This* was the only reality; this beauty. One day we shall wake from the nightmare to the reality again.

At first we felt agonizing worry about parents at home, and our minds were full of horrific pictures of raids and gas, but reassuring cables arrived and the mails, although they began to be erratic, did not cease altogether as we had feared. Everyone settled down to the "phoney war" period. Letters from home became more and more important. The mail 'bus passed Joan Steele's house a quarter of an hour before it reached Lumut. So if she had any home mail she would ring me up to let me know, and then I would hang out of the window waiting for the Customs peon to bring up my letters. Stuart also generally rang up from the office to shorten the suspense if there was any mail. This was disturbing to my work, for Kandasami, Yahya and Sareh and Mat still came to sit for me. Kandasami brought three small Tamil children for me to paint one morning. He led the string of them by the hand looking little more than a child himself, pathetically thin and leggy, with great calf eyes and wide smile. There was a child of nine in a scarlet dress with frangipanni flowers in her hair; a tiny girl with a fierce, fat face and a pigtail which stuck straight out behind her head; and lastly a little boy of six with enormous black eyes. They smelt dreadfully. They scratched their legs, arm-pits, tummies and heads until, by auto-suggestion, I felt in exactly the same state myself. Kandasami had to act as interpreter as they didn't understand Malay and I was but vaguely aware of two words of Tamil: "*ingedi-angedi,*" which means, I believe, hither and thither (a most expressive phrase and one which was useful to describe the erratic movements on the roads of some of the Tamils themselves—after the toddy shops have opened), and the other, a favourite word in Tamil, was *nalagi*, meaning to-morrow. They use it so frequently when asked to do a job that they are sometimes, rather unkindly, called the "*nalagi* people."

In October when the *bulan puasa*, the Mohammedan month of fasting,[1] began I found I could not use Malay models as they were too exhausted to sit. By strict Mohammedan law they are not allowed even to swallow their saliva, nor must any food or drink be taken between six in the morning and six at night. During the night they eat large meals and consequently their life is so disorganized with lack of sleep and digestive troubles that the *puasa* is a depressing month. They go about looking listless and miserable; they cannot do their work properly; they stop playing badminton and their courts get weedy and unkempt in a few days. They become run down and ill. This was what happened to Mat. After about a week of fasting he became very unwell and developed lurid spots which he immediately took to be small-pox; he certainly looked ghastly. Stuart took him in the car to the hospital at once. It proved only to be chicken pox; but he was kept in an isolation ward and became more and more lonely and miserable. Every time Stuart went to speak to him through a window he was worrying about the car and how we were managing without him. He brooded on all manner of things; he had been married to Sareh for ten years and they still only had one child; should he marry again and increase his family? One son was a poor family . . . would he be out in time for *Hari Raya Puasa*—the

[1] The Ramadan.

feast day which occurs when the first new moon is seen after the month of fasting?

He *was* out for *Hari Raya*; but he was a changed man. He left Sareh and little Mat and went up-river to a Malay wedding where he met and fell for a woman named Puteh. She was pale-faced and plump; her eyes were round and dark with kohl. Shortly afterwards he confessed that he had taken a second wife. He knew it was crazy on his wage, but as he said: "*Tuan*, what could I do? *She* fell in love with me. . . . *Banyak susah*. . . ." Very difficult indeed. Sareh, beautiful, golden-skinned Sareh, was a wise woman. She was not going to stay and be overshadowed by wife number two, so she packed up her things and went home to Krian. I went out to say good-bye to her: "Blessings on your going," I said. "Blessings on your staying," came the traditional answer. I was very sorry to see her go, with her sweet serious face now so sad.

Then the pale, plump Puteh took over, bringing with her elaborate, silver-embroidered velvet hangings and puce-coloured curtains. Mat had an enormous old iron bedstead which he had bought in Krian when he married Sareh and of which he was not a little proud, as most Malays sleep on mats on platforms raised off the floor. Sareh's plain cotton coverings were taken off the bed and Puteh re-decorated it with ornate velvet hangings; it was all very new and wonderful and Mat was much impressed. But Puteh had a young niece, an ugly child of ten or so who frequently visited her. She ran about Mat's little garden; she picked all the camelias off his tree by the garage; she screamed in a shrill voice; she giggled whenever she saw Mat until she began to get on his nerves. Then two more little female relations appeared, tiny children, and they all settled down to live with Puteh in Mat's quarters. There was no longer even any room for Mat in the family bed —he was forced to sleep in an old long chair in the garage, cramped in beside the car. This lasted for a few months, then one day there was a scene. One of the giggling little girls had broken the last of Mat's favourite coffee cups. Their silly faces and stupid laughs and Puteh's cowlike eyes were too much for him. He raged; he turned them all out and he wept. Finally he came to Stuart and said he was going to ask Sareh to come back; he had discovered he could not possibly live without her;

they had been through much trouble together. This was what we had been hoping to hear.

As it happened, Stuart was about to do the north coast patrol in the *Rimau* up to Kuala Krau which was the northern limit of his beat. So he offered to take Mat, there and then, so he could visit Sareh in Krian. We left Lumut late at night, there was a waning moon; but it was as bright as day, too bright and too beautiful to want to sleep. We overtook a junk sailing fast and swung the searchlight on her. Sleepy faces appeared and men handed over the papers. The moon shone through her ragged lattice sails and flung into sharp relief all the intricate jumble of her rigging. It looked a jumble to me. The Chinese attitude to such things as scaffolding, tools, rigging, ladders, all of which seem important to the western mind, appears to be casual and haphazard, often dangerously so, but I do not believe the quality of their work suffers. I was just getting to sleep on deck when we overhauled another junk which Stuart searched. After that, sleep was difficult; the moon shone across my pillow; the wind flapped the stays madly and a big ground-swell got up. When finally I did fall asleep it was only to be woken every now and again by crashing, rending sounds as we smashed through old fishing stakes in the inky blackness that followed the setting of the moon. These stakes run out in the shallow waters for miles and some are half submerged. It was very dark, but for the wonderful stars. I loved seeing the Plough, even though it appeared to be upside down to my English eyes and one would have to be transported many thousands of miles north to see it again the right way up. . . . I slept until the east began to glow and the sea turned a cold, steely-blue; I rolled myself in the blankets then and snuggled down to watch the dawn. The pitch of the boat was short and sharp and I felt as if I should slide off my canvas bed and shoot in between the rails at any moment. The huge glistening ball of the sun swept up out of a particularly craggy and dramatic peak. If one were not so accustomed to the miracle of dawn the majesty of such a sight would make one think that the end of the world at least was at hand.

Stuart had finished his job at Kuala Krau and Mat kept us waiting; but when he arrived back from Parit Buntar in Krian, wearing his best clothes of purple and fuschia, he looked radiantly happy. His arms were full of papayas, presents for us from Sareh. All was well; as we hoped she had promised to come back and would return in a month's time. Puteh was duly divorced; but poor old Mat had to pay $52 alimony which, at the rate he paid it, would take him two years and two months. . . . That was happily settled but when we got back there had been disturbances at the Customs quarters. Yahya had nearly been knifed by one of the married men who alleged that he, Yahya, had been making love to his wife. Numerous frictions like this were constantly brought up for arbitration. . . .

Alice and Henry, who had given us Cleo, used to come down a good deal from Taiping, as Henry was supervising the laying of a telephone cable from Pangkor to Lumut. When they came they brought their young son, Robin, to be painted. He had a small, wedge-shaped face, with dark green eyes, blond hair in a fringe and very long lashes. He was a grand little fellow, not at all an amah-spoilt child. When we had finished painting I sometimes went over to Pangkor with Alice. One day, on the way across the island to Teddy's house, we saw a python about twelve feet long tied on a pole with two men to carry it. It had just eaten a couple of ducks—which fact was quite obvious. It must have been longing to disgorge them—if a python has any longings. The men expected to get about four dollars for its skin, a poor price we thought, judging by the cost of such a skin in the shops. When we reached Pangkor House we told Teddy what we had seen; but he was not much impressed as two men were able to carry the python—*he* was only interested, so he said, in the forty-footers which need six men to carry them. . . .

Teddy knew a good deal about snakes. He had been bitten by a black krait from whose bite few people recover, and he had seen the hamadryads' nuptial dance, a fearsome and wonderful sight. He suffered from some kind of trench feet, contracted in the last war, and had to inject himself with ampoules of cobra venom. He spoke of a new extract of hamadryad's venom which was being tested as a cure for leprosy and possibly for infantile paralysis.

Teddy had the best Chinese Boy I have ever met. His name

was Ah Chong; he was very quick and intelligent with a swift sense of humour and a delightful smile. He was, I should think, the perfect servant.

There was a big samsu-distilling gang on Pangkor just then and Mrs. Teddy was a little scared at the mysterious noises in the night and the intrigues going on. Stuart had quite a lot to do rounding up that gang. So while our husbands worked, Alice and I watched the Indian fishermen, who lived in the centre of Pasir Bogah Bay, drawing in their mile-long net. It was lovely there under the big-leaved trees in the dappled shade; rippling muscles and glistening backs dark against the glaring white sand and the blue curve of the bay. They sang as they pulled, a strange long-drawn chant with an echoing answer from the front ranks. They would have a big catch of whitebait, the fine mesh of the net was alive with them, a threshing white foam.

One evening when we came on to the old split bamboo jetty at Pangkor village there were three or four Chinese fishing sampans in, swarming with half-naked Chinese. I suppose it was the effect of the evening light, but I had rarely seen Pangkor so gloriously colourful. The sunburnt torsos were red like Red Indians' and the paint on the boats glowed a deep venetian red. The men were gambling and playing mah-jong, and some were perched on the masts like monkeys. The whole scene was a rich mass of flaming earth colours and warm reds.

Back at Lumut, our garden was being drastically dug up as drains were being laid. At last "push-and-pulls" were about to be installed and we could say good-bye to the *jambans* and Jeyes Fluid. I had always kept the Jeyes in an old Veuve Clicquot bottle because I liked the contrast between that sleek gold and green bottle and its now strictly utilitarian contents. The beautiful new "push-and-pulls" were dumped, for some unknown reason, in the policeman's garden and there they sat in the rain for a week. Such were the ways of P.W.D. workmen. All three of the Government houses were having them installed, so there were at least nine of these naked-looking objects on the policeman's lawn.

The drain-digging had one good effect which was to disturb the gloriosa superba roots we had long since planted, for they suddenly began sprouting. We gardened a good deal and, when war was declared, began to plant vegetables. The carrots and tomatoes were a success; but it was difficult to raise much enthusiasm over vegetable gardening. The flowers were another matter. The zinnia blooms were now five inches across; we became so enamoured of them we could not even resist gazing at them from time to time during the evenings, by the light of a reading-lamp held from the window; and when we eventually came to sowing seeds by the headlights of the car after tennis, we thought we were indeed real gardeners. But our pride was a little dashed by the policeman's Tamil gardener. He came up the path one evening, when we were admiring our own flowers, to cadge a few plants, and giving our garden a look over, critically remarked that we should never have any real success unless all our beds were trenched *three* feet deep. . . .

That took the wind out of our sails. But it was true. The only good gardens in Malaya all had trenched beds. The soil is so bad it should be deeply manured and nourished.

From his own flame-of-the-forest trees, Bertie brought us magnificent seed pods eighteen inches long; in two years the trees grew from this seed to eight or nine feet. The carnations really were lovely, the envy even of the Padre who was a great gardener. Also the roses, of which we might well be proud, for they were flourishing specimens judged climatically. We had fun making a rockery, with granite left over from P.W.D. efforts, brick paths and new beds, and Dr. Menun brought a honeysuckle plant which was sweet-scented and home-like.

Caesar would come in from these gardening evenings with pale blue plumbago flowers hanging rakishly from his mouth. The flowers were sticky and clung to his whiskers, but if he had chosen them they could not have looked better as they exactly matched his eyes. One evening we followed him down the steep drop below the terrace, where the hill fell away to the *kampong*, and so discovered a little path winding round the escarpment and through the edge of the jungle to water catchment tanks in the hillside. Large night-blue butterflies as big as birds fluttered in front of Caesar as he strolled along; when he thought we had gone far enough, he cried anxiously; brave as he now was about the jungle, he did not like to venture very far from the house. Under the jungle trees, among the thin, snaky roots and flat stems, there were blue ferns like shot silk. We dug up one for the garden, but it swiftly lost its blue sheen although planted in the shade of a temple tree. . . .

Once or twice at sunset, a weird creature appeared on the top of a dead tree-trunk in the scrub and bush near the garden. Its tail was long, its head small with ears like a cat. It crouched black against the angry western sky for some time and then suddenly glided off into the trees below. We concluded it was a flying lemur. It was difficult to find out about animals in Malaya; they are very rarely seen and disappointingly few people seemed to know anything much about them.

There was a more common creature, however, that I at least came to know only too well—the scorpion. Kandasami caught the first one I saw; it was as big as a crayfish, quite six inches long and jet black. I killed several myself after that in the bathrooms.

Then one Sunday the policeman took us over to Emerald Bay on Pangkor Laut in his launch. The bay lived up to its name and was very green and still that day. I got stung on the arm by a scorpion which was on a bit of driftwood from the tide line. Stuart sucked the place promptly and painfully and we swam back to the launch. The old serang was very concerned; he wetted his fingers and touched the sting on my arm invoking Allah and looking up to heaven as he did so. The policeman then had a go at it. He had no medicines on board and nothing but gin, which he insisted was good for scorpion stings—to be used both externally and internally. So with these varied administrations I suffered no ill effects at all; in fact I got very happy on the policeman's gins and it was altogether rather a cheerful day. . . .

On the way out we had spotted a crocodile swimming across between the islands; I was surprised to see one so far from the river mouth. It repeatedly surfaced, as if daring the serang to follow and apparently jeering at us with its yellow fangs showing. There were turtles about too, a whole shoal of sea otters gambolling like porpoises, one lonely hornbill flying above the jungle and many exquisite white terns fishing in the bay.

X

KANDASAMI'S DRUNKEN SPREE AND THE CHINESE SINGERS

THE HARI RAYA HOLIDAY was followed shortly by the Hindu festival of Tivavali. Kandasami, resplendent in a new mauve shirt, was drunk long before midday. The roads were full of *ingedi-angedi*, gaily dressed Tamils, and even the chickens seemed more screwed than usual, flying madly across at the approach of every car.

Parties of Tamils, including two of Lumut's dustmen, came up to the house to dance in the hope of collecting a few dollars. They wore vivid garlands round their necks; some carried brass pots from which towered trembling pyramids of flowers. With these balanced precariously on their heads they danced and sang in the garden, beating little hide drums and twirling rattles. Their dance seemed to be a rough combination of rumba cum black-bottom. Really nothing to do with this, except that it concerned Hindus, was an extraordinary dream I had, extraordinary and so beautiful that I could not account for it. My imagination in waking hours certainly could not reach such a fantastic Arabian Night's vision. I saw a crowd of young Indians, very magnificent, in a great hall, each holding in his hands the head of a classically lovely young Indian girl by her long black hair. There was no blood and the scene was so strangely beautiful that I felt no horror. I knew I ought to be afraid but the contours and expressions of their faces, most especially the dead faces of the girls, were so aesthetically satisfying that I felt nothing but delight at the perfection of the vision. . . .

To come down to earth again; after Tivavali, Kandasami's drinking bouts grew more frequent. One of these, although it might have been disastrous, was rather a comedy. We heard people shouting in the garden and going to the window saw

Kandasami standing in the middle of the drive yelling at Ah Seng in the wild high voice Tamils use when drunk, or angry, or both. Ah Seng had his coat off and confronted Kandasami with clenched fists, while Ah Chi was looking on, waving a tea-cloth as she always did in an emergency, her funny little face puckered up with excitement, crying: *Pukul dia! Pukul dia!* "Hit him! Hit him!" to Ah Seng, while Kandasami made wobbly passes in the air.

Stuart went down to arbitrate as usual. It appeared that Kandasami, having been drinking hard most of the day (there was some festival on), had met Ah Seng in the village and tried to borrow ten cents. Ah Seng apologized, but said that having just lost eighty cents he could not afford to lend, especially as Kandasami owed him fifteen cents already! Kandasami was infuriated; he dashed up to a policeman and shouted that Ah Seng was accusing him of theft. Ah Seng, very much annoyed and on his dignity, marched off home up the hill followed by Kandasami wildly yelling insults all the way.

Stuart patched up the quarrel; Ah Seng went back to the house and Kandasami, still a little *ingedi-angedi*, staggered around, attempting to water the garden. So we went out for a walk, and left him to it, unwisely. We got as far as Downing Street, when a shouting, bleeding figure overtook us, dancing with excitement in the roadway, bleeding all down his black and muddy legs. It was, of course, Kandasami, now swearing loudly that Ah Seng and Kuki had attacked him with sticks. Stuart took him into the Police Station to make a report and had him sent to the hospital. He was not to be allowed near the house again that evening. We returned home. Large lumps of the rockery were lying about the drive and Kandasami's watering tins and carrying stick were scattered all over the back garden. Ah Chi was looking very grim and Ah Seng calm and extremely cheerful. Apparently Kandasami had started arguing again, and Kuki, on telling him to shut up, was immediately attacked with the carrying stick. Ah Chi, always very protective of her family, had stepped in and snatched the stick from Kandasami's hands. Kandasami had then challenged Ah Seng to battle; but Ah Seng (who was well built and had been a champion boxer in Hainan) said it would have been "like hitting the wind" to hit Kandasami and had merely chased him round the garden. Kandasami then started hurling the rockery at Ah Seng, falling over himself with rage, and finally fled down hill on his bicycle. But—he fell off ignominiously outside the policeman's house, and had thus sustained his injuries. There were witnesses. . . .

He returned very sober and chastened the next day wearing a long sarong down to the ground to hide his wounds. He was given another chance, but shortly after this episode there was a fresh outburst. A terrible din issued from the *kampong* below the house one night and the Police rang up to inform us that Kandasami, drunk again, was causing a riot in the *kampong* and chasing people. It was hopeless; we said he must go unless he would reform; he did so for a while, but finally decided he could not possibly stay on *without* getting drunk as he had no relations in Lumut and, thus being lonely, simply could *not* do without his toddy. That was honest anyhow. So off he went to Ipoh to his uncle. Tamils seem to have absolutely no head for drink. I was sorry to see him go because, between these disturbances, he was such a good model. But Stuart had a wonderful idea of trying out six gardeners simultaneously for one week in order to pick out the most suitable model and best good worker. However, this ambitious scheme never came off; a good thing perhaps as the garden would have resounded with shrill Tamil voices and tipsy squabbling. The next gardener was old, hideously ugly, but very amiable and quiet; his name was Ramasami and he had a plump, kindly-faced wife and a vast family of cheerful children, who sometimes helped him in small ways with the garden.

Russia entered Poland. . . . And the German war machine rolled on. It still seemed very far away and the war at home still in its strange quiet before the storm. The sinking of the P. & O. *Rawalpindi* was much felt by many Malayans; a familiar ship of many voyages. . . .

With the local Volunteers Stuart took part in target practices with a solitary Lewis gun at Sitiawan; but as yet there were no regular camps. Work and life went on much the same as before. Glorious days of colour and peace. An opaque, rose-pale mist hid the hill-tops at dawn and the jungle was swiftly bathed in translucent gold from the heights to the valleys; and at night

Venus often shone so brilliantly that she cast a reflection on the sea as bright as that of a young moon.

There were portrait commissions in Taiping, days crammed with work and tennis and talk. The sky at sunset there was full of flying foxes, flying high up over the little town of "Great Peace." Later they would have made us think of bomber formations, but then they were just interesting.

I also visited the Turners' Estate "Over the River"; they had been twenty-five years in the country, struggled with malaria and knew what loneliness meant. The country there was beautiful, on the fringe of the *ulu*. Even for Malays the *ulu* has the glamour of mystery and far distance. It is the place where planting has failed and "the ridges of abandoned rice-fields have broken down, where there are no fish in the tiny pools, where the gibbon swings from the branches and apes howl to the moon."[1]

"Over the River" there were wild-pig and pigeon and sometimes a tiger. The tigers did not visit Lumut much, but in one very dry season a family of them came down the ravine by our house to the village and snuffled at one or two doors. Next morning their pugs were found round the club; evidently they were needing a drink. Very rarely we heard them coughing in the long grass just below the garden at night. Anthony was missing for a while and Ah Seng was afraid the jungle wild dogs or the tigers had got him. But he returned safely once more much to Ah Seng's joy. Ah Seng admired him very much; I suspect he considered the other cats were a little too crazy and undignified.

At the Turners' Estate I was taken to see a Malay beauty with the idea of painting her. She was only twenty-two, but already considered rather *passée*. In the end she could not be spared from work, as every available tapper was needed just then to deal with the higher war-time output. She was still lovely, with a high, clear brow and wide, smooth cheekbones, wide-set eyes and perfect full lips.

Mrs. Turner and I crossed a dyke, balancing on the pole bridge, and climbed up the ladder of a little *atap* house to meet some more Malays. A beautiful little girl crouched in the dim room; she was ill with malaria; her hair in a dark untidy cloud

[1] Anonymous Malay poet.

Beach from North Headland—Pulau Rumbia

K. S. and Stuart

round her damp, oval face and her small naked body hunched in a Kelantan sarong of green and silver. We squatted in the tiny *atap* verandah and talked to the child's old grandmother. I did sketch a few houses that day while Mrs. Turner nobly dashed round getting an umbrella to hold over me, and keeping off and chatting to the crowds. The house I unfortunately chose had a very primitive draining system—simply seepage through the bamboo floor on to the ground beneath—which finally overpowered me.

Two very backwood Malays did come from "Over the River" to sit for me in the studio, but they were more trouble than they were worth; an old woman named Gemma and a little girl, Teh. When told to come as usual at 8.30 a.m. they arrived at two o'clock one afternoon and said they had gone to sleep by the roadside waiting for the 'bus. . . .

The contrast of the old, lined face next to the young, smooth one was very attractive, but the models were exactly like shy little animals. When Cleo came to inspect them, as she did all my models, and stared at them, they merely sat and stared back at her without a flicker of interest. So Cleo turned round, made an expressively brief comment to me in her Siamese voice and left the studio in disgust.

At one sitting the child Teh had hiccups and each time she yawned, which was often, she also hiccupped solemnly. Whenever I turned my back to refill my palette she rushed to the window to spit with gusto—I suppose I should have been grateful that she didn't use the floor. They could never by any chance remember the pose. Gemma went on talking all the while in her distractingly difficult *kampong* Malay, asking me numerous personal questions; and, to add to my troubles, they both wore the small yellow jasmine flowers in their hair which always seemed to have a soporific effect on me, so heady was their perfume.

A band of Chinese singers called the Wu-han Songsters was touring Malaya at the end of 1939, collecting for the China Relief Fund. They were young men and women of the student type fresh from China. When they came to Kampong Koh, a large Chinese village in the district, we went, rather as a duty, and received a very pleasant surprise after the first round of speeches was over. The Europeans were seated in the front rows and from such close quarters the bawling-match speeches were absolutely head-splitting. Two extremely cheerful Chinese delivered the same speech almost simultaneously, one in Mandarin and one in Hokien. How anyone followed it, I do not know. A few phrases were spoken in English "for the benefit of our foreign guests." It was all about Generalissimo Chiang Kai-shek and the Relief Fund. I was struck at the time by the similarity of his propaganda to what we were then longing to say for the benefit of the U.S.A. "People of the friendly nations, you must realize that peace is indivisible and isolation impracticable. So long as Japanese aggression is not checked, peace in the Far East, and indeed in the world in general, cannot be maintained. The upholding of world justice and the sanctity of treaties and the protection of the well-being of mankind and the heritage of civilization are common tasks that fall on the shoulders of every human being. . . ."

I was amazed at the way the Chinese publicized people's donations. At the beginning of the evening a boy of about fifteen came on the stage and the announcer said he had given three dollars, his whole month's earnings, to the Relief Fund; he was cheered and clapped. He was followed by a very thin, poverty-stricken-looking Tamil dressed in dirty rags; he possessed a small estate, it was announced, and had given one hundred dollars. He received a great ovation under the cover of which one of our planter friends leant across and whispered to Stuart that it was that very Tamil, now looking so desperately poor, who had but recently sold him several acres of "the small estate" for one thousand nine hundred dollars. . . . However, it was all in a good cause.

Later the stage was decked with long strips of paper bearing in Chinese or in English the names of contributors and the amounts; most embarrassing to the western mind, especially if one happened to be short of ready cash—as we always were!

After all this the Wu-han Songsters appeared. There were about eighteen of them, the girls in very simple pale blue cotton Shanghai dresses and the men in white drill. Some of the girls were like those I had seen only in drawings of old China, with very slanting eyes, finely modelled features and small cherry mouths, strikingly different from the average rather blunt features of many Malayan Chinese who mostly came from South China. They had lovely voices; we had expected the harsh strange singing that one hears in the theatres; but this was the singing of New China, and although that spine-shivering huskiness still lingered in the voices, it was modulated by an increased scale and richer harmony than of old. The songs were mostly to do with the war; but very few were war-like. There was an atmosphere about these singers that, apart from the beauty of their voices, stirred us all; their youth and patriotism perhaps. They sang the Song of the Guerrillas, which I have never forgotten, of the guerrilla farmer-fighters of China, hushed and whispering music, throbbing with a relentless determination; the song of peasants who creep through the dark to ambush the Japanese.

When the singing was over, there followed another hour and a half of raucous speeches in Chinese. Our heads were splitting; we could not politely leave and we hoped for more singing but it was not forthcoming. We got away at last at eleven o'clock though the show was starting afresh with a play, which we heard afterwards was extremely grim and gruellingly realistic with sounds off of a Chinese girl being raped by Japanese soldiers in a hut. . . .

Later when the Wu-han singers reached Penang, the Chinese communists there seized the opportunity to stage a demonstration. I believe there was nearly a riot: the police had difficulty in subduing the mob as they had put their children in the forefront.

The Chinese were splendid about their Relief Fund; some of the younger ones in Malaya have never been to China, but their patriotism is a real living thing. Many had relations there still and had sometimes gone back even during the war. I admired, too, the way they celebrated the anniversary of a tragedy. It seemed to me a highly practical form of exhortation; the anniversary of Japan's attack on China, the seventh day of the seventh month, or "the double seven," was kept with flags flown from every Chinese window; the little Lumut street was gay with the red and blue and white of China's "sun shining in a blue sky on a red and fertile earth."

Ah Seng was acting in a play in aid of the Fund, but he bashfully refused to say what part he took. The day after the first performance one of the smiling brothers, Eng Wah, said to Stuart: "What a pretty girl Ah Seng made in the play last night!" So that was it. There was a bright green Shanghai dress hanging up to air in the back garden and I could not resist saying to Ah Chi: "What a lovely dress! Did Ah Seng wear it in the play?" But she stood by her brother and denied it stoutly. He was most anxious we should not see the play, so we did not embarrass him by appearing in the audience, though we caught a glimpse of the stage from the road one night and Ah Seng in bright green with red cheeks and lips; certainly a lovely girl.

About the same time the Malays gave a play in aid of the Perak Patriotic Fund. It was very amusing; but it lasted for well over four hours which was exhausting and confusing as they squeezed *entr'acte* within *entr'acte*. So the main play was a little difficult to follow: according to Malay custom there was a dancing or musical turn or even one act of a three-act play sandwiched in between each scene. The Malays were excellent at burlesquing the Tamils. There was one delicious scene I still remember; a slightly intoxicated Tamil in a rickshaw was engaged in aimless argument with a road sweeper. It was amusing because Tamils speak Malay exactly as if it were Tamil with the same sing-song intonation, and the Malay who took this part got the accent to perfection, and the more the audience shrieked the more excited and the more "Tamilly" he became.

The "heroine" of the long play had omitted to shave recently, which was unfortunate; but the hero, one of Stuart's own men, was well cast. The play seemed interminable; it grew as it progressed, being more or less impromptu and when we left, long past midnight, it was still going strong.

The Europeans' Patriotic Fund efforts were not so ambitious; but consisted, in the Lumut District, of raffles, Bomb Funds, and so on. In the bigger places plays and the usual dances and tournaments were held, causing an enormous amount of expenditure on petrol and drinks which seemed not quite the right approach; however, useful sums were sent home from Malaya.

Just before Christmas we went to the mangrove streams at Lekir, a dead-end of a place beyond Kampong Koh, to pick

Malayan "holly" for the pudding. The holly grows in the mud and is prickly and shaped like the English variety, but not so dark. The Steeles dined with us that Christmas night; the house was full of red roses, white clematis and carnations; there were scarlet and gold Chinese candles on the table. Afterwards we listened to the King's speech and the quotation which was to hold so much meaning in the coming years. The smiling Eng Wahs sent a fat turkey, two blue and white jars of excellent ginger and a bottle of gin. In fact we were showered with gifts, and Christmas was more like the already fabulous ones of Edwardian days at home. In this and many other ways Malaya had not progressed beyond pre-Great War standards and traditions. Sareh brought a lurid cake she had made herself; it was covered with almond paste and sugar rolled in snaky coils of emerald green, orange and puce. Its appearance was alarming and it weighed like a brick. Mat brought a live duck, some fresh papayas and an elaborate wire contraption of his own making. It was painted bright blue, entwined with minute pink paper roses and numerous tiny electric lights. It was meant, he explained, to enshrine a photograph. It was gay and quaint lit up at night on the verandah like a little bush of fireflies in the dark. His friend Abdullah, one of Stuart's men, came with an enormous paper rose-bush in a flower-pot and a bunch of rather amazing knitted bananas made by his wife. I cherished those bananas; they were almost Surrealistic and recalled a fur tea-cup and saucer I had seen in a Surrealist exhibition; but the rose-bush, which was a horror, embarrassed me; I could not get rid of it, as Mat would know if I did. Luckily Cleo and Caesar also took a violent and instant dislike to it and tore it to shreds during their play.

But I liked the care and thought that had gone into the making of all these quaint, childish things. The Malays are not nowadays an artistic people; apart from some of their silver work and heavy woven sarongs, they have had no real art since their Hindu days—Islam has killed it. I felt at times as if there was something about the country—probably due to its climate—that made for laziness, inertia, lack of originality; almost a barrenness. . . .

XI

MAXWELL HILL. MALAYAN FOOD AND TALK

MRS. TURNER had invited us to spend that Chinese New Year holiday at "The Cottage" on the summit of Taiping Hill. The Chinese New Year falls a little more than a month later than that of the Gregorian calendar and is the chief Chinese festival. In Malaya the holiday lasted about four days, although the actual preparations and celebrations of the Chinese themselves often extend over a much longer period.

Cleo was just about due to have her first family. So, going by the book of words, we "introduced the queen to her box." Her box was very elaborate and lined with soft scraps of silk and paper to scrabble in. I hated leaving her just then with only Ah Chi in charge. Kuki and Ah Seng were going away for the New Year to visit relations in Penang and Ah Chi would join in the village festivities. We ourselves felt so excited to be going away on a hill holiday, the first since we had arrived in the country, that we opened a bottle of champagne and the servants had a glass each to drink to their New Year: those were definitely the days before war-time economies came in. We started long before dawn the next morning; it was cold and dark, driving through the rubber. Strings of silent tappers trailed along the roads wearing lights strapped to their foreheads. We drove to the foot of Taiping Hill where the Tamil porters ordered by Mrs. Turner were waiting for us. As she put it, we were her guests from the foot of the hill. It was still cold in the heavy shadow of the hill; in our ears was the cool clear sound of the water dropping from the cliffs into the pools below. As I was the lighter, smaller chair-men carried me; but though small they were incredibly strong and fast on their feet. They took almost vertical short cuts at such a dash that I lay on my back with my legs precipitously higher than my head.

Every few minutes the carriers grunted in unison and at that signal the chair and I sailed precariously over their heads as they shifted the carrying poles from one shoulder to another. From this job the trapezius muscles had become developed to such an extent that they sloped steeply from neck to shoulder in a hard lump.

The jungle was cold still. The sunlight slanted down on to the leaves, in places shining so brilliantly on a branch or single leaf that the whiteness of it dazzled one's eyes, set as it was against the cool dark depths. The path wound past slabs of mossy rock and over trickling streams; as we got higher there were flowers new to me and the trees became less dense. The first clearing at two thousand feet was filled with sunlight and for a few minutes reminded us of Switzerland, for there was almost a sting in the cool morning air; the little houses of wood looked faintly like chalets and the flowers were gay. We stopped at a small Rest House to which Mrs. Turner, with her far-reaching hospitality, had sent down patum sandwiches and beer. Then we plunged into the jungle once more and the grunting chair-men raced us up the paths and round the hair-pin bends. We overtook, in great style, a very fat man being carried by five chair-men with an extra one, trotting astern, to shove and exhort.

The next clearing, called Maxwell's Hill, was a mass of flowers. The neat green terraces and lawns were bordered with roses, dahlias, montbretia, gloriosa, honeysuckle and morning glory. We decided to walk from there and our host came down to meet us as we puffed up the last long eight hundred feet to The Cottage.

It seemed to be on the very top of the world as one came up over the edge and saw it against the sky, surrounded by banks of brilliant salvias and nasturtiums. It had a charm completely of its own. Mrs. Turner came out to welcome us, and fussed around with an air of amiable proprietorship. Wrapped in warm coats we sat on the verandah and savoured the deliciously sudden climatic change. At four thousand five hundred feet one looked down from the very edge of the terrace on to Taiping far below with its red roofs and avenues of trees, its club, prison, church and great white patches of tin mines all sizzling in the tropic heat. The coast visible from Penang to

Telok Anson was veiled in a gold-blue haze. I experienced then that strange feeling, so strong up in all Malayan hill stations, of being, temporarily, utterly aloof from the ordinary life below, in an unreal world, not of the tropics nor of anywhere else. It was as cool as an English summer, the flowers were English and one had almost an English energy. It was a curious feeling as if one were caught between two worlds, snatched up out of the tropics into a kind of No-Man's land.

There was a roaring wood fire in our room; a large bunch of blood-red dahlias made a gay splash of colour on the old stone mantelpiece. And Mrs. Turner had filled other vases too with daisies and violets and golden rod. There was no need for mosquito nets over the beds; there was the luxury of a hot-water bottle; wood and metal were chill to the touch; the water in the Shanghai jar was tinglingly cold; one's skin felt cool and dry. How delicious to be cold again for a little while!

There were other guests besides ourselves. We played tennis on a court below the house surrounded by blue morning glory. The mist came down in the afternoons and people retired to their rooms and wood fires to sleep. After a large homeside tea we played croquet on the lawn, where, beyond a bed of blue salvia, the world ended abruptly, or we walked up Gunong Hijau (Green Mountain), a peak a few feet higher than The Cottage. There I saw the weird cups of the pitcher-plant and was shown the pugs of the Hill rhinos, which I confess scared me a little. They looked so very fresh and new in the mud. These rhinos, a mother and daughter, were reputed to be extremely friendly; in fact the Tamil cook at The Cottage swore they frequently called at the back door where he fed them with scraps. I was not banking too much on their friendliness, however, and had no desire to meet them especially when the mist was wreathing around as it did at times, blanketing the paths and trees in damp swirling whiteness. From Gunong Hijau on clear days one could see across to the great central ranges, and down to the Kuala Kangsar valley and to the fantastic limestone hills and inland islands of Ipoh.

As I went to my room on the last night a black snake slipped under the door, evidently attracted by the warmth of the wood fire. It was so dark in colour that I feared it might be a krait;

it was not: but the limp corpse was soon flung over the terrace, down towards the sparkling lights of Taiping, laid out so neatly thousands of feet below.

The next day we walked the nine miles down, getting hotter and hotter as we descended into the tropics again and our spirits sinking accordingly. It was raining at the bottom, a soft, hot rain. Our car, left at Alice's house, had broken down, so she very kindly put us up for the night. When we did leave for Lumut, we took with us Adam, another of her pure-bred Siamese kittens. He was tiny but had a tremendous voice, out of all proportion to his size; he screamed blue murder at Cleo (whose kittens had not yet arrived) and hid under the side-board all day, raging.

The house at Lumut was clean and shining and full of flowers, and in my room there was a vase of the indescribably fragrant tree blossoms which Ah Chi always put up, especially for homecomings. Ah Seng presented me with a large pink and white sugar cake from Penang and a bowl of oranges. Ah Chi, walking shyly behind him, carried a live chicken. These were their generous New Year presents.

I had jokingly said to Jean, who was coming to stay once more, that she would just about be in time for Cleo's confinement, and with her experience of cat families, would be a useful midwife. It so happened she was. We fetched her from Ipoh and arrived home soon after midnight. Cleo rushed to me as we came in and promptly sat down on my feet and groaned. I paled, inexperienced in these matters as I was:

"Jean! It's started," I said nervously.

We all three rushed upstairs and popped Cleo in her box on the back verandah. She had torn the chair covers and ripped up the sheets on the beds; poor little cat, she was very scared. Stuart and I were alarmed by all this violence and Cleo's terror; but Jean remained calm and issued instructions. When the first was born, Cleo, the uninitiated, started racing about the back verandah.

Caesar was very intrigued; he sat and watched anxiously, but kept well out of the way. Cleo was caught, put back in the box and the rest of the event proceeded according to plan. . . .

Meanwhile Adam was becoming an amusing young cat; he inspected my models in the traditional manner and if he did not like them he said so in a clear voice. One day the sharp leg of a cockroach became stuck in his tongue. I have never known an animal more patient and brave, as Stuart removed it. It was quite a tricky operation as the thorn-like leg was deeply embedded in the tongue, which was only the size of a postage stamp; however Adam never uttered a moan, but he became hotter and hotter as I held him. It took three-quarters of an hour to remove the forked leg. Adam then drank two saucers of milk and purred loudly and cheerfully.

He was a sporting wee fellow and enjoyed fights with Caesar, who was at least six times as large. Sometimes, exhausted, they lay on their backs in the most impossible attitudes boxing gently. Adam talked more than any cat I've known for his size; he did not say "hullo" as the others did, but always "He-ll!" He evidently took a poor view of life. The Siamese darks, so pronounced in him under the eyes, gave him a cynical expression, but in reality he was madly full of spirits, altogether too human and angelically attractive to live, as events proved so sadly. He soon became a gardening cat like Caesar. By now, so Stuart declared, one had only to say to Caesar: "Come and look at the golden pumpkins," or the gladioli or the melons or whatever it was, and he would canter off in the right direction. He was certainly an active gardener.

But both he and Adam seemed bent on demolishing the mosquito net which Ah Chi patiently mended with her minute criss-cross stitches. She grumbled about it occasionally, but was very fond of the animals and took a great interest in them, especially in Cleo's families. She called Cleo *Mem Kuching*—Madam, or Lady Cat. There was something about Ah Chi and Cleo oddly akin. Both a little pathetic, but lovable; both with a strong, fighting mother-instinct and a matter-of-fact attitude to life and its vicissitudes. But Ah Chi was superstitious: one day I discovered small hard lumps in both beds beneath the under blankets. On investigation these proved to be cachets of rather sweet-smelling black seeds neatly sewn up in scraps of silk. At first I was puzzled, but then it dawned on me: Ah Chi was practising a little artless witchcraft. So I questioned her as to their origin, but she dissolved into bashful smiles and became too overcome with shyness to answer, in fact she ran away down the covered passage-way to her room.

I could not help being touched and amused by her naïve solicitude in family affairs. . . .

To a certain extent I used local food and Chinese dishes; but I came to believe more and more as time went on that the Cold Storage food and European meals were better for one's health, so I limited the quota of oriental dishes to one or two a week. One of the favourites was *mahmee*; a Chinese dish made of noodles, strips of thin omelette, fried prawns and crab, decorated with sliced lettuce or beans and flavoured with a very savoury soya sauce. Jean always insisted on eating this with chopsticks; in fact she refused to eat it any other way and on her first visit to us we had to wait looking hungrily at our *mahmee* while Mat went down to the town to buy the chopsticks as we did not possess any—personally I found chopsticks rather laborious if I was hungry. People used to give *mahmee* lunch parties and at one, I remember, among the guests was an extremely uppish girl fresh from England visiting her father who was a planter. It must be explained that she went to a Chinese dressmaker in Ipoh whose name was Chun Mee. This English girl had already made one or two rather devastating remarks and electrified us with the bald statement that she could learn how to run a rubber Estate in one week—*easily*. So after all this I'm afraid it was not without malicious satisfaction that I overheard her thanking our hostess for "the delicious Chun Mee."—Poor little dressmaker.

Nasi goreng was another good Chinese dish made of fried rice, cubes of fish, hard-boiled egg, tiny squares of bread fried a golden brown and raisins. Whenever I ordered this, for some absurd reason I always wanted to say *Nazi Goering*. It was quite an effort to twist my tongue to the right words while Kuki looked blankly at me. Kuki had a really wonderful touch with eggs and could whip mountains of frothing white for puddings and sweets. Eggs were small but cheap, and Chinese "old eggs" of immemorial-antiquity, which were eaten with curry, were four for twelve cents or about threepence halfpenny each: these, cased in black preservative, were bought in the village. Kuki did the marketing every morning early Some European women in Malaya did their own, but it never seemed to me worth while getting hot and exhausted so early in the day and ruining one's morning work just for the sake of knocking off a few cents. One could always check up on prices, and Kuki was extremely honest; we were very lucky in having such good servants. He would come puffing up the hill in his white topi, pushing a bicycle loaded with beans, bananas, Chinese oranges, spinach, rice, eggs, sugar and fish from the market, or crabs and prawns (sometimes nine inches long) and a quacking duck or a squawking hen on the handlebars. The meat, bread, cheese, butter and fruit, other than local, came from the Cold Storage, and we got from the Hill vegetables which could not be grown down below along with delicious tree tomatoes that look like Victoria plums. The little Malayan bananas were good, very sweet, creamy and tasty, not coarse like the big varieties.

Sometimes I had fish sent over from Pangkor and very good most of it was, fried in butter, or with stuffed green peppers, or as a *moleh*. One morning an enormous basket of whitebait was sent up to the house and emptied in a pyramid under the covered way. I heard the servants laughing so heartily that I went out to see what was happening. They would not or could not explain the joke; but later I gathered that whitebait was considered "coolie food" and they were deeply amused that we should *want* to eat them. Ah Seng asked if he should bone and decapitate them all.

We had curry once a week, as a rule on Sundays; prawn or fish with eggs and vegetables was the best; each thing served in separate dishes, the saffron-coloured rice first, every grain of which was separate and dotted with raisins. Besides the main dishes were the *sambals*, the "little eats," in a big segmented dish; these could be varied in all sorts of ways. Generally they consisted of coils of cucumber in a special sauce, chopped tomato, banana, grated coconut, Bombay duck, fried nuts and perhaps a few quarters of an orange, mango and banana chutney, chili paste and Chinese old eggs. A Malayan curry should be followed by *Gula Malacca*, which is a sort of iced tapioca jelly served with coconut milk and palm sugar—a rich syrup with a unique faintly burnt flavour, which is cooling and delicious.

For a long time I had a horror of curries because of the

regular curry parties which, beginning at twelve o'clock with beers and gins, trailed through the hot afternoon to four or even later. We got out of curry tiffin invitations unless they were from the newer school of thought that insisted on sitting down to lunch not later than two. There was always plenty to do on a Sunday, the one clear day of the week, so that these long-drawn-out parties seemed a waste of time; apart from the boredom, and the miserable effect of gin in quantity after beer, followed by an enormous curry. I must say that this rather tedious custom appeared to show signs of dying a natural death, or at least of modification. But I am told there has always been a newer school of thought and yet the Blimps held the field.

The young Engineer went on transfer not long after Chinese New Year and an older man came in his place. Stuart and I took to him at once. Roger Bacon had travelled a good deal, was widely read and very much alive. He did not, like some of our guests, point to the big Degas print and say to me: "Is that one of yours?" . . .

Even after home leave he looked pale. He was frailly built and there were dark shadows under his enormous blue eyes. He had been in Malaya before and knew what to expect, but he possessed a fighting spirit.

Down in Singapore I once heard a Naval Officer remark cynically that Malaya was "a slough of mental despond." Roger had rather similar ideas and we had lengthy discussions, the three of us. Were we the decadent victims of luxury as war reporters were to declaim? We had cars, but in the United States of America every artisan has a car, and England was moving the same way before the war. We had servants, but the war must have taught many people that even in a cool climate servants are not exactly a luxury, as our industrious but least luxuriating forebears—the Victorians with their servants galore—knew well.

No doubt Malaya's damp heat tends to produce mental tiredness. But many people say that in a strenuous place like Singapore government servants and merchants worked several hours longer than their counterparts in London. Yes: but Malaya has produced no great artist, no great author, we argued. However there have been few Europeans in the land,

and it is doubtful if even Shakespeare's genius could have blossomed in the perpetual dank heat of the palm house at Kew. Is it the heat, we wondered, that has kept the Malays from pursuing the very great sculpture which their near relatives, the Javanese and Cambodians, did centuries ago under Hindu tuition and Hindu inspiration? Perhaps wave after wave of foreign influence has kept the Malay from ever attaining the homogeneous pattern of civilization necessary for great literature and great arts. Islam has certainly given its civilization a pattern, but it is a mediaeval pattern, and it is a civilization that has definitely banished art in compliance with the Second Commandment: "Thou shalt not make unto thyself any graven image, nor the likeness of anything that is in heaven above, or in the earth beneath, or in the water under the earth. . . ."

Another point: we found it disconcertingly difficult to read poetry in Malaya. Could it be that poetry—a refuge in grey cities—is eclipsed by the vividness of the tropics? But, Roger said, elsewhere in the tropics—in Africa and Australia—he had never experienced this strange unreceptiveness. Perhaps it was that we missed what we had been accustomed to in Europe—an infinite assimilation of ancestral thought in the atmosphere itself. No ancestral voices spoke to us in this hot-house of a climate. We debated also if a lack of heavy mists and fogs deprived us of the mood for the shades and subtleties of poetry.

The English and the Chinese are imbued with poetry inspired by their respective countries, both full not only of traditional learning but—bearing out the argument—of fogs and mists. Although the English profess to hate fogs, the Chinese apparently rather appreciate them at home and abroad, as Chiang Yee says in his book on London[1]—"It is interesting to know that we Chinese have been born to the love of fogs for thousands of years." Chinese artists are especially aware of the mellowing effect of mist.

Malaya although often very beautiful cannot be called mellow. She is not softened by fog that envelops and mystifies, nor veiled in heavy mist: her thick greenness is but briefly obscured by steam or an opalescence rising from the jungle at dawn, all too swiftly stabbed by the fierceness of the sun.

[1] *The Silent Traveller in London.*

Although the physical and spiritual atmospheres of a country are so interwoven in their effects on the mind as to be indefinably one, perhaps it is really the metaphysical enrichment by antiquity which contributes most to this combined atmosphere and makes reading poetry a delight. In some countries poetry is a natural pleasure: it flows and rolls sonorously. As it does for instance when you lie on an Italian hillside looking down, with Shelley's ghost on the waveless plains of Lombardy far below. You can point to where the Romans marched and made their roads and struggled through the Alps that tower behind you. Their white roads mark too the chalk hills of Sussex, adding to the great tapestry, the pattern of our civilization. If we live deep in the soft English countryside, with its bosomy curves and golden fields beside the hoary Cam, the imagination is steeped in receptiveness. But for the European sojourner in Malaya the life-lines back to his intellectual sources are too long.

In spite of all this Malaya has charms to compensate for spiritual deprivations. Its beauty is always there, but not by any means consistently obvious or crudely unveiled. It is not only a beauty of flaming skies and silver nights and brilliant flowers. The soft dark magnificence of the cloud ranges—an infinite variety of heaped and billowing shapes—and the piled and sombre citadels of storm are alone worth going ten thousand miles to see. It is a country of violent change, of tremendous chiaroscuro, literally and spiritually. It was quite possible to love it one hour and hate it intensely the next. Except when the white heat of noon flattens and blanches everything there is little uniformity in the weather from day to day. The changes come so swiftly—from blazing sunshine to torrential downpour, from almost suffocating stillness to wild gales—that moods alter accordingly. Living as you do practically out of doors all day long—the houses being so open—you react swiftly to each rapid change. Little wonder it is a nerve-wracking country! But no one state lasts very long, so each change is bearable and frequently exciting.

Curiously enough these extremes of dazzling light and overpowering heat, storms and sudden coolness and the absence of definite seasons, made time go quickly. I believe regularly stressed contrast is necessary to create rhythm. It is the spaced rhythm of the seasons at home that gives variety to English life and at the same time monotony. This appears to be a paradox, but in reality it is, I believe, true; for although one may find seasons disturbing, as I think they are, they mark progress and so make time go slowly.

In little ways the swiftly changing extremes were bewildering. For instance, before dinner the verandah-room was often filled with a heavenly sweetness of pigeon orchids wafting off the jungle, or the scent of tuberoses from a vase by the western windows. The breeze came that way at dusk and the perfume would drift across the room for an hour or so and it was delicious. But when later we came up from dinner the wind would have dropped, the flowers have closed and the room was filled with a fearful stench of jungle civet-cat, while a toc-toc bird outside called monotonously in the heavy stillness. The contrast seemed typical in this land of violent extremes.

With Roger also we blandly tore to shreds the social systems and customs and built them nearer to our own ideas. One of the habits we contrasted with the cheerful bustle of parties at Home was the sitting-down and staying-put at Malayan parties. New arrivals would rebel, until the men's collars wilted and their backs were "a muck sweat." Old stagers, smiling quietly to themselves, sank down under a fan, in deep disdain for youthful caperings. A fan and a *s'tengah*, that was the end of the average exile's desire. Some of his critics in fact went no further than the bar at Raffles Hotel to get them. "This country saps one's energy," Roger ejaculated. "Ambitions go to pot. There's no mental stimulus, no plays, no music, no art."

"I know," said Stuart, "but we have our canned music and there are *some* good films! The lack of picture galleries leaves a big gap, but masterpieces can't be risked out here—at the mercy of white ants and mildew."

"There are no supermen," I grumbled. "No big writers, painters or musicians, scientists or engineers."

"We're a very small community to produce supermen," said Stuart, "and anyhow we see one another at too close quarters to magnify anybody. But, who knows, Malaya may one day find its scope."

"If its not strangled in red tape," I ventured.

"Oh!" Roger retorted, "I believe red tape here is a very

thin red line compared with the hydra-headed proto-tape in Whitehall!"

We were talking before the average person in Britain was alive to Malaya's existence, that is outside the circle of those who buy tin and rubber shares. If Malaya was spoken of at all it was nine to one it would be called "Malay," which should be either used as an adjective to describe things pertaining to the country or as a noun meaning a native of the country, but *not* as its name. He probably understood that Singapore was important, but only in a vague way. So little interest was and still is taken by the British at home in our possessions overseas that later on one was sorely tempted to draw the bitter conclusion that the losses were deserved. . . .

When in Malaya I received a letter from an educated woman in England addressed ". . . Malay, India. . . ."

"Complacency is the worst danger anywhere," Stuart went on. "Yes," Roger agreed. "And it's much more menacing in Malaya than at home where there is more competition. Here not only the official has security of tenure; the merchants and the planters are picked men too and seldom lose their jobs."

"Better to rule in hell than serve in heaven . . ." I remarked.

"That's another point," said Roger. "The ruling class has long had a tradition of dogs and sport and clothes and so on. And a comfortable tradition gives way slowly before serious intellectual interests."

"And the intellectuals get miserably discouraged—poor devils—too far from the source of their inspiration," said Stuart.

"I think some people here, particularly women, are unhappy and have become shut away in themselves perhaps because they try to live in one place with their hearts in another—in England," I suggested.

"I've been reading Rebecca West's book, *The Strange Necessity*, Roger said. "She makes the point that unless they're satirists like Shaw or Wilde, the Anglo-Irish, Anglo-Indian, and let's say the Anglo-Malayan, move in a world that has no common shape and they have each got to build a new world of their own. As she says, Kipling started off gaily and turned himself into a Eurasian and into a Hindu. Then he grew tired of the pretence and lapsed almost into silence."

"Even the cosmopolitan Jews hung up their harps on the

willows of Babylon!" Stuart observed. "They couldn't sing as exiles in a strange land."

"And the moral is—what?" asked Roger. "When you enter a sheep-pen, bleat; when you enter a byre, low. That's the Malay's philosophy. The man who is happy in exile is the man who takes the line of least resistance. Accept everything that comes along and do your job. And 'drink, for you know not whence you came, nor why'!"

It is said that Malayans drank too much. At the time of the fall of Singapore, some people in England said that the "whisky-swilling planter" was the cause of the Malayan calamity. To Malayans—if they can forget their bitterness—that is so utterly ridiculous as to be ironically funny. But this bitterness may never wear away if Malayans from Japanese prison camps heard even the whisper of such puerile condemnation. Anyone whose country has been invaded, especially if he has been assured countless times that he and his family are amply protected, will understand only too well.

The habit of drinking whisky and soda (*s'tengahs*) in the evening was prevalent. *S'tengah* stands for a half measure of whisky and soda, it comes from *satu tengah* or *sa-tengah*, which means "one half" in Malay, and is not "stinger" as it is sometimes mistakenly written in novels about the East. The habit, a natural outcome of thirst and exhaustion, was quite a nightly ritual, especially among older people who probably felt more easily played out. But there seems no reason, beyond the imagination of some novelists, why Malaya should be more infamous for indulgence than any other hot country where people are thirsty. Probably no one who has not lived and worked in the tropics can know what it means really to sweat and to feel as limp after it, as if the small fierce sun had drained every ounce of energy out of one's body. As the evening *s'tengah* assuaged the weariness of the hot day, and perhaps covered up a certain lack of vitality, its need can be understood. Of course there were some who abused this need, and one did occasionally meet a real soaker; but without exaggeration it can be said that the majority of people were temperate.

Pahit[1] parties were often boring, but then so are a great many

[1] Pahit—in Malay meaning "bitter"—had been evolved to indicate any short drink, so that "pahit party" in Malayan jargon had become the tiresome twin of "cocktail party" in English—or is it American?

cocktail and tea parties in England: drinking whether the drink be tea or spirits is deadly without the gaiety bred of interests in common. This mutual boredom would have been inevitably the same in any very mixed community—at home or abroad—where all types and conditions were thrown together, quite irrespective of tastes and ideas.

People in Malaya—a land of furloughs and transfers—had perforce too many acquaintances; real friends were all the more gratefully appreciated.

XII

HOLIDAY IN SUMATRA

MARCH WAS EXCEPTIONALLY HOT, even for Malaya, that year. So we were more than glad we had planned to take our local leave then. Government servants received two weeks each year beside all the Chinese, Malay and Indian festivals and our own Occidental holidays. We had saved up our first year's quota so as to be able to take three weeks' leave. We had been hankering after the Dutch hill station, Brastagi, in Sumatra. For a long time we had toyed in our usual optimistic manner with plans for a holiday there. It was not until we received a gloriously unexpected and fat cheque from Stuart's generous-hearted Mother, that Brastagi suddenly became a real possibility instead of a vague enticement. We made our plans accordingly.

One blazing day early in March, Stuart's relief took over the district. When we had lunched him and his wife and told them whom and what to look out for in the district, we crammed our always too numerous luggage into the old car and were at last ready for the long drive to Penang. I was holding Adam in my arms as we stood in the hall seeing to the last minute arrangements, when Ah Chi seriously enquired: "*Mem* take *kuching* Adam too?"

She was left in charge of the cats, which she loved, always showing a motherly interest in Cleo's babies. She stood with Ah Seng and Kuki lined up on the verandah, and as we drove away, they flapped their hands at us in the easy-going modern Chinese salute, which is a cross between a royal wave and something more military, a rather cheerful gesture which I always liked. The cats sat about on the steps looking quite dejected. They were puzzled and anxious as we did not often go away, especially with so much luggage. They had done their utmost to get packed into it.

That was one of the hottest drives I remember and the car, whose springs were beginning to show their age, had to be nursed over every bump. It was good to see Jean as we entered Parit Buntar. She was playing tennis as we drove past the club, but signalling to us she dashed across the road to her house and regaled us there with long cold drinks and friendly jabber.

Penang Island looked as lovely as ever as we reached the last lap and came out into the open paddy fields of Province Wellesley. The Straits were very rough that evening and it was difficult to manœuvre the car on to the heaving ferry-boat. In Penang we had rooms overlooking the sea at the E. and O., filled with the sound of waves and lisping casuarina trees. We revelled in the luxuries of civilization and the thrill of being on the verge of a holiday in a new country.

The next day was a wild rush of last moment shoppings; having my hair done, meeting friends, and trying not to let the shops go to our heads in our dangerously extravagant holiday mood. We succeeded in getting down to the harbour in time and I was surprised at the sight of the funny little Straits boat we were to cross in. She was so small I did not see how there could possibly be room for any cabins, and I thought we would have to sleep on deck in long chairs. While we waited on the quay for the little ship to come alongside we watched the rest of the passengers. Rather to our relief there were no other Europeans, so we should not have to make polite conversation. A group of travelling musicians attracted our notice. They were shifty-eyed Sumatran Malays with three very beautiful, very naughty-looking girls with smooth luscious faces, loose but lovely mouths and vacant black eyes. Their luggage was intriguing; even more numerous than ours, but more excusably so; they had gaping fibre suitcases, baskets of food and fruit, carpets to sleep on, umbrellas, guitars and mandolins.

On board we discovered allotted to us a minute cabin in which we could move one at a time. There was, after all, one other European passenger on board, a cheerful, red-faced Scot who raised our envy by saying he was on his way home. He was going across to Belawan Deli to pick up the Dutch mail boat which no longer called at Penang. We had a lengthy dinner with him and the captain, a silent, embittered man.

Soon after dawn the next morning we crept into a dull, muddy river mouth lined with glaucous-looking mangrove swamps. At Belawan Deli the boat was besieged by screaming hire-car drivers. Starting with fabulous sums for the drive into the hills, they knocked off five or six guilders every time you so much as batted an eyelid. With this method, Stuart reached a reasonable sum merely by looking coolly surprised and keeping calm. We were then swept ashore into a big open tourer and were driven at a furious pace along the great wide road leading to Medan, the capital of Sumatra. Jehu had not a chance in this race. It was evidently a habit of the hire-car drivers to race each other along that stretch of road. With fearful abandon they overtook each other, sometimes three abreast. The spare man or odd-job boy stood up in the front seat clutching his cap on his head and goading the driver to further efforts. Feeling reckless we rather enjoyed it. After a while we were passed by another car in which sat the red-faced Scot who waved his hand airily. This gesture caught our driver on the raw. Bending over the wheel diabolically he shook hell out of his machine and we managed to beat the Scot's by a short head into Medan.

I was surprised to see Europeans riding bicycles and going about more as we would in our own climate. The Dutch live differently from us in their colonies: they accept the country more as if it were their own home—permanently, and not, as we are inclined to do, as a place where work has to be done with England as our permanent home and background. One thing which struck me as typical was that all the notices were in Romanized Malay with, of course, Dutch spelling, whereas in Malaya the notices are all in *Jawi*, that is Malay in its own borrowed Arabic writing. It was not the English policy to allow *Jawi* to fall into disuse. Only a slight point, but one on which critics of imperialism are confuted. From the colonizers' point of view, not necessarily from the inhabitants', the Dutch attitude to life in the tropics seemed good. Less of a *pied à terre* outlook. Their houses looked more solid and better designed, their hill stations are better developed and, from what we saw of their towns, they had far more entertainments. They were real settlers in the deepest and more permanent sense of the word. It was interesting to see something of this great Netherlands' island, as big as Italy, which lay so near to Malaya across the Malacca Straits. Somehow they had achieved an atmosphere of the Continent. But what is Malaya beside Java and Sumatra?

Netherlands' India can be compared only with our India, not with little Malaya.

By this time our spirits were high, and we were both in the mood to be excited by everything fresh and new and, above all, different.

Before we could set out for the Brastagi plateau we had to visit the brother of an acquaintance we had recently made in Penang. This man turned out to be such a grumbler that he was almost comic, though had our spirits not been high, he might have been depressing. He started off almost by condoling with us for going to Brastagi. "Of course yee knoo it's tarribly coold up there; the food is shocking too—och, shocking. Noo coold storaige yee knoo, yee have to eat water buffalo and laike fish, and the *expense* . . . !" Here words almost failed him.

When he had polished off our trip to Brastagi as not worth the money it would cost, he gave us the sweetest smile and insisted on directing the driver to take us round to his sister's bungalow for a wash and a drink before going on. His sister welcomed us hospitably in a most charming bungalow, sat us down and then started off in much the same manner. Brastagi might have been hell and Medan its gates, from her dire warnings of the discomforts and most of all of the expense. She never spoke without saying how terribly expensive so-and-so was—material at so many guilders a yard, servants at so many a month. We sympathized heartily.

"And even the beer has gone up now," she moaned automatically.

Stuart hastily put his glass of beer down beside him and tried to ignore it. We dared not look at each other. I could see he was becoming pale with the effort of keeping solemn throughout, so I said we must go, and presently we made our exit quite straight-faced and, I hope, gratefully and undishonoured.

Once more on the road the reason for the odd-job man soon became apparent, for we were hardly out of Medan before we had our first puncture. Punctures were quite frequent after that and on every drive we took later. We drove through miles of flat country, past a great many coffee and tobacco plantations. It was not for some time that we could see the central plateau rising up to the east. The ascent was sudden when it came, through steep jungle-covered hills; and the temperature fell rapidly as we looked down on the flat country in the heat far below.

It was good to come out of the jungle on to the open plateau at Brastagi village. Batak women sat under a shelter in the market-place selling flowers; a mass of vivid gerberas, rich banks of carnations and sheaves of thick, creamy white lilies grown in the rich, dark volcanic soil of these uplands. The exhilarating cold, the profusion of colour, and above all the sight of the open country stretching away to the horizon made us hilarious. The car swept up the hill to the hotel with its banks of pink begonias. Young fir plantations smelt fragrant and untropical in the hot sun. There was scarcely any jungle to be seen, and behind the hotel, rocky-bare and smoking faintly against the blue, was the volcanic crest of Sibayak.

We ate an enormous and excellent lunch, regardless of whether it was cold storage or not, and shared a bottle of Burgundy to warm us. The sun was shining, but we felt the cold at first; it took two weeks to get absolutely acclimatized. The view from the hotel windows was refreshing, surfeited as we were by landscapes clotted with jungle or eternal rubber trees—although at Lumut itself we were exceptionally lucky in the wide estuary view. A few odd sugar-loaf hills stuck up out of the rolling plain which sloped away gently to the unseen lake of Toba Meer.

The hotel bathrooms were of the sink and dipper kind. The evenings were always so chilly one had to climb into one's sink to warm up. This was a rather precarious feat as the whole arrangement stood on a wobbly stool about four and a half feet from the ground. I could just fit into my sink if I wedged my knees under my chin, but Stuart had to leave his long legs hanging out. In the middle of this performance one invariably became entangled in the chain and the water would begin to run away. When we discovered there were no fires in the hotel we thought with longing of the roaring wood fires of "The Cottage" at Taiping Hill. Our wet-blanketing friend of Medan scored a point and I went about wearing furs at night until thoroughly acclimatized. However the place *looked* warm with its fine Brussels carpets, panelling, red damask walls hung with richly oleaginous Dutch landscapes, and really attractive lighting caged in great wrought-iron balls. The Boys, all Javanese, were very smart in *batik* head kerchiefs and short *batik* sarongs of sombre colours worn with white drill suits. The tails of their headgear protruded at jaunty angles or were precisely even according to rank, condition and degree, the butler having a style of his own. Our own table Boy, Djamari, was extremely intelligent and willing. I made a sketch of him later and he talked a good deal to Stuart while posing. He, like the other Javanese, seemed far more alive than most Malays: his long eyes lit up with interest as he talked, the lines of his face were lean and clear cut. He told us he had been Boy to Peter Brooke of Sarawak who had been at Brastagi on his honeymoon recently. Stuart had first met Peter Brooke at the London School of Oriental Studies, so we were interested. Djamari spoke also of the Bataks, the hill tribe of Northern Sumatra, formerly fierce and dreaded, but now some of them are Moslems and some Christians. In spite of the missionaries there was something dark, earthy, rather sub-human and indescribably pagan about them—Djamari obviously had no liking for them. I was told that the children were remarkable linguists, talking Batak, Malay, Dutch and even English.

The colours they wore were in striking contrast to the transparent flower-like colours of the Malays; rich, earthy terra-cottas, dusky crimsons, rusty blacks and indigos. During the day the women went about stripped to the waist with yards of heavy, dark cloth folded on their heads as a protection from the fierce sun. In the cool of the evening they took this headgear down and wrapped it round their stocky little bodies for warmth.

After dinner at the hotel every night there was the ceremony of the liqueurs. The most imposing Boy was a hefty creature we called the Demon because his expression was that of an amiable Satan; and it was his business to wheel round a trolley on which was a vast array of liqueurs, everything imaginable from kümmel to Napoleon brandy. The catch was an enormous flat black bottle of "*Fine de Maison*" and we fell for it. Second only to the Napoleon in place of honour and served in outsize brandy glasses, warmed ritualistically over a little flame, it turned out to be nothing better than the usual very ordinary brand, which tastes best disguised in ginger ale and after a strenuous game of tennis. It was an expensive ramp (shades of Medan!) but such an elaborate and artistic one that we forgave it and, after our own initial lapse, delightedly watched each newcomer fall for the Big Black Bottle.

The first breakfast was a Dutch sort of breakfast, and good. The rooms were full of sunlight that streamed across the beds of pink begonias and flooded in under the gay striped awnings. Besides all the usual things, omelettes and ham and so on, there was black bread with cheese and butter, or rye bread and cold sausage, but best of all were the golden gingerbreads eaten with butter and honey. I tasted too my first *Buah Susu*, "milk fruit," as the Malays call the passion-fruit. You cut the top off and eat it like a boiled egg, with sugar. I think it was by far the most delicious of all the new fruits I had tried.

From outside on the terrace we could see the other volcano, Sinaboeng, away to the north; a perfect cone smoking gently in the golden morning air. The warm scent of the firs was sweet and homelike, and we thought how wise the Dutch had been to plant them and not Australian tree-ferns as in Malaya's hill stations, where the jungle has been cleared. The sugar-loaf hills were like islands in the plain; each had a cap of dark jungle on the top exactly like jam on a suet pudding.

We felt limp in the legs from the height and unaccustomed to the delicious cold, though the sun's rays soon became very hot. We staggered down to the village and gazed our fill at the blaze of colour in the flower stalls. There was a school for Dutch children near, a charming brown building in deep-roofed Batak style with red painted eaves. It was good to see children of the ages of seven to seventeen again; we had almost forgotten what they looked like; so very long in the leg. There was a little Dutch bar in the village where we discovered one could get an excellent *rum groc warme*. After one of these our knees were limper than ever, so we hired a gharry to take us up the hill to lunch; these little vehicles took the place of the rickshaw here. They were drawn by Batak ponies and adorned with tasselled awnings and gay tin-a-linging bells. We arrived pleasantly to the tune of tiny clattering hoofs and tinkling bells in a dreamy glow of *rum groc warmes*.

As was the custom there, we retired to our room after lunch until tea and crisp, nutty biscuits were brought to our bedsides at four o'clock. What a pleasant and deliciously lazy custom! After the sleep and the tea our legs seemed to have recovered normal strength, so we put on shorts and walking shoes and dashed out, full of a sudden new energy now that we were becoming acclimatized.

The warm fir-grown hillsides sloped up to a high jungle-clad ridge, behind which towered the smoking crags of Sibayak.

Arum lilies grew wild in every tiny *sawah*, the miniature valleys, where rice was cultivated beside the streamlets. There were feathery groves of bamboo, lanes smelling of elder and mimosa, market gardens of carnations. The paths were strewn with passion-flowers and fallen passion-fruit.

The next day we tackled the big jungle ridge, plodding up past the flowery *sawahs* to the hot fragrant pines and finally into the damp chill jungle. The thick mossy banks were spangled with a heavy dew. A star-shaped flower rather like an edelweiss grew palely profuse, and a few wild begonias gleamed among the leaves. The trees were magnificent, unspeakably fantastic; hollow, draped in moss and lichen and festooned with lianas. The path zigzagged on the narrow spine so that we could see alternately out over the open plain to Toba Meer or across to Sibayak's smoking crater.

It was cold up there on the ridge at about 5,600 feet and the leeches were large, but we could deal with them. Our energy was rewarded by a really dramatic view. Some of the trees had been cut away and it was possible to see down on to the valley floor, a sheer thousand feet below. Bananas grew beside a river which wound through neat strips of paddy fields: in the middle of this smooth green perfection was a circular corral of tall bamboos enclosing a Batak village; isolated, secret and dark like its inhabitants, its high-roofed houses huddled together on the rich brown earth. Barricaded behind great bamboos, the village was an island in a tender green sea of growing paddy. I felt I was gazing down on something very primeval, forbiddingly inviolate.

XIII

TWO VOLCANOES

A DAY or two later we started on our first real walk; our objective was the 7,980-foot volcano, Sinaboeng. To do this climb in comfort before the sun was too hot, we had to wake at four-thirty in the morning. We felt very noble getting up at such an hour. It was bitterly cold and pitch dark. We drank tea out of a thermos and ate bread and butter and honey and then crept along the empty passages shivering, even in layers of clothes, and out of the silent hotel to the car waiting below. The guide, huddled up and wearing his sarong like a cloak, sat beside the syce. The road wound crazily and was violently bumpy. I felt extremely cold and rather sick; but we could see the Southern Cross and every now and again the great dark mass of Sinaboeng with a star hung just above as if thrown up out of the crater. After three-quarters of an hour we reached the foot of the mountain. The road was blocked by a great rock which had fallen recently, so we had to get out and walk the last lap. It was so icy cold that I sat in the car while Stuart and the guide, a Malay-speaking Batak whose name was Lehu, took the breakfast out of an ungainly basket and put it in our rucksack, with the coats, sketching things and camera. Lehu swathed in his sarong, but wearing only cotton shorts and tennis shoes, cheerfully shouldered the lot. Stuart told him to take the lead, whereupon he set off at a good round pace. We thought afterwards he must have misunderstood Stuart's words about "setting the pace" for meaning we wanted to go fast: however, at first we were so cold we were thankful to do so.

We went up through a little coffee plantation and into secondary jungle, mostly bamboo and long wet grass, which gave way later to jungle trees. As we entered the trees the dawn was beginning. We looked up and saw the bare crest of the mountain above us. Up and up we went at the same speed. We crossed what appeared to be a vast rocky watercourse littered with debris, which we heard later, when Lehu had the breath to speak, was not a watercourse, but the track of the last eruption in 1937. It was very beautiful; the great jungle trees loomed dark and eerie festooned with the fantastic ropes of millions of lianas. Steps led on up, cut precariously in the edge of the ravine. Then the track descended into another ravine; it was heart-rending to lose all that height; on and up again. A pulse beat in the back of my head and my heart pounded so much that I could cheerfully have lain down and died. In the correct "mountaineering" style we blew off heartily and quite unmanneredly at intervals. Neither of us could speak. I thought I had better save what breath I had, and Stuart told me later that he had felt as ghastly, but had tried to console himself that if he felt as he did I must be feeling worse! In foolish pride neither of us made any attempt to tell Lehu to slacken the pace.

By then the sun had risen. The whole naked ravine side, seen through the dark trees from our dim path, shone like pure gold. The ravine had been swept bare by the boiling sulphur water of the eruption; huge trees, lianas and great tangled roots hung down torn and dead, but golden in the dawn. I was still feeling rather sick, cold and hot by turns, but aware of the great beauty. Soon the track became almost vertical through a mossy tunnel of gnarled trees. The steep steps were natural ones formed by innumerable, entwined roots in the rich loamy earth.

"How long have we been walking?" I panted.

"Forty minutes," answered Stuart, and we were amazed, for it seemed much longer.

Knowing the walk was supposed to take four hours I made a mental calculation and said fearfully:

"Surely it *can't* be three hours and twenty minutes more?"

We groaned in unison.

The sunlight was growing brighter and the open ground seemed nearer. After a while we sat down to rest in a wee glade like a miniature platform with a view over the sunny jungle. It was charming and elfin, like an Arthur Rackham drawing. We had a pull of cold black coffee from a beer bottle, one of the most welcome and refreshing drinks I've ever had, and Lehu suddenly announced we were only half-an-hour from the top. I thought at first he must mean half way; but he kept on saying we were *very* hard walkers. He seemed much impressed, and it was some time before we heard the end of this mad achievement, quite unintended on our part!

While we were resting an earth gnome commonly called a sulphur worker, in dun-coloured rags and tattered *kopiah*, passed by on his daily trek to the crater.

After the coffee and Lehu's announcement, our spirits rose with our bodies and we fairly soared up. The track became so steep out of the stunted trees that we had to hoist ourselves up by roots and branches; some of the "steps" were three feet deep.

When at last we came out of the trees, the sun was hot and golden and glorious on one's body. We turned round to look down. The plain was swimming in the early morning light; Sibayak was smoking peacefully and far, far down below lay Lake Kawah in the jungle, like green glass in thick moss.

We felt excited and exhilarated. The air was cold, the sun hot and the shadows fresh like cool water. We plugged on, mad with excitement, through the azalea bushes which smelt lusciously of honey. There was a thrill of expectation so that we could not help but dash up that last bit over the almost bare earth to see something neither of us had ever seen before, something very wonderful, and, to us, unique.

When we did reach the crest and looked down, the sight that met our eyes was beyond our hopes. It was six-forty-five then and I sat down at once to draw.

We were on a narrow lip of a path looking down into the old sandy-floored crater. Beyond this to the north was a second ridge lower than ours, smoking and limned in lemon-yellow sulphur dust. Great clouds of steam came hissing up from the depths of the shadowy pit beyond; the smoke rose white against a warm cobalt sky. Beyond this towered a castellated pillar of rock; its chiselled soaring lines were lit sharply by the slanting early morning brilliance. Every now and again the steam was blown across it tantalizingly but enhancing its perfection. Those infinitely lovely perpendicular lines were a paean of beauty in the freshness of the morning.

Below this ravishing pinnacle the rocks fell away in wild, jagged contours to a dark col. We sat in awed silence, but managed to consume for our breakfast an enormous quantity of cold sweet black coffee, which was excellent, cheese and ham sandwiches and several eggs.

"These eggs smell bad!" I exclaimed throwing my first two into the crater.

"No," laughed Stuart, "not the *eggs*, it's only the sulphur!"

Even as I drew, the serene beauty of that pillar faded and grew misty as the sun mounted. We had come none too early. We walked on to the highest knoll covered in scrawny azalea and bilberry bushes and sat there for a while to sketch Lehu. Although he was a Batak, and his teeth were filed, he had not the rather sub-human look of some of his race. He was a cheerful little fellow, stubby-faced and merry-eyed—bright currants of eyes. He sat for me on the very highest point of Sinaboeng, in his old blue-check sarong which blew in the wind like a cloak, as he gazed out over the plain.

We went down on to the yellow smoking ridge between the two craters. It was alive now with numerous earth gnomes, hammering and chiselling away among the fumes, delving out their sulphur. We choked on the bad-egg smell as the fumes and smoke got in our throats. We stood there in the heat and watched the little men climb nonchalantly up out of the crater, out of the smoking purple rocks, to empty their sacks of hot yellow stones at our feet. They were each armed with knives and pestles. They pounded the sulphur stones to powder which they carried down the mountain every day in small dumpy sacks on their heads. We watched them later tramping down: silhouetted against the sky, one at a time, on the lip of the crater they looked more than ever like wild, half-human, earth people.

By now the whole plain was swimming in heat. Small puffs of white cloud floated about below us. At ten o'clock we finished the last drop of coffee and started down. The way was so steep and the roots so numerous that we could not look about us much. We leapt and slipped and jumped down precipitously. When we reached the bottom, Lehu led us to Lake Kawah where we squatted on logs and stones in the shallows to wash our hands and faces in the delicious cool water.

"We have just crossed the fresh pugs of a tiger," he remarked.

I was most annoyed at not having been shown the marks, but perhaps, like the Malays, he would not use the dreaded name of tiger when still in the jungle precincts. The Malays call him *Tuan*—lord—if they have to speak of him within the jungle where he is master. This one, said Lehu, was one of many, not as a rule man-eaters. However, even if he was rather a tame tiger, I was disappointed at not having seen his pugs. We got into the car and rattled off home. There were half-naked Batak women in the fields pounding grain with enormous pestles. Elaborate arrangements of strings were erected to keep the birds off the ripening crops.

Back at the hotel we felt heroes in our hob-nails and had a glass of Voorburg—a citron gin with pomegranate—to celebrate, and after a huge lunch, which included a really excellent turtle soup, we slept blissfully until tea-time.

That evening we noticed a solitary Englishman, a newcomer, fall for the Big Black Bottle ramp. We became great friends and although we never saw him after that holiday, we both feel we have a lasting friend, and we shall, I hope, meet him again one day. He had flown from Calcutta and was going on business to Singapore, but when he heard of Sinaboeng he decided to come back. Apparently only "mad dogs and Englishmen" bothered about that peak, but we were in good company with Allan Biggar. He was a little lame, but that did not deter him in the least and a few days later he went up the mountain with a friend of Lehu's for a guide. This man had heard of our shocking race up and went into eulogies over it to Allan, though he must have felt some sympathy for Lehu with that rucksack full of beer bottles. Poor Allan was under the misapprehension that we had gone right down into the extinct crater. So not to be outdone by us, he toiled down there and was quite hurt when he discovered his mistake.

The next expedition was to Toba Meer, the great lake to the south. The drive across the sloping plain was lovely. It was good to be in open country and watch the sapphire cloud shadows racing across the hills and see the beautiful patchwork of the paddy fields in the valleys. The road down into Harangol, the fishing village at the northern end of the lake, was very rough and steep. We crept down behind a native 'bus which repeatedly stuck at unpleasant angles on the hair-pin bends. There was plenty of time to savour the view over the Harangol Bay and the miles of blue hazy plateau and vast lake beyond.

Adam—with temple flowers and spider lilies

From a charcoal drawing by the author

From a charcoal drawing by the author

Even the almost sheer sides of the mountains here were terraced for paddy. This produced a most lovely effect; thousands of tiny bunds outlined the contours of the hills with perfect neatness, a masterpiece of irrigation, which would make even the Swiss open their eyes wide in admiration and they know how to irrigate mountain crops. I should think Harangol, although cool, must rank, at least on market day, as one of the smelliest places on earth. It was market day then, and it stank. We agreed that we had never before seen people so qualified to please the anthropologist; even I towered almost head and shoulders above them as we walked along the water front, while Stuart looked like someone from Mars. The stench of mud, excrement, sweat, betel juice, durians and dog was overpowering. We discovered another thing about Bataks that day; like the Igorots of the Philippine Islands they eat dog flesh and were busy buying the horrible-looking carcasses in the market. Rather nauseated and having seen enough we struggled out of the crowd and retreated to a small pretty Rest House where the trees hung low over the water. From there we watched the long boats coming in, like "Coral Island" war canoes black with men. They were racing in the craziest, splashing, oar-flashing, zig-zagging way with a great deal of shouting and noise. We were the only Europeans there that day. We took a motor-boat out on the lake for a while but its beauty was spoilt by a plague of tiny flies like miniature drugged mosquitoes; we were covered in them. We were glad to leave Harangol with its stinks, dead dogs and flies and on the upland road at Gunong Pisau, one of the sugar-loaf hills visible from the hotel, we turned off to see the Pisau-Pisau waterfall. There the river, flowing from the plateau, fell three hundred feet or more from a narrow wooded gully to the paddy fields below and pushed out a little delta into the lake.

It was very beautiful and quiet up there with a perfect view of Toba Meer. The folded, flat-topped hills fell like cascades of thick green velvet to the vast, glassy stretches of blue water. A strange country of plateau carved up by writhing ravines, fold upon fold, unreal in the hot sunlight, like modelled hills. When we had gazed for some time we walked back to the car. An old Malay was waiting for us there with a bunch of pink and striped carnations, dark crimson gerbera, red gladioli and in the centre one perfect arum lily, its sentinel pistil intensely gold and powdery in its white sheath. All these were crammed into a long slim vase of unpolished bamboo. The bouquet was very lovely and Stuart bought it for me. The old man smiled with pleasure, his manner so gracious and charming that even though he was paid for the flowers he had the air of bestowing a gift. And so it was, for what money can really pay for fresh flowers in a white bamboo stem. . . .

We were more than ever struck by the racial contrasts when we got another close-up of Batak people that same day. Walking at dusk we found ourselves near a Batak village *kampong*, the high pointed roofs looked old and darkly primitive behind a bamboo enclosure. It is curious that these people, although so much less attractive and less civilized than the Malays, build far better houses and seem far more advanced agriculturally, especially in regard to the irrigation of their crops. Perhaps it comes from the tonic mountain air and from their very clannishness, their self-contained, self-sufficing mode of living. Their houses with steep sway-backed roofs are perfectly thatched and the walls are painted in pastel colours made from clays. When a patriarch dies in a house, it is said that another smaller roof is erected over the old one, so that some houses have several tiers of roofs which gives an attractive pagoda-like effect.

We did not go inside the *kampong* for it was getting dark and we had been advised not to enter without a Batak guide. There were notices in the roads in Dutch and English requesting Europeans on no account to give money to the Bataks. The Dutch have had a good deal of trouble, I believe, in the past with this people. As we walked back to the hotel we encountered droves of silent men and women returning from their work in the fields. There was none of the smiling childish inquisitiveness of the *kampong* Malay. We were made to feel aliens and not very comfortable ones at that, as the dark, stunted figures in their sombre clothes went swiftly by in the narrow dim lanes. They glanced at us coldly with their small black eyes; they were anxious to get back and shut themselves up in the enclosures of their ancient *kampong* with their pagan rites. Like the Eskimos, they are said to have had a way of getting rid of their old folk. They made them cling to a high branch which was shaken until the unfortunate ancient fell to the ground. The idea was that if a fruit will fall from a shaken tree it is over-ripe and therefore ready to be cast down. They are also reputed to have used the dead bodies of Malay babies for compounding medicines; for three weeks after the death of a child the Malays must watch the grave carefully in case Bataks come to dig up the body.

On another occasion, earlier in the day, we went to see Kampong Brastagi, the original native village. The houses were beautifully made and I longed to draw them, but the moment we passed the barricade we were surrounded by a howling mob of boys and youths clammering ferociously, not whiningly for money. Under a high, barn-like building on stilt legs the women were at work, pounding grain. Even in the brilliant daylight there was a most unwelcome atmosphere about the place and quite frankly I was glad to be out of it, and free from the hateful swarm of youths who stuck as close as leeches.

There were to be extra festivities at the hotel over Easter. By now we found we were becoming rather broke, as the Scot of Medan had so gloomily prophesied. So we decided to have a quiet few days before the week-end, and, appropriately, though we had not exactly realized it was Holy Week, we went on the water waggon, and cut down our expeditions to local walks.

We walked off the map and lost ourselves in *verboden* water catchment areas. Hundreds of wooden steps led up beside the pipe lines only to peter out in silent, dense, wet jungle; other paths lost themselves in warm-scented fir trees and long grass, or led to little hollows where a few natives worked among hibiscus flowers and lilies in watercress beds; all very fragrant and warm and still. We came back past the passion-fruit vines and through small dappled groves of bamboos like Chinese sepia drawings. No wonder the Chinese love the bamboo—to them a symbol of purity—with its surpassing loveliness and grace. In the built-over parts of Brastagi, the Dutch houses and holiday bungalows clustered round a large hill; very modern houses with delightful gardens and wide views of the plateau. We were envious comparing all this to our own hill-stations which, by the very nature of Malaya's hills, are inevitably more cramped and shut in.

After this quiet time we had a crazily hilarious Easter. We started off with a ride before breakfast on some skittish Batak ponies and continued with a round of golf and then a swim, after which Stuart and Allan did gymnastics on the bars in the blazing sun—Allan in a topi which somehow remained on his head. There was tennis after tea and finally we danced, sustained by Château Yquem, until four in the morning—when we ended up with a walk in the moonlight.

Not unexpectedly we were a little under the weather the next day, which was Easter Sunday. Sunday mornings at Brastagi were always entertaining; the Dutch from neighbouring houses came up to the hotel for apéritifs and lunch. It was good to see so many Europeans: there were French, Czechs, Dutch, and over Easter, one or two English and a few Americans. Some were very smart, others still in shorts and some of the girls in slacks. There was dancing and it was all rather gay and entertaining. But on this particular Sunday we drooped, in a thick haze of cigar smoke, exhausted by our ridiculous activity of the day before and wondering fretfully why Dutchmen like cigars so very much. . . .

In the sun outside on the terrace an Indian was playing with sleepy snakes and eating fire. The snakes may havc been doped, but the flames were genuine enough. Having eaten his lighted cigarette he produced, with stertorous breathing, clouds of smoke from his nose and mouth, followed by sheets of flame. As far as I remember the smoke did not come out of his ears as well, but it might just as well have done for it was all magic to me.

By this time there were some other English people in the hotel, a rather stand-offish couple. Allan had been cabled for again, to go to Shanghai this time, and he had to go down to Medan first about his visa, but he would be back in time for our trip. We three had planned to go up Sibayak together on the Wednesday. We were getting very fond of him with his stock of dryly humorous little anecdotes, his love of books, and above all, his lively spirit. We recovered to enjoy the dancing on Easter Monday, and on Wednesday morning we got up at half-past five. Lehu was our guide once more, or rather porter, as this was a simple walk and very different from Sinaboeng. Neither was the crater as dramatic, for there was no sudden approach to its lip. It was bigger in area and much older; its countless jagged edges seemed to indicate that there had once been an infinitely higher crest now much worn down. It has never erupted within living memory.

We breakfasted on the crumbling shale, and I tried to sketch while Allan and Stuart experimented most intriguingly with eggs and beer bottles. Having drunk the coffee they held, and eaten as many eggs as we could, Allan insisted that it was possible to squeeze a shelled egg into a beer bottle if you heated the bottle. Lehu was very much amused at the craziness of Europeans and showed all his filed teeth in a broad grin. In the midst of these quaint experiments, the stand-offish couple from the hotel appeared suddenly over the crest. As they marched by they bowed in a Dr. Livingstone manner and honoured us with a stiff "Good morning." They gave Sibayak's ancient eerie crater one bored glance and then turned back on their tracks, striding purposefully in the direction of drinks-before-lunch, with heads carefully averted from our bad behaviour. We all heaved sighs of relief; the mountain top was ours again to explore and sketch and heat our beer bottles on as we wished. It was very cold; we were glad of jackets and pullovers, and it was good to get down into the shallow crater where the air was warmed by the sulphur holes all around. Under the wildly cleft face of a cliff, one particularly large hole emitted horrible shrieks, as of the tormented from the bowels of the earth, and steam, as from the cauldrons in which they broiled, shot forth in hissing blasts.

When we came to descend again we discovered to our surprise we had been wandering about up there for three hours. On the way down I noticed layers of brilliantly coloured clays in the bank beside the path, bright yellow, a deep maroon and a lovely china blue. Lehu told us the Bataks used these clays to paint their houses, but the colours dry very much lighter and of course lose that startling pristine freshness.

There were one or two parties of Chinese trippers ascending, all very trim and cheerful in white shirts and shorts. Back at the hotel we agreed, over a bottle of Niersteiner at a very late lunch, that Sibayak was a more tourist-haunted mountain, and the loneliness of Sinaboeng reigned supreme in our memories.

A day or two later we had to pack up and go down from the

plateau into the heat once more. The boat was very crowded at Belawan Deli, but we managed to book a couple of long chairs and watched the coolies loading rubber. The heat and stickiness at sea level were such that these men could literally wring out their clothes: even as we watched, one man pulled off his singlet and wrung a stream of water from it. Down here again we began to realize the benefit of the holiday. One felt more mental energy; the heat had not to be endured determinedly, as so often on long drives and journeys, and we discussed our plans for the future with renewed zest. The cabins were quite unbearable, even with the fan on at full blast, so we slept on deck in the long chairs, quite peacefully until appalling noises from the engine room, like the rattling of a thousand milk cans, woke us up. Then the moon rose, distorted to a red-gold ingot behind the clouds, and the sea was like oil, fading into a dark smudge of heat, so still that even the stars were reflected in its glassy surface. I slept to wake again at the beginning of the dawn and in a delicious sleepy coma watched Penang Island slipping by, lemon-coloured lights palely winking on the Hill and towering cumuli high above. The boat entered the Straits at the northern end, because of the minefields, I imagine, and during breakfast steered a strange course down the narrows. She anchored in the offing as there was no room alongside, and after an hour we at last got ashore in a grilling hot tender. Mat was waiting for us with the car and a spray of pink carnations, complete with celophane and festive satin bow, a welcoming present sent by Jean.

We got back before dusk to the house on the hill at Lumut, to which it was always so good to return. The first thing we saw was a row of beautiful gladioli against the cream wash of the house, white, mauve, delicate pink and flaming crimson, the flowers of bulbs planted barely eight weeks before, and zinnias, sown when we left for Brastagi, were already in bud. All the cats came out to meet us, the kittens skipping about, Cleo talking hard, Adam frisking and Caesar plodding faithfully along. We were exclaiming with pride over the gladioli when Kandasami (who was still with us in those days) arrived on the scene hot and panting, but wreathed in smiles. Having seen the car passing through the village he had at once run full speed up the hill so that he could show off the garden.

XIV

MAY 10, 1940

INSPIRED BY THE CHANGE of scene and the renewed energy acquired at Brastagi, we started a new routine, getting up at five-thirty and working before breakfast. It was not too good before dawn, very damp and chilly and the mosquitoes were still at large. The cats did not understand it all and in consequence insisted on an additional breakfast.

By now Adam was in a delightful leggy stage with a short, clean-smelling coat like a bull terrier. His debaunched face was bony and quaint. He was a lovable, excessively matey, little creature. His fights with Caesar were well worth watching; they generally took place at bath-time round and round the bedroom, ending in hopeless entanglement in the mosquito net. Adam would put his seal-coloured ears back until his face was a furious small wedge, a foxy-face, then he would shriek with excitement and Caesar pounced. Adam dodged by turning a somersault in mid-air and off they went hareing round, wrestling, jumping and boxing, while we stood transfixed with laughter. Occasionally, Caesar paused and glanced in our direction obviously hurt that we should see fit to laugh, but Adam was always too preoccupied to notice. He boiled with excitement and his tail fluffed out to treble its normal size. He was socially minded: the only one of the cats who deigned to appear at parties.

While we were away, the European population of Lumut had increased by three. Roger's wife, Margaret, had come out from England bringing their two small sons. It was most interesting to meet her and hear about England in war-time, the black-out and all the other strange new conditions. We besieged her with questions, for she was the first person we had met from home since the outbreak of the war.

The news from Europe grew steadily worse. Everyone felt an appalling weight of anxiety and helplessness. On May 10,

1940, the Bishop of Singapore came to Sitiawan to take the Whitsun monthly services. Nearly the whole district, about twenty-five people, turned out for evensong. It was a sweltering, dead-still evening; there was not a breath in the palms; the tiny church was sunbaked. Across the aerodrome the sun sank behind the distant hills of Lumut in an angry west. When the sermon was finished and the last reedy hymn sung, the congregation waited outside, as was the custom, for the Bishop and Padre. It was then that we heard the first rumour of the invasion of Holland. Everyone was very quiet and sad, for although we were more or less expecting it the news stunned us.

That night we dined with Roger and Margaret; two or three other people were there as well. It was a weird night, intensely hot. After the angry sunset the sky had thickened in a swift and lowering purple dusk, streaked with forked and sheet lightning; the trees blue-green in the livid flashes had lashed madly to and fro in the wind, while the thunder rolled along the tops of the hills. And now, while we all sat round and listened to the crackling wireless the storm was still raging.

One of the guests, a man, who had been all through the last war and never ceased to talk about it as the adventure of his life, was crouched over the set, flushed with excitement. At one unpleasant moment the lightning flashed through the room, crackling demonically in the set and was followed by such a crash of thunder that we instinctively ducked as the whole house shook and rattled. The man by the wireless raised his ecstatic pink face and chortled gleefully: "Like a bomb . . .!"

If it had not been for this man's ghoulish attitude to the events shaking the world, that moment and, in fact, the whole evening would have been too poignantly dramatic. The "phoney war" was over, we were all now intensely conscious of the reality: Brussels, Amsterdam, Luxembourg, so near to England. . . .

The heat and oppression of that terrible night weighed like lead; the threat to England was now clear; fear clutched us. Heavily we said good night to Roger and Margaret and went home sadly.

The tension was such that it became impossible to continue our pleasant home routine of work and play. Every day at lunch-time Stuart and I hung round waiting for the news to come through and, to keep from fidgeting, we played darts incessantly. There were things of solace; even Cleo's kittens were a help, their delightful antics would evoke at least a hoarse chuckle from the palest of pessimists. Cleo watched them through half-shut eyes with pride, as they explored the sun pools cast on the floor through cracks in the shutters.

Night after night I dreamed of parachutists, figures in field-grey and the people of Belgium. When one cannot help actively in any situation I believe perhaps the mind attempts to rectify one's inability in sleep.

Europeans who had children at school in England now faced the question of whether it was wiser to bring them out to Malaya at once or not. The Steeles had this problem now, for Barry, their son, was at home; for months this constituted one of their greatest anxieties, as it was for many other parents. Was it better to wreck the child's schooling and possibly his health and to risk the long voyage or to leave him in England to face—only God knew what . . . ?

I was lucky. I could go on painting to distract my thoughts. I made studies of Yahya's beautiful hands—most Asiatics' hands are slim and tapered—and I had several new models. Among them was one of the local Malay police, Sergeant Desah, solemn and kindly-looking, rather like an amiable monkey in his khaki pill-box cap with its black pom-pom on top; Ismail, the club Boy, neat and extremely dapper in silk jacket and sarong, and Stuart's Chief Clerk. The latter I chose as being a fine type of Chinese, and I wanted a study of one for a composition. He had an extremely good head and profile. One suffocatingly hot day I was working at a sketch of him and grumbling about the heat. As he sat there the sweat was dripping off his face, and he merely remarked that it was "a warm day." I have rarely heard such an understatement.

The more I saw of the Chinese the more I liked them. In Malaya they seemed in many ways to be closer to the British people than any of the other races, most especially in their love of family life. In the delicious cool hour before sunset, the Chinese families strolled about in front of their shops, or squatted on the grass, gossiping contentedly. The young fathers played with their children; pudgy two-years-olds staggered about clutching their rice bowls against their chests; the sturdy mothers carried their youngest astride their hips. The infants wore comic, wee caps of scarlet wool with gay pom-poms on their square, shaven heads.

We discovered a quarry along the Sitiawan road with an exciting colour scheme. The high walls were of bluish-grey stone washed with the red of the laterite. Against this sun-flooded, light background Chinese coolies worked in dark clothes, the women in ultramarine jackets, scarlet scarves and black trousers, and the men in drab blue. The women, friendly and inquisitive, came to see what I was doing when I had set up my easel. When they saw themselves they were convulsed with giggles, their red-brown sunburnt faces crinkled up with infectious mirth. They called to each other in their shrill clacking tongues to come and see.

There was a very lovely little Malay girl in the village, the daughter of a minor Government official, one of the Sultan's many distant relations. She was called Raja Puteh. Her father was a jovial old roué, the very man, in fact, who had chosen the *Ronggeng* with such gusto; he agreed to let her sit for me and she arrived one morning with Ismail leading her by the hand and an escort of two small boys. She was extremely beautiful and completely self-assured. Her face was oval; she had really black eyes, a neat nose and small curling mouth. The day she came was unlucky. Early that morning a tank had burst in the roof and flooded a bedroom. The house was full of workmen noisily clearing up the mess. While she was posing there came a second deluge from above, this time through two ceilings and down into the studio, a few feet from where I was working. Ah Seng and the coolies crashed around overhead, moving furniture, scraping and banging and making a tremendous hullabaloo, while all the time the water was showering down near us. Raja Puteh never moved her disdainful head or registered any emotion whatsoever either of interest or alarm. I took this for an example of equanimity and tried to follow it. When it was time for her to go, Ismail came to fetch her, stepping elegantly out of his shoes at the door. I knew I could not offer her money, so I had bought some chocolates for her, but she was much too proud to accept them and walked gracefully from the house, a dignified scrap of humanity. Ismail cheerfully pocketed the chocolates.

One evening when we were gardening, the Customs Charge Room rang up to say a "battleship was arriving." We rushed in to change out of gardening shorts and clean ourselves up to welcome the Navy. What an excitement a battleship arriving in little Lumut! I visualized something like the *Rodney* at least on the sky-line, but when, five minutes later, we got down to the Customs there was only a small submarine chaser and she was already at anchor.

"Hm," said Stuart, "the Charge Room were not keeping a very sharp lookout!" This was long before the days of coast watchers.

It was the Malay District Officer's duty to meet the Captain. So we returned to the house. There followed some confusion as to *who* legally represented the Naval Intelligence in Lumut. Finally the Captain came up to the house to put a report through to Singapore; he would not stay and left at nine o'clock asking us to go on board in half an hour's time. Naturally we took it to mean dinner. It was a crazy evening.

Down at the jetty the ship's launch was ready. It was an unexpected pleasure to hear shrill cockney voices again. I experienced a sudden sharp pang of nostalgia for London; how strange and yet familiar those Londoners' voices sounded in the warm still air of the Malay night!

The little ships in Malaya sometimes took twenty or thirty Malay ratings on board for training, though how this was done when no one on board spoke the language was beyond my understanding. One of these Malays shouted an order in his own tongue:

"*Angkat tali!* Go astern *sekarang!*"

And in the darkness a despairing English voice cried:

"Wot the 'ell? . . . Wish oi could speak the bloody langwidge!"

On board we had a drink with the Captain, and were taken up on the bridge to gaze at the canopy of stars; sprawling Scorpio, the loveliness of the Southern Cross, and, low in the north, the Great Bear. We grew more and more hungry; but there was still no sign of dinner and when, at nearly eleven o'clock, back in the tiny wardroom, we were offered yet another drink, it became apparent that it was not going to materialize. So we made our farewells. The problem still remains: unless he was dieting or had dined well before six how did the Captain manage to get back to the ship from our house, bath, change into mess jacket and eat his dinner in that scant half-hour? . . . We wanted to laugh and talk about it going ashore in the launch but the presence of the Londoners restrained us. One got into the habit of saying anything and everything in front of boatmen and servants up-country, as it was very rare that any of them spoke English.

Ravenous by this time, we shot home and raided the ice-box. Fortunately there was crab in aspic and we ate the whole thing there and then, much to the envious astonishment of the cats, who had dined at their customary hour.

About this time the cat household was swelled by the arrival of Minnie the Moocher, Taffy's cat and the mother of Caesar. Taffy was going home on long leave. We were down in the village shopping one afternoon when an excited Chinese rushed up gabbling something about a cat. Then I heard a familiar Siamese voice talking anxiously and there a few yards away, perched on the very top of a mass of crates and cases on the railway lorry was Minnie in her box. She was the living image of Caesar, so much so that when Kuki saw her he exclaimed delightedly: "*Sa-rupa* Caesar!" Not like Caesar, but the *same* as he.

The servants had heard from their relatives in Hainan at last; everyone was miraculously alive in spite of the Japanese occupation. To celebrate the good news, Ah Chi wore flowers in her hair and Ah Seng's face was one large smile again. But just then there was a bad bout of malaria in the district, and Ah Seng went down with it first.

Ah Chi appeared one day with red marks like bad burns on her throat. I enquired what had happened but she could not explain. I soon learned that when the Chinese have headaches, toothache or sore throat or any other ailments, they pinch their own throats or foreheads in the primitive illusion that it will concentrate and draw forth the numb ache. It may have acted as a counter irritant, but the self-inflicted pain must have been acute to produce such dark red marks. Our Chinese servants were always more unwilling to go to the hospital than the Malays or Indians. Mat would go quite readily and so would the Tamil gardeners. They seemed to have a faith in medical treatment and actually asked for anti-tetanus injections and for any cuts to be cleaned properly. But the Chinese from whom one might have expected a more enlightened attitude, had a deep-rooted fear of doctors and of the operating theatre in particular and of "being cut" as they put it, so it was always with great difficulty that I persuaded them to see Dr. Menun. It was the same, of course, when they all had fever; they did not want to take quinine and it was necessary to take ours in front of them, when the malaria was bad, before they would take their own dose.

The Government anti-malarial department was taking a great deal of trouble to discover what infected mosquitoes existed in the locality. At one time there was a "human bait" sleeping for several nights in the garden within a double net; but he failed to entice the "bad" mosquitoes. One was apt to forget his presence—and the curtains were never drawn in our house. He was only noticeable when, now and again, he lit a lamp inside the folds of his white nets which looked then like some weird ghostly thing seen on All Hallow-e'en.

The terrible news from France of the advancing Nazi hordes was coming through. That was early in June while we waited for Stuart's mother (henceforth known as Zia) to arrive from East Africa; she was on her way to visit us, regardless of raiders and U-boats and quite undaunted at the age of seventy by a few thousand miles of open sea. She arrived at the hottest time of the year. We went up to Ipoh to meet her off the mail train from Singapore; her very blue eyes were shining with excitement and she was wearing a little red hat over her snow-white hair. White hair is not often to be seen in Malaya, the servants were much impressed by it and remarked upon its venerableness. On the drive back she told us how the purser on her boat, a Dutch line, had turned out to be a fifth columnist and had been arrested at Singapore, and likewise a Swiss woman passenger, who had proved to be a spy. So her voyage had not been altogether uneventful. Ah Seng was still in hospital with fever when she arrived, so the house was not looking its best to welcome her; the wine at dinner was corked and Minnie and Anthony were celebrating prolonged and noisy nuptials in the garden. Such is the way when you want everything to be at its best. But the anxiety about England was so great that nothing else mattered very much.

Then came Dunkirk, France fell and Churchill made his historic speech. We out there asked ourselves: "*Whose* blood, sweat, and tears?" The tears we could share; but we felt more than ever conscious of our inactivity. It did not seem right that we should have unlimited supplies of food and drink, clothing and cigarettes, when in England these things were rationed or unobtainable. It irked us. All we could do was to send home regular parcels of sugar and tea, jam and cigarettes, cheese, dried fruit and chocolate.

Every Bill passed in the Straits Settlements still had to be reconsidered in the Federated Malay States and again in the unfederated states. It looked as if there were need for a unified Government for the duration. We wanted to be *ordered* what to do; no restrictions, taxes or rationing were put upon us, at least not for some time, and then only very lightly. At last a definite command did come ordering people to remain at their jobs and not rush home to England to enlist. And so life dragged on.

Dr. Menun, very shyly at our joint request, gave the European women in the district lectures on First Aid. Then came the news of two months' training for the Federated Malay States Volunteer Force and Stuart arranged to go to camp. Another Customs man would come to take over.

The Volunteer Camp was on the Ipoh race-course and the first announcements about it calmly stated that there would be a few days' gap in the middle of training so that the races could take place. But later it dawned on the authorities that this was not *quite* the thing in war-time and the races were cancelled. . . .

It was extremely dry weather and a few tarantulas appeared in the gardens. One hot morning Adam came scampering in with a hateful mass of black hairy legs and remains hanging from his mouth. He sickened rapidly; he would not eat and there was little we could do for him. Even Dr. Menun did not know a cure so we rushed him up to Ipoh to the Vet. We were both utterly miserable and I'll never forget that sixty-five mile drive. Adam was limp in my arms like a sick child. We left him with the Vet, who said there was nothing that could be done;

the poison of the loathsome spider had been only too deadly.

That evening we had been asked by some planter friends, Bob and Deedee, to meet their new young assistant and his wife. It was late by the time we got back; but we went to their house as we were, very unhappy, very dirty and very tired. They were good to us in their quiet, but warm-hearted way.

And we met Vanessa and Gerald for the first time, who were later both in Japanese prison camps. She was a pretty little thing with large brown eyes, curly auburn hair and an enthusiastic, unquenchably plucky manner.

This small personal tragedy of Adam's death, although so infinitely unimportant and small beside the appalling events in Europe, seemed to add to the shadow slowly darkening the sunlight.

Then Stuart left for camp and the house seemed empty indeed. People were good to Zia and me and asked us out a great deal so that we should not feel lonely. Even Caesar knew. He scarcely left me, following me everywhere and each night he slept inside the net. People say cats have no affection or sympathy, perhaps Siamese are exceptional, certainly Caesar was as faithful as a dog.

The Jap scare was rather bad at this time, but it did not seem real; the reality was the European war. It did not seem possible then that Malaya would ever be invaded; war perhaps, but not that.

Often Zia and I would go down to the garden by the sea and sometimes the Customs Officer and "Banks" joined us there and talked until late. I remember one particular evening of miraculous beauty. Nature often does her best when life is most gloomy, or is it that perception is quickened by unhappiness as by joy? We sat by the water's edge under the frangipanni trees, as we had so frequently sat before, and watched an almost unbelievably magnificent sunset. It was very quiet; there was a gunboat at anchor in the estuary. A young moon hung over the coloured expanses of the river, and later brilliant lights from the gunboat's portholes were reflected in the black and silver water under the velvety, indigo-blue hills. Every now and again the reflections were cut by the slim lines of a *kolek* coming in from the sea, leaving dark arrowy wakes trailing across the brilliance.

We talked as usual about the war; a conversation and mood in bitter contrast to the scene we watched.

If he was not on duty, Stuart manged to 'phone me in the evenings wherever I was. One evening his call had not come through. Zia and I were sitting upstairs quietly reading after dinner when an Indian coolie appeared out of the night, climbing over the edge of the balcony. Rather surprised we stared and asked him what he was doing. He saluted and replied he was mending the telephone wires. Shortly after this the telephone bell rang and soon Stuart was speaking to me from Ipoh. Having tried to get through without success, and knowing there had been no storm to cut the line with falling trees, he had guessed the trouble, and had called the Lumut exchange and asked them to send a man up to the house at once to put my 'phone in order and that before I even knew it was not working. . . .

The Ipoh camp at the race-course was none too good. The men slept on the Grand Stand; there were no facilities for reading or relaxing after a long day out in the heat on exercises, and at first the food was either too high to eat or so little that the men were always hungry. The food conditions improved slightly later on.

The country surrounding Ipoh where the mock battles and route marches took place was strangely beautiful. Limestone hills and hummocks rose sheer out of rough tin-mining lands, and the swampy places were full of lotus flowers and hibiscus hedges; Chinese temples and private houses sprouted windows and balconies like dream eyries high up in the craggy rocks; a grotesque landscape.

It proved necessary for Stuart to keep in touch with the vital Food Control work of his district which meant he came back to Lumut at most week-ends for twenty-four hours. On the first Saturday he arrived with an enormous bouquet of white carnations, red roses and orchids; he had bought all the flowers in the shop. They filled even the huge cuspidor which I had bought from an Indian pottery shop in Ipoh. It was the biggest vase I could find and when painted cream it was quite effective and more like a Grecian urn than a cuspidor!

Sometimes Zia and I went up to Ipoh to stay and if he was off duty, Stuart came out and dined with us. It was very hot up there with the temperature at nearly 100 degrees some days, and at night after the quiet of Lumut it was difficult to sleep because of the traffic.

There was a fascinating Chinese shop in Ipoh known as the Bird Shop. It was run by a family of hard-bitten English-speaking Chinese. They sold a variety of things from white paroquets and tall tuberoses—like heavily perfumed, plaited silk—to coats and hats and cheap mah-jong sets. Out in a small back-yard was a kind of zoo; unsafe, unhygienic and probably rather inhumane. It was later condemned and the animals were moved to the country. There was a black panther, black as night and, but for the furious slanting golden eyes, almost invisible in his dark gimcrack cage. There were flying squirrels, baby crocs and alligators, lovely hooded Chinese pigeons, two beautiful little clouded leopard cubs, a civet cat, a cat-bear and some mouse-deer; also several Siamese cats which wandered about disdainfully over the jumble of rickety cages.

Sometimes we went to the Chinese Po Gardens to buy new seeds and plants. A plump, sweet-faced Chinese girl dealt out the seed packets and gardening tools with a gentle smile and slow, careful movements as if time were of no importance at all. The garden was formal, stiff with hollyhocks, dahlias and cockscombs in hundreds of pots, so that there was barely room for the car in the tiny drive. The wooden bungalow was hung with torenias, ferns and wax flowers in baskets, and on every creaking step was a pot or two. Inside there were flowers from the hills for sale; English roses, gladioli and golden montbretia.

On the outskirts of the town was another Chinese garden, drowsy with the honeyed scent of frangipanni and oleander. It was a weird, decayed place and lives in my memory only for the wafts of perfume that came from it as one drove past into the smells of the town, and for the strange figure we once saw there. He was an elderly Englishman; although one would scarcely have know it; he might have passed for a Malay, but for the beard and pointed features which made one look twice. He wore Malay dress and his feet were bare. Years ago he had married a Malay, retired and lived as one of them. This was the only case of "going Native" that I saw. He had a defiant air as he glanced at us. There was something at once pitiable and repulsive about him, blending as he did with the surroundings;

that decayed and alien garden, its too heavy perfumes and its damp walls, crumbling with lichen.

All the planters, who were not over age or unfit, and who could be spared, were also at camp. It was very lonely for their wives out on the estates, often many miles off the road down muddy tracks through dark endless acres of rubber. One such girl whom Zia and I went to see, lived eight miles off the road and over twenty miles from Lumut. She was a White Russian, the wife of a good-hearted amiable Scot whom everyone liked. In two years she had made a wonderful garden out of nothingness. There were potting sheds and flowers and fruit and she even grew lemons. Wide lawns led down to the river past beds of apricot Japanese cannas. True, the river was muddy, mosquito-haunted and full of crocodiles, but the effect was good. She was proud of her garden and no wonder, for she had worked hard in it. She was very lovely; with long fragile hands and graceful arms, and a high, fair brow heaped with blonde curls like a crown. She hardly ever smiled.

"Do the crocodiles come up on the lawn?" Zia asked conversationally.

"Zomtimes," she replied dreamily. "We catch them in a trap then—with a died chicken for the bait. . . ."

XV

A CHINESE TEMPLE AND A MALAY HILL

THE IMPERIAL AIR MAIL ceased and six weeks passed without letters from home; that was a long time in those days. Then my mother discovered it was possible to send to America and on by Trans-Pacific Clipper to Hong Kong, and I got a letter at last, much to the envy of our friends.

The fortnightly cables from home that most of us had arranged to be sent were more than ever welcome now. There have been some accusations of disloyalty or indifference regarding certain parts of the Empire—it is a pity the accusers could not have watched the lines of anxiety deepening in English faces in Malaya and seen the grey hairs appearing during those weeks after Dunkirk. As for the Jap scare, it was of secondary importance: nothing mattered but what was happening to England. Some people were convinced the U.S. Fleet would come to Singapore if Japan attacked the Netherlands East Indies—which seemed to be the most likely move. Whether this was Japanese propaganda to beguile us into feeling "safe" remains to be proved; but it all fitted in with the official blah that was doled out later on. The arrival of the Australian troops and the start of the Volunteer training camps were like a thin camouflage over the helplessness of Malaya, and one may be sure that not a single one of the many hundreds of Japs already in the country were deceived by it; a good many of them were undoubtedly active agents. The local Jap barber, obsequious and kow-towing, who lived in Sitiawan built himself a little shop overlooking the aerodrome where he had a perfect view of its total lack of defence. . . .

The day camp finished, Mat went off in the car at dawn so as to be in Ipoh in good time to pick up Stuart. Zia and I filled the house with flowers; golden brown coreopsis and yellow marigolds, and cannas with cockscombs like bunches of flames. The sweet corn, seven to eight feet tall, was ripening in the kitchen garden, the silken tassels of the cobs were very long now, some silver, some deep crimson. But that evening everything was overshadowed by the news of the first terrible raid on London. I was recovering from dengue, which at the best of times makes you feel as if all your bones had jellified and your head had become much too heavy for your body, and I staggered about trying not to imagine London in utter ruin. It was a bottled-up fear and fury we all felt, a dead weight of depression.

Stuart had brought us back Chinese house-coats from Ipoh: mine was a silver-grey, embroidered with pagodas, and he had found satin shoes that matched it exactly; and for Zia he had chosen a scarlet one to show up her white hair. There was a lot for him to see in the garden; the duranta tree, covered in white blossom, was looking like a wedding cake, and the amazing "Music Note" shrub was in flower; there were new kittens, six of them this time, all Siamese; four of Cleo's lively little devils and two sedate ones of Minnie's. Minnie had disappeared for some hours to have her kittens and the next day Anthony had stalked into the hall and sniffed enquiringly at a cupboard door. There followed a loud piercing squeak. Zia and I looked up startled, to see that Anthony had opened the door and two minute, white, shrieking Siamese kits had fallen out. This was the only occasion on which Anthony showed any interest in his offspring. One of these we called Ptolemy, and kept for ourselves to take Adam's place, and Dr. Menun was to have the other. All Cleo's were already booked as usual.

At tea-time every day the kittens laboriously hopped down the stairs like small rocking horses one after the other, meandered out into the sun and streamed across the garden stopping to sniff the fallen petals and delicately test the reaction of some minute creature in this wonderful new world they had found. They were endlessly enquiring and diminutively gay, and as always a consolation and a distraction from anxiety.

There were other lovely things to watch such as the Keng Hua opening at midnight. This is a Chinese flower which blooms and dies during a single night. As it opened its white petals tinged with pink, it seemed to bow its graceful head and then shook free the mass of fragile stamens within the indescribable heart. Watching it bloom was like listening to a Yehudi Menuhin solo. . . .

Ah Seng had fever again; Mat was ill with various kinds of unpleasant parasitic things, as well as a poisoned foot and infected hands; the normal cure for which was German and, of course, unobtainable; and now Ah Chi too had dengue. It was then the Chinese Moon Festival, so we went down to the town to buy Moon Cakes for the servants. We hid dollar notes in the cakes as the women of fourteenth-century China once hid messages to help the rebels against the Mongol tyrants.

Before Zia left we went up to Penang at Hari Raya. We had some good parties at Lumut and we took her to the islands. Once when the launch bucketed more violently than usual she nearly slid overboard; there was a very high wind that day; it even swept two loaves of bread out of the cabin; but Zia never turned a hair. Nor did she when some poisonous scarlet centipedes dashed from under the flower pots she was tending, nor when she heard the tigers coughing below her window at night, and their alarming growl, *aum*, as the Malays so onomatopoetically call it; nor yet when there was a very unpleasant double murder on an estate Over the River. So brave was she that we considered now was the time to return the hospitality long owed to a certain rather difficult and trying character.

This was a planter of the old school, who lived in the next district and rather liked to think he ruled it. We met him when we were politely returning our first call on some neighbours, conventionally attired and on our best behaviour. In spite of all we had heard, it was impossible not to gape, when in he stalked. His feet were bare, and he wore emerald green pyjama trousers and a loose Malay jacket which contrasted in the most startling way with his red hair and ruddy face. The voluminous folds of his silk suit hardly concealed the Falstaffian and fascinating curves of his figure. Some of the younger men were almost scared of him and his conversation, which was able, so it was mooted, even to wreck careers.

Zia's presence made the *pahit* party quite successful. We were kept busy, for his thirst like his figure was memorable.

Besides the green costume he also affected a rose-coloured one cut on the same lavish lines. When Zia first saw him, some weeks before the party, he was wearing this. As we flashed past his garden in the car he was standing on the lawn under a temple tree.

"Oh!" exclaimed the astonished Zia, "Who *is* that tall woman in the pink evening dress?" . . .

Another party which lives more pleasantly in the memory was given as a farewell by two planters who were sending their wives off to Australia, nominally on leave, but fundamentally because they were convinced the Japs were coming. Most of us there were keen gardeners and the party ended in a delightful way. Armed with torches we followed our hosts over the lovely garden and were laden with cuttings and seedlings. In the dramatic torch-light the great clusters of yellow cassia flowers, like giant laburnums, and the pale ixoras looked more luxuriant than ever before. Vanessa was there I remember, dancing about ecstatically with armfuls of cuttings for her new garden.

In November, after a series of little farewell dinner parties, Zia went down to Singapore to wait for a boat to the Cape and we drove with her as far as Kuala Lumpur, where we stayed a night with Derek. The drive down was one of the wettest I ever remember. There was a cloud-burst in the Slim River valley and, quite blinded by the rain, we dashed through a wash-away on the road. Sheets of water flew up and flooded the wind-screen. Soon afterwards, over a shallow valley a thick and most brilliant rainbow appeared, hanging under sheets of rain. The effect was wonderful, the grey clouds, the mist and the vivid chunks of colour: no blue was visible, only red, gold, yellow and emerald like jewels in all that green wetness.

We stopped for tea at the Tanjong Malim Rest House, on the Perak boundary, a hot, dirty, characterless town, which I never liked, with its shabby Rest House tucked away behind the Chinese shops and the hideous meat-market. In Kuala Lumpur the next day, Derek took us to see a big Chinese temple set in the heart of many acres of rolling hills used for a Chinese burial ground, a bit of China in Malaya. The temple itself was hidden in old rubber trees and surrounded by other buildings. Left carelessly to rot under the trees was a heap of carved, gilded panels and figurines which had been torn from the old temple for some unknown reason. All were delightful and some most beautiful. In a pool of water on one deep panel floated a leaf, or so we thought until I stopped to pick it up;

it was part of the carving, almost Grinling Gibbons-like in its realism. Another panel fifteen feet long and eighteen inches wide depicted scenes from a legend. Little men in castellated turrets gazed down on travellers arriving in courtyards on prancing horses from the plains—the expressions on their faces were perfect: scorn, laughter, cunning and hatred. This panel was in deep relief; the scenes interspersed with plaques of birds, flowers and leaves. There were a few inferior bits of tracery set in a miniature temple gateway, but on the whole the workmanship was very fine indeed, and far too good to be wasting there under the dank rubber trees. Beyond these lovely things and also in the darkness of the trees was a school; here we stopped short, hushed and fascinated by what we saw. A man, a young Chinese, dressed simply in white European shirt and slacks, was dancing alone, without music in the bare school yard. His technique was as lovely as an accomplished ballet dancer's; he had perfect control of his slim body; the slow, strange inflexions of wrists and ankles and delicate hands were most beautiful to watch. He seemed almost in a trance alone in that cool dark place. It was as if we were interrupting something very ancient and consecrated. The young man never stopped his gestures and arabesques, nor looked in the least self-conscious when he became aware of our presence. Presumably he was rehearsing for temple dances which, I believe, Europeans are very rarely permitted to see.

The temple was surrounded with half-built courtyards and served by a miserably incongruous entrance in the back of a tin shed, typical of Chinese haphazardness. Once inside the sunken paved courtyard, with its trees and painted roof-tops and pantiles, dragons, and flying, pagoda-like eaves, all was quiet and peaceful. An unseen gong beat rhythmically; a few children wandered about on a verandah; a gaudy Buddha, in the shed with the unprepossessing tin back, gazed across at the main building. We went up the steps and over the high lintel into the temple. It was full of multi-coloured banners, joss sticks and brass gongs; some of these were shaped like barrels and others, painted vermilion and gold, were like gargantuan seed pods. There was a brass pagoda, crowded with many gods and tiny bells; the great Buddha towered above the altar. At th back sat a forbidding black-faced god with countless arms like Siva. There was another courtyard here with steps leading to an inner shrine. Suddenly several sexless-looking beings appeared from a balcony and the largest and most alarming of these waved us away; but they had no objection to our being in the main temple. They had shaven heads and wore black gowns; they were Bhuddist nuns.

The whole place had a strange appeal about it with its air of secrecy and its garish red and gold beauty. When we came out again into the courtyard, there was an aeroplane overhead high up in the burnished sky, a symbol of the age we lived in, a contrast with the agelessness of the symbols we had seen.

That short time in Kuala Lumpur was heavy with farewells, to Zia who went off on the night mail to Singapore, and to Derek who had recently got married and was about to sail for England and long leave. People were still being allowed to go home for furlough then, but it was necessary for Malayan Government servants to sign a document pledging themselves not to join the services while on leave. And Derek's wife never succeeded in getting a passage out again and he returned alone in 1941.

Farewells are depressing and emotionally exhausting so that Stuart and I were glad we had planned a few days holiday in the coolness up Fraser's Hill; it had been Zia's idea really and was a wonderful parting present from her.

We left Kuala Lumpur the following morning. The hill road was trying for the old car and we took it cautiously. This was the last journey in her, as Stuart had found someone to buy her, and a little red Ford Prefect was already waiting for us at Lumut. It is absurd how fond one becomes of a car and we felt quite sad that this was the Hillman's swan-song, as far as we were concerned. The mountain river tumbled noisily down from the hills beside the twisting road; there were Chinese women panning for gold, washed down from Raub, in the shallow water, their red and blue garments made bright splashes of colour among the white foam and grey boulders. But when Stuart attempted to photograph them they took off their huge coolie hats and squatted down behind them, hiding their faces, coy and inherently superstitious of the Evil Eye. The coolie-class Chinese are famously superstitious. They will endure and encourage the most ear-splitting screams from the axles of their barrows or carts because they imagine the noise will frighten away the bad spirits. I met an American woman missionary once who had adopted a small Chinese girl as her people had turned her out. She was in fact outcast simply because her "heart line" ran straight across her palm; that, said her relations, was the hand of a murderer and they would have nothing more to do with her.

Fraser's Hill was one of the oldest hill stations in the country; a neat, polite little place, rather cramped on its narrow jungly ledges. It was veiled in mist when we arrived, but the next morning all the peaks were sticking out dark and blue from a sea of cloud below. A great white sea of vapour, whose waves lapped the islands and creeks, dashed up the bays and inlets of the mountains. And there under the cloud, unseen and far away, lay the whole of the hot country miles below cut off from the hills and soaked in rain. Again I experienced that feeling of being in quite another world, not, as one feels in Switzerland, *above* the world—but in a totally different land, isolated and unreal.

It was a brief, peaceful holiday; the war seemed sinfully far away. We felt proud to be English, very proud, but rather as a parasite might be of the beautiful creature it lives on. In a small way anxiety was a part of our sharing of the burden; but it was very small compared with the personal suffering of the people at home. We were ashamed of our peace and isolation and feared that when we did eventually go home we should be like visitors from another planet. . . .

We did little but walk and read and sit by the fire in the evenings to play chess, which we were beginning to learn, and we would warm an occasional bottle of red wine among the logs drying on the warm hearth.

There was a diminutive golf course in a narrow ravine and someone with a cruel sense of humour had built a row of small shelters from which people watched the golfers. This proved popular and highly entertaining. I felt I should never dare to play again; I am sure no other game is so revealing both of characters, and figures, as golf. . . .

When we got back to Lumut, it had been raining and the garden was gay with pink zepherantes, a little crocus which flowers briefly after rain. Ah Seng came out to greet us with a long face. Anthony, his favourite, had been missing for some days. Then one morning Stuart received a 'phone call: a black cat had been caught at the Rest House and would be executed shortly if it was not ours. We retrieved it; it was, of course, Anthony, beautiful Anthony Hitam, growling with rage at the indignity of being caught in a cat trap, a trap baited too with half a chicken, but so furious was Anthony that he had not touched a morsel.

Apparently "Banks" had complained of too frequent cat choruses at night in the Rest House roof and the trap had been set at his orders. Some weeks after Anthony's adventure the Rest House cat was delivered of five black kittens in "Banks's" cupboard, on a pile of his dress shirts. He made pointed remarks to us but we remained quiet on the subject. The virile Anthony, that old reprobate, was quite probably responsible for all the numerous black cats now appearing in the village.

Of Cleo's and Minnie's new Siamese kittens, two were worthy of especial note, Robert and Ptolemy. Robert was so called because he was going to Roberta, a girl I had recently met during camp. Her husband, Niel, a keen volunteer, was a planter. She was an unusual person, youthful, tense, rather elfin and yet outspoken and frank, and quite crazy about animals. So she deserved Robert, a kitten of character and determination.

Ptolemy had large green-blue eyes, a big dark tail; his coat was soft and silky and the colour of Cornish cream. He was a really beautiful little animal and among the other kittens looked like a king playing with the rabble. He seemed to arch his head back on his furry chest until he had the taut look of a T'ang horse; his face was pointed and very serious. He was quiet-voiced and good; he never had the character of Adam or of Caesar; but he looked an aristocrat. When he lay with his head sunk back on his T'ang horse chest, front paws out flat on the ground and, incredible as it sounds, hind paws and tummy twisted round to face the sky, he seemed absolutely boneless. In this extraordinarily amusing attitude he would sleep blissfully during the hot afternoons. He was passionately devoted to his elder brother, Caesar: he was also good friends with Robert. Poor Robert had a bad time when he left to go to his new home. He was offered a lift up to Ipoh, but escaped from his box and got lost on the way in the roof of a planter's bungalow. Stuart had to go and fetch him home. Once home, Robert leapt out of the car, and the other cats rushed on to the verandah steps to welcome him back. He and Ptolemy literally fell on each other's necks and romped about with joy. Both the mothers and Caesar then washed the frisky prodigal. Finally he went off in a large box with windows, a built-in scratch-pan and a can of milk, but again he missed his connection in Ipoh and had to wait all day in the Volunteers' Mess before Roberta could fetch him.

I had one or two rather trying commissions at this time. One of Dr. Menun's assistant Indian doctors asked me if I would paint his mother's portrait.

"Certainly," I said. "When can she come for sittings?"

"She is dead," he answered.

My heart sank; was I to paint from the corpse? I looked blank and murmured conventional sympathy.

"I have a photograph," he said. It was enlarged from a small snap and so blurred that the features were almost indistinguishable, but being broke as usual I accepted the commission!

The second trying commission was a portrait of one of those people who must have a beat-up or burst every Saturday night and could only sit for me on Sunday mornings. . . . He always arrived late. He was an infuriating sitter and he knew it and will not mind me saying it—he mocked both himself and me in a husky voice; but his eyes were as clear as a baby's. No one knows how he did it.

As an antidote to all this I chose some new models: a young Chinese nurse, pale and prim against a background of black silk; and the hospital peon, he was a Sikh, of course bearded, huge, solemn and magnificent in an orange-coloured turban. He might have passed as an elderly and aristocratic sage, but he was only a messenger boy—a young man in his early twenties. When the sittings were finished I gave him the usual fee. But he must have thought I had intended it for the hospital, because he came back the next day and graciously returned it, politely but firmly refusing to take any payment at all. A pity as consequently I did not like to ask him to sit again.

XVI

TRAGEDY AND A SEA PATROL

JUST BEFORE CHRISTMAS that year the first trial black-out was arranged in the district; it was in fact quite an eventful day as the afternoon was marked also by a boat-race. This was not as frivolous as it sounds, because for war purposes it became necessary to ascertain which of the four Government launches was the fastest.

The two Customs boats, the D.O.'s tubby launch and the slim Police launch were tied up alongside each other at the sun-baked jetty. The D.O. was late; we waited for him, tossing gently on the fast-ebbing tide. The great river danced and sparkled in the sunlight. The casuarina trees by the Rest House were dipping and sighing in the freshening breeze; over the Chinese roofs of the town towered the three cone-shaped hills of Lumut. It was a familiar landscape. Half the population was already gathered on the jetty to watch the race. A Chinese youth was performing on roller skates, but there were no ribaldries directed at him from the crowd as there would have been in England; he was showing off in peace. A gramophone was playing Chinese music in one of the shops across the green. It was peaceful, gay and friendly. I looked up the hill to where the roof of our house showed red above the other houses and thought of the garden, and the cats waiting for us, and Ah Chi, freshly bathed and neat sitting on a box by the kitchen door, patiently picking the clinging "love grass" seeds from the socks she washed so well.

Then we started the race. At first the Police launch forged ahead, but on the mile course the *Rimau* overhauled her and won easily, while the D.O.'s launch wallowed laboriously in the wash, and the little *Kerita* lay far astern.

For Lumut a boat-race and a black-out were almost too much excitement for one day. The black-out was a primitive arrangement then, which, strange to say, we rather enjoyed because it was novel and relieved the monotony. The electric power was simply turned off at the mains. The Europeans and some Asiatics each took a beat and patrolled the village. We started off down the hill accompanied some of the way by Caesar; the night was so dark that the heat clung round one's face like warm velvet. The population padded about the streets talking in hushed voices; their white clothes glimmered ghost-like in the blackness. A few had shut themselves in their houses. Here and there a dim tell-tale glow showed through the broken shutter of a shop. We nearly hanged ourselves on the wire washing lines in the back-yards, and stumbled dangerously over the gaping stone drains. When we drove to Sitiawan, the old *kampong* appeared to be a mass of lights and we began to curse the Malay lack of co-operation; but as we drew closer we saw the lights were only myriads of fire-flies in the trees. . . .

Christmas Day was much happier than we had expected. Before dawn we drove into Taiping with the Steeles to church. The jungle road was chill and dark at first, but presently the sun came up out of the trees. The slanting rays fell across the wet paddy lands at Bruas, the mist rose off the jungle, and great buffaloes trod ponderously forth to wallow in the mud.

Back at Lumut we had a drink before lunch with the Bacons and watched their children playing in the swimming pool in the shade of a great clump of tall bamboos. Margaret had decorated a Christmas tree for them with candles and snow and baubles; it looked unexpectedly exotic, while the hot sun blazed down outside.

That night our very good friends, the Steeles, came to Christmas dinner once more, bringing generous armfuls of presents. I had decorated the table with stagmoss and a large green glass bowl of local fruits: yellowish-green sugar-cane, green pineapple with the bloom blue on it, green and yellow bananas, gold and scarlet rambutans, dusky purple mangosteens and little yellow and green and gold mandarines. Bertie insisted on chewing the sugar-cane, which really only intended for decorative purposes was decidedly stringy. It was good to hear Joan laugh again, as, for a short time, she forgot something of her anxiety; her dark brown eyes were screwed up with infectious laughter into little half moons of mirth.

At the New Year it was decided by Government that Food Control was of first importance, and so Stuart was not to be called up for any more Volunteer training camps, which were now to be held every six months.

About this time we both had to go down to Singapore to see a specialist. We spent one day there; but in that short period had the extreme good fortune to meet two of the kindest and most generous-hearted people I've ever known. The Hiltons were shipboard friends of Zia originally and until now there had been no opportunity to meet them. Bung, as everyone called him, was a Surgeon-Lieutenant-Commander, R.N.V.R., in the Singapore Naval Base. They were at the station to meet us in spite of the fact that the train arrived at 6.30 a.m. After breakfast, like real up-country cousins we toured the town, saw the famous Change Alley where cheap-jacks sold all kinds of goods for next to nothing, and in Raffles Place gaped at the European shops which seemed wonderful to rusticated eyes, especially Kelly and Walsh, the one up-to-date bookshop. I was impressed then, with the sight of pill-boxes in Raffles Place, and at a few other odd corners. Marjorie took us down to the native waterfront; the great roadstead was full of junks; the pearly sea stretched away among hundreds of islands to the hazy sky.

The Chinese quarter was built of tall storied houses which flowered with washing hung on poles from every window, like a thousand banners down each narrow street.

We drove through the tumbledown rabble of a Chinese slum and along the notorious Lavender Street, a strange approach to the luxury of the big swimming club by the sea; then up to the Gap, a rough open space high above the net-work of islands and the sprawling town. There are countless islands stretching to the horizon; at night their lights flickered like a million fire-flies across the sea. The white cupola of the Supreme Court, the tall spire of the Cathedral, the masts of Fort Canning and the thirteen-storied Cathay building were easily distinguished landmarks. Just below the Gap is the incredibly rococo house of Mr. Aw Boon Haw, a self-made millionaire, manufacturer of the famous Tiger Balm, a cure for every imaginable ill.

Singapore town was a curious place that I personally never

cared for very much, even after many visits. For years I had longed to see it and somehow I was disappointed, but I should imagine it was a place more than most that one needs to live in and to explore at leisure in order to appreciate it fully. There was little that was Malay about it; it seemed to be inhabited almost entirely by the British and the Chinese and, unlike Penang, it had to me no particular character or charm of its own. It was a melting-pot, a polyglot place built out of a mangrove-swamp where the true Malay had never lived. The servants spoke English in the clubs, houses and hotels; here Malay was no longer even the lingua franca.

When our business was done, Bung drove us the fourteen miles across the Island to the Naval Base, that bare, ugly place of raw new houses, barracks, shadeless roads and oil tanks above the calm, perfect anchorage of the Johore Straits. The land across the narrow Straits overlooking the Base was owned by Japanese rubber firms. How easy their job of spying must have been and how they must have laughed among themselves! From a hill we looked down on to the famous floating dock and an enormous liner alongside a wharf. No names could be mentioned then but I thought she was the *Queen Mary*—as it has since been revealed, she was.

The peace of Lumut was lovelier than ever after Singapore.

There had been a further addition to the household: Ah Chi's little daughter, Ah Sah, aged eight, had suddenly arrived from China. A bright-eyed, brown-skinned imp with a shy lively smile. She had come with friends from Hainan where she had been forced to hide in the jungle to escape from the Jap bombers, but she showed no trace of her ordeals. Although Ah Chi was delighted to have the little girl back safely, she took it all very calmly and it was only then that she told me she had also a married son of sixteen, who was still in Jap-invaded Hainan.

One perfect blue and gold morning a dreadful thing occurred. Stuart had only just left the house. I had arranged a vase of white and scarlet flowers to paint and was stretching a canvas when Kuki rushed in and pointing vaguely down the hill said:

"*Tuan sudah mati . . . !*" The Tuan is dead . . . for a few very bad moments I not unnaturally thought he meant Stuart had crashed. Tremblingly I ran outside; all the servants were standing under the temple trees on the edge of the garden looking down the hill. Kuki then explained he meant the *tuan* who lived down there in the next house, the Policeman. My nerves were so shaken by the original shock that at first I was slow to react: probably it was only a servant's tale, the Policeman was most likely taken ill and now unconscious. When I had 'phoned Stuart, who got on to the doctor and the police, I rang Margaret and together we went to see if there was anything we could do . . . there was nothing. He was dead. At first we thought it was murder; the case of the murders Over the River was still dragging on and it might well have been revenge; but undoubtedly he had taken his own life. To those who knew him best it was an appallingly unexpected thing. I write of this tragedy only because it seemed part of the increasing shadow. In a small European community such a thing shakes everyone to the core of his being; it has a far more personal and terrifying aspect than it would in an English town. That a man could suffer so much without showing it to a soul, live among them all with a smile on his lips was a challenge that opened dark vistas of the imagination.

Very early the next morning he was buried in the English churchyard near Ipoh. It was a clear morning, brilliantly beautiful. The distant mountains rose above the town in misty-gold perfection. Looking at them one instinctively felt the help that comes from the hills—such superb tranquillity could hardly exist in this world if there were not something else to follow. The guard fired the volleys over the grave, by a strange coincidence at the exact hour at which the Policeman had shot himself the day before. . . .

Chinese New Year came as an outstanding relief from routine and that particular one lives in my memory as something very perfect and complete—four vivid days of peace in sharp contrast to the horror of what had occurred so recently. The Chinese shops were very busy; full of brown gelatinous cakes, dried sharks' fins and fungus for the New Year feast. The Eng Wah family were more smiling than ever. We received an invitation to a New Year dinner from Mrs. Deong Leong; as a sea patrol had already been planned Stuart could not go, but Mrs. Deong shyly tempted me with wonderful descriptions of

From a charcoal drawing by the author

Chinese tin-mining coolie girl

From a charcoal drawing by the author

Yahya

From a charcoal drawing by the author

From a charcoal drawing by the author

her bird's nest soup and exactly how it should be prepared, even to the number of hours it takes to wash the feathers from the nests.

Although I regret missing her famous soup and the memorable, if somewhat formidable, experience of a Chinese dinner, that week-end was well worth it.

Ninety pounds of ice were put on board to last for the four days at sea. At the end of that time the remaining tins of food and bottles of drinking water and beer were awash in a chilly pond in the ice-box, all that remained of the huge block.

On Saturday afternoon, office work done, Stuart took the launch down the river, inspected all the junks and tongkangs in the Strait and, as it was too rough in the serang's view to go north, anchored in the Dutch Fort Bay, at Pangkor, for the night. Stuart and I cooked the supper in the galley. The frying-pan was in a bad state as I had quite forgotten Malays will not touch pig's fat and had left it uncleaned after the last trip some months before; it was soon cleaned up with emery paper and we achieved an excellent meal of sausages and bacon. There was nearly a disaster when some waste rag under the primus caught fire; the flare was alarming in the confined space of the galley, but it was put out and the supper was undamaged.

It was a cold night with a wind blowing; but the next morning Stuart did the patrol up north, and at midday the serang agreed to chance it, to do the southern beat and make for the islands anchorage, as the wind seemed likely to drop. All the junks Stuart inspected on the way south were festive with Chinese crackers and joss sticks; each grinning crew had a large duck, either about to be slaughtered and waddling about on deck, or just being prepared for the pot; plenty of vegetables too for the New Year dinner and I expect, had he been able to find it, some chandu hidden away cunningly.

The swell was dying down with the wind and the friendly hump of Rumbia lay right ahead. The moment the *Rimau's* anchor splashed into the green fathoms between the arms of the bay we went ashore to bathe, and in the late afternoon climbed up to the saddle where we had long wished to build a bungalow. About two hundred feet above the sea this narrow strip ran out to the headland. From it one looked down on the north side to wild rocks and waves and on the south side to the delicious curves of the bay, the *Rimau* rocking gently in the clear green water; the lovely line of the white sand fringed with palms and the rising steepness of the multi-coloured jungle behind. We desired so strongly to possess this piece of Rumbia that we tried to buy it, but were told we should have to take the whole island on a ninety-nine years' lease, which was not quite what we had wanted. The headland itself was already like a garden; small palms with delicate greyish stems and many flowering shrubs grew there. Back in the jungle it was cool and still; there were glimpses of the *Rimau* framed in trees as she lay at anchor in the dazzling water. There was a rough stone gully twined with roots where white flowers grew and tiny bulbs sprang from the trees themselves. We scrambled down this and came out by the sea. There were fresh iguana tracks on the sand.

We were hot and sticky from scrambling about on the hill and the evening bathe was more luxurious than ever; the water caressed one's skin like the finest silk. And we met an extraordinary fish. He would not leave us; small, striped green, brown and silver, he was the most ridiculously friendly fish I've ever come across; in fact I will never say fish are cold-blooded again. He ran up our arms and snuggled into our shoulders lovingly. When we stood up he swam in small circles round our legs, and if we walked into the shallows he followed, almost on to the sand. He allowed us to pick him out of the water and pass him from hand to hand and all the time he lay and regarded us with his black and silver eye. He was so absurdly ingratiating we could hardly drag ourselves away from him; but it was getting chill and finally we had to go. He drifted away disconsolately with his head hanging to one side, an absurd, forlorn wee fish.

When we were back on board just before sunset the crew went ashore to bathe and played on the sand like children, throwing coconuts at each other, Yahya like a young god among them. It was odd to think that he could probably have made his fortune in Hollywood, almost without saying a word. It is rare to see such a specimen of physical beauty; his skin was a kind of golden ochre with a dash of Venetian red. To watch him made me wish more than ever that I was a really first-class painter.

After dark we took the dinghy and pottered round the bay. There was so much phosphorescence that every stroke of the oars made a whirlpool of diamonds. Our fingers showed black against it as we scooped up handfuls of the liquid stars.

I woke up in time to see the sun rise over the ultramarine mountains of the mainland, and after a bathe and breakfast we got under way. Soon the islands were spread out astern as we headed into the sun to catch the boats sailing up the muddy-mouthed Perak River to Telok Ansun. The blue-green of the deep sea changed abruptly to thick, brown-stained water as we drew near the low-lying mangrove coast. We were out seven hours. The sea was silvery with the heat at noon, the glare struck off the water, while the islands floated dreamily on the horizon, enticing with their memories of cool greenness and deep shade. There were a good many junks about that day; in all, twenty-two were inspected during the whole patrol. We returned to the Rumbia anchorage at tea-time; the cicadas' song rasped over the water as we entered the bay and the two martins flew out to greet the launch as usual and fluttered in the shade of the awning. At night when we put the mosquito nets up on deck they got very much in the way, but they never left the *Rimau* for long until she weighed anchor. We bathed lengthily and deliciously at the very peak of the high tide; the water was up almost to the jungle. Failing to catch any fish for supper we cooked some eggs and groped in the cold slush of the ice-box for a tin of fruit; cool peaches slid down well. We turned in on deck early, before nine o'clock; the martins had already gone to roost in the tarpaulins.

Rimau pitched a good deal in the night, which woke me eventually and I saw the sea was alive with phosphorescence. Later, rain on our faces woke us both, waves were breaking then, glimmering silver waves, and each raindrop sent up flashes of silver fire. Half asleep we staggered out from the nets and made a dash for the saloon; it was wet there too; but there we spent the remainder of the night more or less asleep half rolling off the narrow seats. After all these nocturnal disturbances we woke too late for the sunrise.

That morning we left Rumbia regretfully. The martins swooped back to the Island as the *Rimau* moved slowly out of the bay.

On the way home we explored for the first time the Robinson Crusoe-like beaches of Pulau Lalang. The sand was glaring white, but delicious in the shade of the nipah palms which were thick with their heavy red-gold fruit, not unlike pineapples. In their shade were turtle-wallows ringed with trailing purple convolvulus. I hoped to see a baby turtle emerge, but had no luck. Bêche-de-mer wallowed in the shallow water and there were tiny brilliant fish. It was very lonely and very far away. A timeless place that slept in the sun with the bloom of creation still untouched upon it.

We returned to the dinghy and rowed back to the *Rimau*, anchored in deep water in a crescent of the islets. In this lagoon-like place the sea-bed was patterned with coral and rock shapes with patches of sand between as green in the depths as fire opals.

As the *Rimau* approached Pangkor on the return she overtook an old fishing junk, a tatterdemalion thing. Her sail against the sky was like a pair of ancient Dutch trousers, all patches, and she was hung from stem to stern with silver-scaled fish drying in the sun, curtains of fish reeking to high heaven while the crew sat under them grinning cheerfully. Another junk we overhauled had a sail made entirely of flour-bags laboriously stitched together.

Lumut seemed very hot and curiously brown after the sea-born freshness of the islands.

One of Dr. Menun's Indian colleagues took the First Aid examination; it was held in a small ward at the hospital high up above the estuary. There was a strong breeze blowing through the room and all the time white pigeons kept drifting down and down outside the window as if falling into the vivid blue of the sea. There was an extreme homeliness about that examination; only three of us went in for it. Dr. Pram was a complete contrast to Dr. Menun; he was not in the least shy and he adored a good laugh.

"Now," he said to Deedee, "please name some of the delirant poisons"—ether, belladonna, alcohol, etc.

Dead silence: Deedee's black-lashed, china-blue eyes stared innocently at Dr. Pram as if seeking inspiration.

"Can't you recall *one*?" His dark face was suffused with

seraphic smiles as he hinted: "Sometimes they cause ECSTASY . . .!"

The huge black eyes rolled heavenward. Still Deedee looked completely blank, while Margaret and I were convulsed with inward laughter; it was particularly funny as Deedee herself always boasted that she was the proud possessor of "hollow legs." At last Margaret could bear it no longer.

"Are you T.T., my dear?" she enquired.

"Oh! Alcoholic poisoning, Dr. Pram; how silly of me!" Deedee chuckled.

I should think we all lost a mark or two over that hilarious question, but we passed the examination successfully.

One morning shortly after this, while my mind was full of First Aid, the air was rent with piercing shrieks. I rushed out; there was Ah Chi's little girl, Ah Sah, apparently on fire; clouds of smoke and heartrending yells were issuing from her while Ah Chi dashed about wailing and flapping her inevitable tea-cloth. Now is a chance to practise my first aid, I thought, so trying to keep calm I ran and seized up the studio rug and returned full-speed to the rescue. However, Ah Sah was not on fire at all! But she was surrounded by a cloud of enraged hornets, and Mat and Sareh were holding smoking coconut husks near her to drive them away. The child was badly stung; I doctored her, and Ah Chi, like a terrified mother hen, shut both her infants in their quarters, while the whole garden was alive with hornets. The cats, I think, were wisely out somewhere. I retreated to the house, but was soon chased out myself and finally took refuge with Mat in the garage, which was dense with the smoke of the burning husks. He too was badly stung, but seemed rather more amused than annoyed by the whole incident and grinned philosophically in his habitually cheerful way.

The cats appeared from their hiding places when the smoke and the shouting died away, and flopped languidly on the tiles to cool their sun-drenched bodies. Caesar was busy washing Cleo's ears while Ptolemy gambolled round them both, cheekily dabbing at their lashing tails. We had been worried about Cleo for some time as her eyes had become half covered by the inner lid; this state was catching and now both Caesar and Ptol were infected also. The remedies having failed, there was nothing more we could do but drive them up to Ipoh to the Vet for an operation. They were put in boxes on the back of the car. Some forty miles from Lumut I began to feel anxious about them and at the Blanja Bridge we got out to see how they were faring. Cleo and Ptol complained softly of their journey; but Caesar's box was empty! He had forced the bars and jumped out. Caesar, the faithful affectionate paragon of a cat! Stuart and I looked at each other in dumb dismay; he might be anywhere along that forty-five miles of jungle and rubber. Coming back that night we strained our eyes to see; every white culvert in the grass took his shape and every shining eye in the trees might be his. The Police Patrols and the Customs men had orders to watch for him. For a long time there was a hope that he might make his way home; but he never did and we missed him sadly. It was miserably depressing to see Stuart doing his garden inspection before breakfast unaccompanied by that prancing familiar figure.

The cat household was much diminished now as Minnie, Ptolemy's mother, had died suddenly one evening, and with the others in hospital, only old Anthony mooched around, tougher and more hard-bitten than ever. We visited Cleo and Ptolemy at the Vet's after the operation, and they welcomed us with cries of joy. When we left Ptolemy's shrieks were piercing; he could not bear to see us go; he stood on his hind-legs and scrabbled at the cage door; his face was puckered as he beseeched us to take him home. They came home soon after, and on arrival systematically searched the entire house and garden, in a way they had never done before, obviously looking for Caesar.

XVII

CHANDU SMOKERS AND A VISIT TO PENANG

THE BRIEF "autumnal" colourings of February, when a few branches of the rubber trees turn russet and there is a brownness about the landscape, passed swiftly to the blossoming of March. The bougainvillaea, purple, red, orange and rose, were in full bloom with the pink oleanders, the white glory of the frangipanni and the creamy froth of the *těmbusu* trees.

There was a great deal of extra work; a rush of food shop registration and prospecting for coast-watching stations. A sense of security now pervaded the country born of the propaganda issued. Every town seemed full of husky looking Australians, the sight of whom was certainly encouraging.

Since the tragedy next door the small local community had changed: a new young Policeman had been appointed and "Banks" had left. The new "Banks," Stephen, was a slight, neat Scot with a deep voice, green eyes and a wide, cheerful smile; he shared the house next door with the young Policeman. Billy seemed young to handle the big uncompleted murder case; but, large, cheerful and burnt pink by the sun, he was a very amiable soul who took it all in his stride. Stephen, unlike his predecessor, who was nearly the undoing of Anthony, loved animals. He had a spaniel named Sally; she had belonged to the former Policeman so, lest she should mope, Stephen would never leave her alone in the house.

One evening during another trial black-out, Stephen was sitting with us in the garden, the best place in a hot-climate black-out. It was past ten o'clock when Stuart decided it would be a good opportunity to see if any lights showed up from the sea, a job which had to be done some time. So the *Rimau* was ordered to come alongside and we set out with Stephen and Sally down the dark river. At first the night was calm. A few fires in far-away *kampongs* shone in the water; but on the whole the people had blacked out well. Then the wind rose and as the *Rimau* reached the wide river mouth she began to roll. Until then I had never fully comprehended the phrase "as sick as a dog." Poor Sally, that trip was hell for her! And trying for us all ultimately, because north of Pangkor a deep swell got up so that the *Rimau* had to anchor in the lee of a small island for the rest of the night. I slept through most of the bucketing until my canvas bed suddenly gave way and unkindly flung me on the deck.

Just before dawn the wind dropped and the rain fell: in despair Stephen and Sally took shelter in the saloon. The *Rimau* crept home up the estuary. The pale light revealed a rather wan Stephen asleep on the seat with his head pillowed uncomfortably on some of our empty beer bottles, while Sally lay limp and exhausted at his feet.

At this time the whole district seemed stricken by illness. Several Europeans were down with obscure fevers and other troubles. Then Roger had to have an operation: exhausted by overwork, he died suddenly in hospital. . . .

This further tragedy so close on the heels of the other again shook everyone deeply. Margaret and the children left the country, and the European population of Lumut, smaller than ever before, was reduced to four.

Life raced on ineluctably. Looking back, it was as if events, both large and small, were piling up for a period of danger: a thin crust of happiness lay over a volcano. The last few months in the country were fuller of new interest to us both than any previously; it was almost as if one felt unconsciously that everything was about to cease and savoured each new event, every happiness to the full. Never had the house seemed more charming, the distant mountains more benignly peaceful and life more vivid. I saw the country and the people again with quickened senses, with a fresh vision. It was the proverbial lull before the storm.

There was more to do than ever. The coast-watching job led to some pleasant expeditions. One Sunday morning in particular stands out. The highest of the three hills of Lumut was just over a thousand feet and seemed a good possible position for a look-out. So, making a picnic of it, with Gerald and Vanessa,

Billy and Stephen and Sally, we started off at seven-thirty in the morning. The jungle, being Forest Reserve, was thin and there were glimpses of Pangkor Island—looking like an elongated Isola Madre in a vast Maggiore—in a sea so flat and blue it might have been a colossal lake. The view from among the giant bracken on the summit was worth the leeches and the sweat. There was Penang faint in the north; the Ipoh mountains inland, clear and sharp across flat miles of mangrove, rubber and jungle; every town and village was veiled in trees, but out to the west the Sembilan Islands lay invitingly in a hot blue calm. We packed ourselves into the tiny patch of shade thrown by the broken trigonometric triangle and ate a picnic breakfast. Stuart, perched on the pole above our heads, took what proved to be a number of excellent photographs, all of which with many others are now lost.

The way down was so steep it was impossible not to run. Back at the house, after showers and a change, we lay about pleasantly exhausted, drinking large quantities of shandy. Poor Billy, pinker than ever, sat down and oozed copiously, groaning that no one would ever induce him to climb a "mountain" again in the tropics.

On another occasion, by ourselves we explored the steep rocks behind the house. They were covered in a black lichen which gave Lumut its name. The sheer surfaces were like twin cascades of jet, where the monkeys played at races. After a scramble we found a ledge from which we could survey the whole village and the magnificent curves of the Dindings River. The beauty of rocks and open places in Malaya was very moving because it was so rare to find. Like toys, hundreds of feet below in the evening sunshine lay the black and white European houses with their red-tiled roofs, the tiny white club, the *padang* where the Malays played soccer with their sarongs tucked up, the leafy charm of Downing Street, the sugar-cake mosque, the modern white Customs. There was a thrill in seeing all these familiar things from a new angle dwarfed by the majestic river set in the green hills.

While we were sitting there Stuart began to talk about his day's work; he startled me by calmly announcing that a leper had come into his office that afternoon to ask for a job. Apparently a cured and discharged leper with a certificate; but it gave me a jolt. Most of the day had been spent in interviewing nine hundred chandu smokers in Sitiawan; an unpleasant job, not only physically so, from having to handle the filthy licence cards, but mentally too: it was depressing to witness the incessant march past of emaciated bodies, prematurely old and wizened and often diseased, craving and sometimes imploring horribly for an increase in their legal supply, which few would be allowed—on medical examination. The next day the process would be repeated on Pangkor and the next in Lumut and so on. This inspection of licensed smokers had to be done once a year in every district. The sale of chandu (prepared opium) from Government retail shops was gradually being reduced, not drastically as I believe was done in some of the French Colonies; but simply by controlling the supply to every smoker and not, if possible, registering any new ones. Would-be smokers had to be examined by a doctor who would state, if they were suffering from some painful and incurable disease, that they might be allowed to become registered smokers in need of a certain amount of the narcotic. Stuart was always extremely anxious not to register new smokers unless absolutely necessary. He formed a scheme with Dr. Menun which worked very well. If a young man applied for a licence and Stuart considered him not suitable, he marked his name on the list with an agreed sign and sent him to Dr. Menun who examined him, and unless he was in the last stages of tuberculosis or something of that sort, returned the list and marked the name with a cross, implying the man did not need the drug. In this way many new would-be smokers were prevented.

One particularly interesting local case was a terrible example of abuse of the drug. A Chinese baby less than a year old was brought to Lumut hospital in a state of coma. The infant was discovered to be suffering from narcosis, and it was over a month before Dr. Menun could say that its system was rid of the poison. Apparently the mother, the busy wife of a fisherman living in one of those crazy bamboo sheds on the quays, had been distracted by the wailing of her offspring. So one day she gave it a little chandu to suck under its finger nail: finding it was soothed, she was delighted and repeated the process *ad lib.* until the child fell into a coma and the mother became frightened. An habitual smoker could always be spotted by his scragginess, the leathery look of his skin and the way his veins stood out across his sunken chest and skinny arms. The life that such men as rickshaw-pullers have to endure makes their craving understandable enough; but what seemed wrong was that the sale of chandu should be a source of revenue, and yet it was difficult to see how else it could have been controlled. In the course of time chandu smoking would have been stamped out, when the older smokers had died and if no new ones were registered. When it had been eliminated the financial gap would have been filled by the income from the fund that was then accruing. In a strict way of thinking the fact that money can be made out of such sales at all is wrong; but the cautious and generally sure way of compromise has always been the British method. Probably it would have worked ultimately. This scheme of gradual elimination gave the people time to get reconciled to the idea, to educate their minds to it and adjust their lives accordingly. Now (since the Japanese surrender) in accordance with the agreement made by the United Nations in 1943, chandu is no longer sold to the public.

A planter's life is often a monotonous one. But for an Acting Estate Manager this is not so, as he gets a move every six months, which means a different estate with all its individual problems of coolies and planting to be studied afresh and dealt with while its own Manager is away on leave.

It was while Niel and Roberta were living on an estate near Ipoh doing this that I went to stay with them to paint Niel's portrait. I gained a new aspect of a planter's life, very different from that of the static Manager who may remain on the same estate for twelve, or fifteen, or more years.

The bungalow was attractive in the old-style rambling way with big verandahs and long flights of wooden steps, all built above the stone-floored garden-room below. The garden was charming, enclosed by a fat hedge of bamboo and full of flowering trees and tall orchids whose blooms showed vivid against a background of limestone hills.

Roberta's ducks and chickens and baby turkeys wandered almost at will into the garden-room, while the ten Siamese cats and one old spaniel lived amicably with them. Roberta's passion for animals also embraced two squirrels from the rubber trees. These lived in her wire-netted bedroom and in the evenings they were allowed in the mosquito-room where they raced madly round the wire and danced over us without a vestige of shyness as we played a not very serious game of mah-jong; they even had sufficient nerve to drink out of our glasses. One afternoon when I was resting peacefully Roberta brought one of the squirrels into my room to amuse me. Hastily I hid everything edible; but while I was bathing before tea he found my travelling clock and when I returned he was busy flinging out the stuffing, with furious little hands and sharp teeth, in tremendous glee.

Roberta was full of apologies. Stroking the small creature's head with long sensitive fingers she said almost sadly: "But you *do* love him, don't you?" There was something squirrel-like about her own little pointed face and huge eyes. Her love of animals was almost fanatic.

In the end Niel, who had the excuse of terracing many acres, backed out of having his portrait painted and induced Roberta to sit for me. Shyly she agreed. The peaceful mornings spent in the garden-room painting her were interspersed with doing the portrait of a child of two-and-a-half years. His mother assumed I could get a good result running about after the boy in his nursery, with a canvas in one hand and a brush in another as she put it. . . . She was difficult to handle and seemed to expect results by miracles. But with Roberta's diplomacy and my pig-headedness we persuaded her to bring the boy for a few brief sittings to the studio in the garden-room.

When both the portraits were completed, Niel brought some Chinese women workers to the house so that I could select a model. I chose a young girl with a simple madonna-like face, a peasant type I had always longed to draw. She wore her red scarf under her great straw hat; such a serious, charming, primitive little face she had. Then two small Telugu boys, children of estate labourers, came to sit; they huddled together, gazing immovably at me with enormous black eyes.

One evening we drove into Ipoh to dine with friends. There was a full moon. The fantastic shapes of the Chinese scaffolding over open-cast tin mines loomed like an enormous film set. Little swamps caught the light, while the rubber trees were black seas of contrast. The limestone hills too repeated the chiaroscuro effect in humps of black and silver, lit here and there from within where lights shone in temples and cave houses. Over everything that night was the heavy scent of tree orchids.

After dinner our hosts took us to a cinema. Transport was being discussed and a fellow guest, a major, offered Niel and me a lift in the Battle Buggy in which he and other officers, including a brigadier, had arrived. Not knowing the regulations, that no woman is supposed to ride in a Battle Buggy, I accepted innocently and climbed into the bouncy vehicle. The brigadier, wonderfully true to type, was heard to murmur: "For God's sake don't let me see!" as he sportingly turned his back.

Soon after this visit I had to go to Penang for a week of treatment. I did not want to go at all especially as Cleo was about to have another family and she liked to have me around at such times. It was hotter in Penang than I ever remembered it: one could do little more than lie under a fan most of the day. The heat was a colourless grey heat so that sky and sea merged softly. There was a sea-hawk lazily fishing; and one pale grey warship in the offing melted into a pale grey sea. Only the red-gold flowers of the tulip tree against the window had any colour.

The town was full of soldiers, mostly Punjabis and the hotel was packed with bored-looking officers. Maybe, had we been able to occupy Thailand then as I believe the Military were itching to do, they would have been less bored. . . .

I spent most of the week trying to get models. In a town packed with types new to me it should have been easy enough. The hotel manager, a Swiss, promised he would find a "really lovely" dancing girl who would sit for me. One evening when I was returning late from dining out he met me in the foyer and suggested going to one of the Chinese dance-halls for me to inspect and approve the selected beauty. It was nearly closing time when we arrived. The young proprietor of the dance-hall appeared; he was rather dreadful, a new-rich, modern Chinese, at that moment very full of brandy. The girl whom the Swiss so much admired was produced. She wore a tight-fitting satin Shanghai dress with flowers in her hair and was passably pretty, but not quite the delicate exotic type one so often sees in the dance-halls and which I wanted. However, it was too late to demur, the band had stopped for the night, and the other girls were all leaving. So the next day this "Taxi girl" duly reported at the hotel accompanied by a giggling friend. Both appeared more or less dumb with shyness. What prettiness the model possessed looked in the light of day a little more adenoidal than I had thought on the previous evening: however I made some sketches of her in the sweltering heat in a lonely corner of the empty ballroom. That was my last day in Penang and then suddenly, with the usual irony of life, models came my way almost unasked.

That afternoon an excellent type of Punjabi Mussulman was brought along by his Captain, but an afternoon in Penang is not the best time in which to do work of any sort, and as I drew the sweat was streaming off me. The Punjabi—arranged by his officer on my balcony—stood to attention all the time, and the sweat dripped off the lobes of his ears. Unable to speak Urdu I couldn't tell him to rest or relax as he would have left, thinking I had finished the drawing. So all I could do was to work like mad, trying not to feel sorry for him; it's a dreadful feeling to become conscious of physical discomfort in one's models, one needs a steely heart. He was a forty-five-year-old veteran, who had retired, but joined up again when the war broke out. A fine specimen of a fighting race.

I had barely finished and was lying exhausted under the fan when Stuart arrived to fetch me home. That was a good week-end to make up for the long, hot week: there was much to talk about and the usually apathetic dance band was on its mettle. First we went out and bought two delightful water-colours by Mun Sen, a Chinese artist who lived and worked in Penang. He was a little, shy man with no idea of the monetary value of his work; his pictures were for sale at a ridiculously low price. He ran a kind of art shop in the Chinese part of the town; but his sketches were put modestly in a back room. Sometimes he himself appeared and seemed overjoyed to receive a little appreciation. He worked in an entirely western style, direct and clear. We chose two, a grey one of a sandy creek and a sunny one of Malays at a food stall under shade-trees.

On the way back to the hotel we met a big Chinese funeral procession. It took nearly half an hour to pass—with its long array of priests and mourners; men in wide flat-brimmed hats and gorgeous robes, musicians, and hired mourners in sackcloth, wailing and throwing out paper strips as they passed to represent money. There were men, women and boys, in every variety of costume of the most vivid colours imaginable, firing now and again an illegal cracker and carrying laudatory banners, white streamers, flags with texts, canopies for the family and a portrait of the deceased, followed by the catafalque and a bevy of rickshaws. The Chinese attach great importance to all matters relating to death and funerals. Their immense unwieldy coffins are a familiar sight all over the country. I remember a coffin-maker's shed on the roadside near Lumut which was stacked with the great wooden boat-shaped things; the man was ceaselessly at work in the yard, hewing and cutting and polishing the wood with a red varnish that preserves the corpse. Chinese burial grounds are always in the most beautiful positions on open hillsides. Some of the graves are elaborate with white stone arms stretching out in a horse-shoe from an ornate slab cut with Confucian sayings. Chinese mourning is a white sleeve-band.

I have a picture in my mind of a village funeral feast at Lumut, a contrast with the great procession in Penang. The house, surrounded with pink oleanders, stood under the old trees by the river side. The family sat at long tables under an *atap* shelter; at the entrance to the house lay the coffin with joss sticks burning beside it. Near it in the place of honour sat an old Buddhist priest—fast asleep.

The corpse always goes to the feast. And at one very rich man's funeral in Ipoh, so the story goes, the family had him preserved in a block of ice. In ice he sat at the head of the table, a grisly paterfamilias; but as the dinner of many courses trailed on, so, horribly in the great heat, the ice began to melt....

Cleo had already had her babies when we returned. And this particular litter of four perfect Siamese was, we agreed, the best she had ever produced. As they grew up they seemed to mill round her with more vigour than any of her previous offspring. She would group them spectacularly in doorways, to show them off to their best advantage like a pride of lions. She adored them, and sat for hours watching them. They had exceptionally chuggy little faces; Lewis and Louisa had square jaws like Anthony, while Brenn and Brenda's faces were more pointed, taking after their mother. We found it impossible to resist keeping Louisa, who had the bluntest, snub-nosed face and was adorable.

By this time Ptol was growing more friendly than ever; he was long in the leg and coltish. Every morning he woke us with a lot of wet kisses on our hands or by calling huskily and imperiously in our ears as he stalked round the pillows waiting for someone to get up and give him milk. His great blue eyes were threaded with exquisite greens and mauves, like the sea in sun and shadow.

Between trial black-outs and coast-watching expeditions, which were sometimes too tough for me to join (when Stuart walked through miles of jungle and ended up by half swimming, half wading in marching boots in the warm sea), we gardened and carried on life much as usual, but all the time with a strange new zest.

Yahya was still the best model. Then one day he had to go to a port where he could study to take his serang's certificate. Regretfully I did my last drawings of him, wondering what sort of a boatman would arrive in his place. Actually Samad, his successor, proved to be quite a useful person—from my point of view as well as the serang's. He was a sturdy Malay who did not pose at all badly; although he had not Yahya's looks, he was well built and quite pleasant to draw.

As I wanted to make some studies of leg muscles I rather tentatively asked him to come in shorts; it was always important to be very careful not to offend the extreme modesty of a Malay. He consented and appeared several times. Then one day I happened to notice him going down the hill after the sitting. At the bend of the road he vanished into the jungle to reappear a second or two later wearing the regulation long khaki ducks. He evidently dared not face the remarks of the crew had he appeared in undignified shorts. The question of obtaining and dealing with models was a difficult one, especially for me—a woman. The old Mohammedan law does not allow the portrayal of living people; but modern Malays seemed to have little objection to it.

Sareh, getting a little matronly now, but still lovely, plump and smooth as a dove, sat for me again frequently. She looked demurely docile and very Malay, posed half-hidden by red and green leaves, fingering a bowl of rice put on a vermilion sarong.

Billy's Malay cook next door had an eleven-year-old daughter who also came to pose. Little almond-eyed Bibi was so painfully shy that it must have cost her a good deal to pluck up sufficient courage even to enter the house. She walked swiftly on bare feet into the studio, with her hands clasped nervously before her and sat down twisted into a posture of static bashfulness. Malay girls grow up quickly and even a few months later she was almost a young woman, flaunting her veil provocatively across her mouth as she sauntered down the hill to school.

XVIII

A MALAY WEDDING.
FROM THE ISLANDS TO SINGAPORE AND CAMERON HIGHLANDS

MA'AROF WAS A NEW Malay magistrate in Sitiawan. Having spent four years in England, he was not so shy of Europeans as are most Malays, and Stuart and I soon became friendly with him. One evening he and his very emancipated, attractive wife were visiting us. They apologized for coming in Malay dress; they need not have, for it was charming; and they explained they were going on to a wedding afterwards. Later they persuaded us to join them, assuring us that the host would be delighted. He certainly did not seem to mind and welcomed us royally. He was *Haji* Din, *Kĕtua* of Kampong Sitiawan, an extremely fat and jovial headman. As a *Haji* he wore a small turban of silk over his *songkok*.

This was his daughter's wedding night! Very excited he rubbed his podgy hands together, bowed and beamed, his shiny black sarong was alarmingly taut across the barrel of his stomach and a huge smile dimpled his moonlike, perspiring face.

The garden of his house was crammed with tables and gaily lit. We were led up the steps of the bungalow where, on the threshold, for politeness' sake, we had to leave our shoes. Here I parted with Stuart, as the men sat in the outer room and the women in the inner one. Mrs. Ma'arof and I were led there and seated on cushions close to the walls. It was very hot and stuffy.

Not knowing how to dispose of my legs, which seemed very much in the way, I sat cross-legged on my cushion. Through the doorway I could just see Stuart grinning at me, as he too sat cross-legged between the D.O.—resplendent in black and silver—and Ma'arof.

After a while, Mrs. Ma'arof informed me gently that only men are supposed to sit cross-legged, while women should curl their legs up under them. The sarongs made it difficult to see exactly how they did this. I tried to imitate the uncomfortable position and soon became terribly cramped. My hostess took pity on me and gave me permission to sit as I wished. Never have I been so conscious of my legs; fortunately I was wearing a long and very full skirt; but I felt extremely large beside all the little Malay women, who giggled gently at my awkwardness.

The room was decorated with pink streamers, stars on strings and numerous crescent moons. A pink curtain of Islamic crescents hung in front of the bridal throne.

Presently I saw the men were being served with curry. When they had eaten, it was our turn. Soup plates full of rice were placed before each of us on a cloth. Bowls of rose-water were passed round for us to wash our hands and mouths. Then the curry. I was not allowed to help myself, but willing hands piled meat and vegetables on my heap of rice. It was a very hot curry. They showed me how to eat it with my fingers, definitely an art; the food is scooped into a ball and shot neatly into the mouth, using the thumb as a lever. The gobbets of chillie and the other ultra-hot bits I was hiding hopefully under the mass of rice, when suddenly a scrawny, greasy brown hand shot out and delved in my plate to find the best tit-bits for me and break them with deft movements of the fingers. What could I do but eat them after so much overwhelming hospitality! After the curry, sweet cakes and luscious pink drinks were handed round. Again I fear I disgraced myself by taking a whole slice of cake, feeling here was something clean and easy to eat at last. What I should have done was to crumble off small portions with my fingers and nibble in a more communal fashion. However, the women were all very kind to me and long-suffering and amused at my gaucheries. After the sweets, betel-nut in little boxes came round and then we all settled down to wait for the bride to appear.

The room became packed with people and suffocatingly hot as all the children and poor relations crowded in. Every few minutes the old grandmother of the bride poked her head into the bride's bedroom and shouted ribald remarks, while the women shrieked with laughter.

In the cooler air of the outer room the men seemed to be getting quite gay on the strictly non-alcoholic pink drinks. I envied them the air as Stuart waved to me encouragingly.

At last, after what seemed hours, the bride appeared. She was a disappointment, as she was not wearing correct Malay dress, but a half-Europeanized garment of a lurid peppermint pink, with a heavy pink veil bound to her head, white stockings and hideous strap shoes. She was led behind the curtain and seated on the throne. A long strip of pink carpet was then laid down and the groom was led in with bent head and downcast eyes to join his bride. The crescent moons then parted to reveal them both sitting there looking painfully nervous. The groom in orange wore the smoked glasses of the Malay dandy and kept his head bowed, precautions against the Evil Eye.

The old man knelt before them and prayed. No one took the least notice of him as everybody was talking and laughing at once. The old grandmother and the bride's mother fanned the bridal pair ceaselessly, and throughout the prayers, quite regardless, the beldam carried on her flow of ribaldries much to the hilarious delight of the assembly.

Then the men came in and were permitted to walk up the strip of carpet to lay their gifts before the couple. The *Bunga Telor* was brought in. This was a really marvellous object, a collection of hard-boiled eggs painted all colours, impaled on long sticks and made to resemble a flowering bush growing in green paper leaves. After this we were each presented with an egg wrapped in coloured paper attached to a little cachet, redolent of that peculiar mousy smell I had noticed before among the Malays.

By this time Stuart was able to rejoin me and we retrieved our shoes and breathed the comparatively fresh air of the night again. But I would not have missed that wedding for anything and I regret losing the drawings I made of it.

Six months had passed since the last sea patrol—the one at Chinese New Year—and the time had come to do another.

As it happened the Straits boat was at the jetty with a cluster of sampans loading rubber into her, so the *Rimau* could not get alongside and had to tie up to the furthest sampans. This often occurred and presented little difficulty when there was no food and gear to take on board. But two days at sea meant food and drink, books, paints and bathing things and often the typewriter as well.

This time, as it was my birthday, there was besides this, the famous cuspidor full of red roses. Stuart had had them sent from the Hill that morning and I could not possibly leave them to wilt in the house.

It was all I could do to get myself on board, climbing in and out of the grubby Straits steamship, jumping down from her deck on to the bales of rubber, which acted like springboards and sent me bouncing at every hop, and finally shinning up the anchor and over the bows of the *Rimau*. Having achieved what I considered no mean feat I sat back to watch the gear coming on board. First I saw Stuart bouncing from one springy pile of rubber to another in the now swinging sampans: he was holding a dish full of butter in one hand and a cold pheasant in the other. He had not risked giving the pheasant to the boatman as—in 1941—it was too exotic a luxury. Then came the *Rimau's* crew, by devious ways, each laden, and last of all the dogsbody who, of course, got left with the roses. Heaven only knows how he negotiated those pneumatic bales, holding that enormous cuspidor.

The last junk was inspected before we reached Pulau Nipis, "thin island," with its narrow spine and fringe of palms like emaciated vertebrae along the very top. The soft curves of Pulau Rumbia lay right ahead and soon the *Rimau* was within the island's arms once more.

As we entered the bay a pair of turtles were mating in the surf off the headland, great primeval-looking creatures. And a devil-fish leapt clear of the water lashing a whiplike tail. Then the martins flew out to greet us again, circling round the boat.

There was a good sunset that evening. Numerous white terns were playing over the jungle, sailing down with pointed wing-tips upturned, and two great sea-hawks swooped restlessly before settling on a tree-top for the night. Then when it was dark the sea suddenly became full of brilliant snakes of fire. We thought they must be water-snakes like those in the *Ancient Mariner*, but the serang said the effect was caused by a tiny beetle practically invisible which leaves a track of phosphorescence in the water; Rumbia seemed to have something fresh to reveal each time one went there; "They coiled and swam; and every track was a flash of golden fire."

It was a cold night and the stars were wonderful, Orion and dazzling white Venus, and when the boat swung, the lovely Southern Cross floated into view. We had twenty fathoms of chain out that night and swung more than usual with the tide, as it was choppy in the anchorage. Once we woke as the *Rimau* began bumping on the coral ledge; she had dragged her anchor, and the Twins and Samad came stumbling sleepily past our camp-beds to deal with the chain.

It was very cold before dawn and several *koleks* were inshore, while the fishermen filled up their water casks at the spring. We pulled our blankets closer and watched the sun come up out of the mountains and the *koleks* leave the island. Then when we felt a little warmth we went ashore and bathed for the last time in that clear, green water.

It is good to know places like those, and when you are in towns and crowded cities to think of them—out of Time, so defeating Time with intangible possessions of shining peace. While among the islands Time, although it hardly existed there except as belonging to the civilization to which we must return, was the constant, shadowy enemy; Time and the unspoken fear that we might never see the islands again. And indeed, although, of course, we did not know it then, that visit was our last.

But now, free of Time, they remain rich and indissoluble in memory. And it is reassuring in years of war and of unrest to think that they do also most certainly exist, not only in a fourth-dimensional world, but at this very moment still untouched in their dateless beauty.

Malaya was always to me a land of sharp light and shade, metaphysically as well as physically. This sense of contrast coloured every event in ordinary life from trivial moods to changes of locality.

It was a far cry from the Sembilan Islands to Singapore, where I had to go twice more for medical treatment. Each time I stayed with the Hiltons. The first time they had a charming house in Johore Bahru, to the west of which is the elaborately castellated stucco palace of the Sultan of Johore. The house, looking across the narrow Straits to Singapore Island, was built in cool Spanish Moroccan style high up on a terrace above the sea. It had quaint wrought-iron balconies, a long arched verandah and a little tower from which in the evenings one could see the dark causeway and the searchlights of the Naval Base reflected in the water. They gave sudden height and depth to the night, their moving white pencils of brilliance probing the sky and patterning the sea.

Bung and Marjorie, with their marvellous hospitality, took me round a great deal. Singapore seemed civilized and conventional to me after so long up-country. I met a lot of people; few appeared to know anything about the Malays and Malaya itself. Except for a month or two at Fraser's Hill or Cameron's many had never left Singapore. I was amused at the questions I was asked about "up-country." Was life very deadly? Did I see many tigers? And so on. It was rather fun to play up to it with stories of crocodiles, murders, mosquitoes and the gloomy jungle.

Unashamedly I enjoyed the rôle of an up-country visitor to the metropolis. We danced at the Tanglin and the Coconut Grove. We swam in the great sea-pool near the Airport, relaxing on the buoyant water for hours gazing at the blue sky and the trees and the 'planes, those already obsolete Brewster Buffaloes we came to know only too well later. We went to the Sultan's Zoo in Johore and saw the *orang-utan*, the jungle man, with his flaming red hair and blue-black face, a fascinating nightmare. We danced at the Raffles and dined in the garden there under the stars. Suddenly I saw it from the tourist's point of view—one of the most famous hotels in the Far East; the little tables under the dome of the night, the soft lamps, the tall palm-trees waving gently against the velvet blue sky, a perfectly correct tropic night. I saw that garden a few months later during an air-raid; it was a well of blackness then; the palms were silver-tipped in the light of the full moon, the bomber's moon.

Two of the little things I childishly liked about Singapore were the red pillar boxes, so easy to find—they were silver in the Malay States and had a way of eluding one—and "God Save the King" played after shows. Two familiar touches that made one aware of the homely solidarity of the British—an attribute not always appreciated.

Later the Hiltons had a tiny bungalow at the Naval Base. Here I painted several portraits including their own little dark-eyed chestnut-haired Penny, and a little Swiss-American girl with a passion for ice-cream.

The Base, with its mushroom growth of bungalows and barracks, was very different from the graceful Spanish house above the water. Some houses live in the memory; all have an atmosphere of their own, I know the Hiltons must often think of the charm of that red-tiled house across the Straits.

To an outsider there appeared to be little secrecy and no great activity, about the Base, and it seemed only too easy for taxi drivers to pass its gates. How different from the Japanese, who did not allow anyone within miles of their great island bases in the Carolines and Marianas. Sometimes at the gates I saw Brooke-Popham passing by, big nose, big topi, big moustache, in a big car. . . .

There did not seem much change in the Singapore life from one visit to the next. A few strands of barbed wire perhaps on the Pasir Panjang (Long Sands) Road and a few more Indian troops at the Base. And people were doing First Aid and busy making artificial but very realistic wounds to strap on "casualties" in air-raid practice. . . .

From Singapore with its shoppings, parties and portraits, I went straight to an estate in the heart of the country where Niel and Roberta were now living.

This house at Sungkai in Perak was different from their bungalow at Gopeng. It was older and, but for one vista cutting through the trees, was completely surrounded with rubber. By then Roberta had induced Niel to have his portrait painted; hence my visit.

It was the same amusing household, dominated by cats, dogs, baby turkeys and squirrels. This time Roberta was rearing chicks and turkeys in an incubator and every night she took one or two of the newly-hatched ones up to her bedroom in a box full of cotton wool. I have a mental picture of her in a blue housecoat of stiff brocade going up the open stairs to bed, carrying her squirrels and her shoe-box full of chicks. We retired to bed early there, for a planter's day begins before dawn. I had a room which, after the smaller more modern houses of Singapore, seemed very spacious, with dressing-room, bathroom and verandah attached, in the good old up-country style. Space is cooling in great heat and the old planters who built these houses knew that.

When Niel had been round the Estate we breakfasted about nine before he sat for his portrait. They had Indian servants; and the ayah, a pleasant, very willing old soul, and a lively young boy whom Roberta was training, took a great interest in the daily progress of their master's picture. So also did Mr. "Pop," a middle-aged planter friend of Niel who was staying in the house. Once or twice when I came to lay out my paints Mr. Pop would be found posing hopefully in Niel's chair and had to be restrained forcefully. He was an amusing person.

He became very plaintive about a nest of hornets just outside his bedroom window; he had already been stung once or twice, but Niel made only a rather feeble attempt to smoke it out.

Then one day at lunch Mr. Pop began making pointed sallies about toe-nails and coloured varnishes. As he was wearing very open sandals himself through which large and horny toes protruded unadorned, I suggested it might be an improvement if he varnished his own toe-nails and stopped being rude about Roberta's and mine. That afternoon, when we had retired to our rooms to rest, Niel crept into Mr. Pop's room and varnished all his toe-nails a lurid red as he slept, but while Niel was finishing up with a vivid "V" for victory on each big toe events turned ironically against him. A large hornet flew in from the nest about which Mr. Pop had complained so fruitlessly. It attacked Niel. Niel defended himself with a fly swatter which broke at the crucial moment. The noise woke Mr. Pop. He sat up in time to see Niel being dive-bombed by the furious hornet which got him on the top of the head. Mr. Pop was righteously but repressedly gleeful; although at tea-time he wore a chastened air and his toe-nails were covered with sticking-plaster. By the evening Niel had a lump as big as an egg on his head and the next day that nest was smoked out thoroughly.

Stuart drove the hundred miles from Lumut to spend the last week-end at Sungkai. There was still enough petrol for that, although it was rationed by then.

A neighbouring planter had promised to try and persuade some Sakai people to sit for me. The Sakais are the aboriginal hill-tribes of Malaya. Some of them used to come down a track from the jungle past the planter's garden and he was friendly with one or two. They brought him gifts of monkeys, baby civet-cats and Malacca canes and were delighted with a present of tobacco in exchange. So on the Sunday he took us five miles or so through secondary jungle to their encampments.

It was very light jungle; in places little more than scrub, with groves of entangled plantains, thorny palms and bamboos, tall black orchids and wild ginger. The wild ginger blossom was like a giant scarlet spider crouching flat on the mud, a formidable fleshy flower naked of foliage.

The two encampments we visited were in clearings in the jungle, only two or three rough *atap* huts in each, raised well above the ground on tall stilts. Numerous dogs and chickens ran up and down the rough ladders. The Sakais crouched on their platform dwellings and looked down shyly at us. They are smaller than the Malays with more heart-shaped faces. They originally preferred the hills, but were beginning to live on the lower slopes. There appeared to be sixteen or so to each hut, and most of them were very ugly, but we met one quite fine pair in the smaller settlement, a pathetic, barren place. The woman was young with taut, pointed breasts. Her hair was piled up in a fuzz of curls, but the front part was shaved into a very neat "widow's peak" which stressed the smoothness of her small, blunt face. But none would let me sketch them. They explained it was unlucky. If I did, some of them would die, as sure as fate: it always happened. Why only a year before someone had made pictures and since then six of their company had died. They shook their heads regretfully. It was a further example of the Evil Eye superstition. These people were, I believe, Senoi Semai.

Two of the hill tribes which inhabit the main range of the Peninsula are the Senoi[1] Semai and the Senoi Temiar, roughly classed by the layman as Sakai, *orang bukit*, or hill people, as the Malays call them. At Cameron Highlands, the biggest hill station of Malaya, Semai were often to be seen filing along the roads in the development area, pathetic scarecrows in the cast-off, antiquated clothing of several different nationalities. The

[1] "Senoi in both Temiar and Semai languages means 'fellow' in the sense of Conrad's 'one of us.'" H. D. Noone, M.A., Protector of Aborigines, Perak.

penalty of living on the edge of civilization was that they had become caricatures of their real selves. But the Temiar people, who kept away more to the north, are a better developed and more virile race. We saw a number of these Semai at Cameron's, on the roads with their long blowpipes, looking strangely out of place, and beside the river in small encampments.

Cameron Highlands was the most popular place for local leave in the country. Still only half-developed and much bigger than Fraser's Hill, it lay about four thousand feet above sea level some twenty miles south-east of Ipoh as the crow flies, but a great many more by the twisting road.

We spent a week's local leave up there, driving from Sungkai. The Highlands sprawled over two small plateaux; on the lower was Tanah Rata with the Convent school, an attractive building in Flemish style, the pretty Rest House, some bungalows with tall chimneys and a row of hybrid shops, Chinese and Japanese photographers, strange neighbours, and the usual polyglot collection of peoples. It was all rather unreal and vaguely artificial: the houses and hotels had sprung up on land so recently carved out of the jungle. If deserted they would soon be but turgid shapes beneath vines and creepers. On this newly-won earth one was more conscious than ever of the struggle between man and the jungle, that rapacious, many-fingered beast. . . . There is something orgiastic and even terrible in the pullulating mass of vegetation, every yard of which must be hacked and sawn and burnt away before even the smallest dwelling can be built. And after that the beast must be ceaselessly kept at bay; it can never be destroyed, but will keep on returning and returning relentlessly. Cease labouring and in a year or two all the man-made clearings would be submerged under that green fecundity.

The second small plateau, Cameron's, was more spacious with two flower-bedecked hotels, the school, a golf course and delightful modern houses whose gay gardens and borders formed bright chequer-boards of colour; all this pretty provincialism surrounded incongruously by forest peaks on every side. Above, still higher, the roughening road led up the Blue Valley, where "real English" cows grazed peacefully; and yet further to tea plantations and raw new houses high up in swirling mists on half-cleared slopes. Beyond, over a range, the track headed east to outlying tea-planters' bungalows, along the river and into the dense heart of the *ulu*.

We spent a lazy week, dancing a little, walking a little, watching fat trout bask in sunny tanks at the Hatcheries, admiring beautiful begonias in the potting sheds at the Agricultural Gardens, drinking hot rum at the Smoke House Inn and gazing with envy at the flowers there; roses and dahlias, stocks and pansies, forget-me-nots and poppies, an English summer, spring and autumn rolled into one. To eat, there were strawberries and real cream and fresh vegetables, all delicious after so many tinned foods.

Mostly we prospected lazily and planned for the three weeks' local leave due to us early in the New Year, but we took one energetic walk up Gunong Berembun, a six-thousand foot hill opposite the Rest House. It reminded us of Brastagi: the track was steep through twisted trees crumbling with moss, and festooned with orchids and swaying lianas; then from a tunnel of stunted bamboos the track emerged suddenly on to the cleared summit. The blue plain lay below, and beyond it our own Lumut hills and the river winding through them to the sea; the Sembilan Islands, enticing even at that distance; and far out on the horizon Pulau Jarak, half way to Sumatra; to the north-west all the limestone hills of Ipoh, and behind us the vast green recessive ranges of Pahang, unknown except to a few surveyors.

It was the last day of that short leave, and we sat there for a long time making plans for the real holiday to come—in January, or so we hoped.

XIX

GARDENS AND CAVES AND JAP SCARES

IT WAS in Ipoh that we saw a walled garden of a kind most unusual in Malaya and in which its middle-aged bachelor owner, Mr. E—— took a justifiable pride. He loved it; he was content to stand and look at it for hours and was delighted when people enjoyed it too. He asked me to come and see it, as he wanted it painted.

When we first visited the place we were struck by its extraordinary, almost nostalgic quality; it was so like an English garden. But Mr. E—— cherished no illusions or homesickness for England: he had planned to live on the east coast of Malaya when he retired and he was building an elaborate scale model of the ideal bungalow he would have there. He was madly keen on his present garden and it was good to see such enthusiasm in a land where interests are often dulled.

In the heart of his neat, well-kept acres lay this small holy of holies, this little enclosed garden close to the house. From the verandah one stepped into a walled space of bright green grass, paved paths, a herbaceous border gay with hollyhocks and sunflowers. It was compact and lovely and very homely; a place to return to again and again, a place rare in Malaya where beauty was big and wild rather than homely.

I sketched until dusk; then when darkness fell we sat in the walled garden and Mr. E—— flood-lit it from the house. The chiaroscuro effect was extraordinarily pleasing. It had been raining and the leaves were wet and shining; under the trees the shadows were densely black with here and there a clear-cut leaf and dramatically lit trunks standing out, and sprays of red flowers falling across the velvet darkness.

Mr. E—— lent us the bungalow later for a long week-end so that I could make further studies of the garden. He went away himself and so we could imagine that charming spot was ours for the time. In our host's absence his Chinese boys waited on our needs with smiling excellence and served delicious meals and cool drinks with admirable speed and timing. There was such an atmosphere of peaceful content about the bungalow and the walled garden that one almost forgot the growing Japanese menace and the war anxiety. It was quiet, well cared for and much loved. Rows of enormous blue hydrangeas peered over the verandah balustrade, and against the dark trees of the neighbouring estate a white pigeon-cote stood out bright in the sunlight.

When, towards midday, the sun flooded into the garden and began to drain the colour from the flowers I stopped work, and we went to explore some Chinese temples in the limestone cliffs, an expedition we had meant to do for many months, but which had somehow always been delayed.

Beyond the town, past the open-cast mines, white cliffs rose abruptly in many crumbling pinnacles and creeper-covered turrets. From among dank beds of lotus lilies steps led up to the caves in the cliff face. At the entrance to the biggest temple were rough basins hewn in the rock, reminiscent of holy water stoops in the porch of a church. I wondered what they were used for and later I saw a priest washing his clothes in one, eminently practical. This temple cave was lofty, but not wide, very much like a cathedral. A delicious waft of incense greeted us. There were altars with bronze gods and goddesses upon them and the usual great red banners hung from the high ceiling. Daylight, cold and white, filtered in from a dream-hole in a gallery placed like a west window; the only other lighting came from wicks floating in dishes of oil and from a few dim lamps. In a kind of side chapel a gold face gleamed mysteriously from behind murky glass in the dusky shadows. At the back of the main shrine the darkness was intense. Blindly we groped our way through a black tunnel to emerge into the candescent sunlight of a completely enclosed grassy plot. Overhanging cliffs towered up to a blue sky on every side, unscaleable except by an expert mountaineer (though roots and an occasional palm and long creepers found a hold here and there miraculously). What a hide-out it must have been at one time. The strange garden, still and quiet and lost to the world, was roughly terraced into three tiers; on the lowest was a crescent-shaped lotus lily pond. One old priestess ambled round telling her beads;

a few Chinese boys wandered about quietly. Close to the cliff facing the pond was a pantiled house: as far as we could make out from the cheerful priest we encountered later in the temple, this was where the priests themselves lived, but it was also used as a club.

This same priest, when we returned to the big cave, took us up a steep, rock staircase to a gallery where we could look down from the dream-hole into the dim temple, grey stone, cinnabar red cloth and gleams of gold. The gallery led out to the cliff face, cut with narrow paths and small crumbling terraces. A snake basked on the hot white rocks, its vivid blue tongue darting wickedly like an electric flame. The old man showed us new temples full of gargantuan figures, crudely painted, unfinished and over-poweringly big for their caves. Several had a black swastika painted on their clothes or chests, but the old priest assured us these were only religious symbols of good omen and that all the temple people wore them; he himself had one tattooed on his forearm. The crooked cross is after all thousands of years older than the Nazi régime.

Before we returned to Mr. E——'s bungalow, we explored one more temple, a smaller, humbler place. The approach was picturesque in the extreme. A white bridge led over a pool of pink lilies to a courtyard. In this courtyard a weird young man with long wild hair under a tall Tibetan-looking hat was bargaining with a Chinese vendor. The vendor was selling tiny birds and chicks, while a baby civet-cat climbed about his shoulders. Just inside the temple door at a small stone altar stood an old priest clothed in sombre grey-green, two pig-tails projected from beneath his round hat. His prayers were wafted up in the blue smoke of the joss sticks as he laid gifts on the altar; dishes and trays of food, pink and white sugary stuff, noodles, fried fish and vegetables, and two gay paper jackets, one of emerald and the other of scarlet. The slanting light from a doorway suffused the scene; the whole was a symphony in greyish white with deep shadows relieved by vivid colour.

On one side of the altar was an ancient bronze pot for burning incense, and the paper clothes for the dead, and on the other, in typical Chinese manner, were a couple of bicycles. . . .

The main body of the cave was a nightmare; like one of those heterogeneous, confused scenes that are so impossible to describe on waking. There was a rotting wooden gallery crammed with altars, and below was a muddle of pictures and tables, torn banners and even bottles of fizzy orangeade which the Chinese love. We skirted the gallery and followed along a dark platform above a malodorous pit full of water with a horrid suggestion of dubiously torpid shapes. With heads averted we passed hurriedly by and came to another large cave. Unexpectedly this opened on to sunny undergrowth on the opposite side of the hill, so thin was the wedge of cliff at that point. Hundreds upon hundreds of steps led up to tier after tier of wooden floored landings, all with that nightmare essence. Chill, barren places, dim and unpleasant with the lost, half-memories of centuries. Although most caves had wide views across the sun-filled valley, or peepholes in the inner wall overlooking the road, a thousand years seemed to separate them from the world outside. It was good at last to shake off this atavistic feeling and return to the present, as we emerged the heat of the sun struck burningly, the steps were dazzling white, and the hot road stretched like a dry bone to Ipoh. We thought gratefully of the civilized charms of Mr. E——'s bungalow.

When we eventually went back to Lumut, Louisa came dashing out to meet us with her face bound up in bandages. As usual with the cats, she had become ill in our absence, and, like Caesar, she had developed a boil which had burst. Faithful Kuki had taken her to hospital, had had the wound lanced and cleaned, and what is more, had waited patiently for four hours to get it done while Louisa fretted in her basket. She was sweeter than ever, extremely friendly and good-natured. The next day I took her along to the hospital again to have the wound dressed according to Dr. Menun's orders. The whole hospital compound was in a hubbub with several Malay policemen and a very excited murderer careering about; he was suspected to be insane, and as we got out of the car, Louisa and I narrowly missed running into him.

Louisa was the only one of Cleo's last litter now left, as Brenn and Brenda had gone to the Russian girl, who had built them a special mosquito-proof "house"; and Lewis had sailed on the Straits steamship to Customs friends in Penang. There was some little trouble about his landing there as he should have

Noon—Pulau Lalang

From a charcoal drawing by the author

Gurkha soldier

had a Vet's certificate, but the Vet being so far away Dr. Menun had written him out a permit instead. We received a card from our friend in Penang saying: "Customs Officer Lewis arrived safely and I greatly approved of his cabin trunk." (It had a built-in scratch-pan.) "Had a spot of difficulty getting him ashore as his Lumut certificate was admired but not accepted . . . however everything ended well!"

Louisa and Ptolemy were excellent friends. We attempted to induce them to pose with bribes of liver; Ptolemy, however, walked off after he had eaten his share, but Louisa was more obliging. With her soft fragrant fur and supple attitudes she was a delight to draw; she had beautifully marked seal-dark stockings, tail and ears. Her small face was so blunt-nosed that, unlike all the other cats, she could not learn to shovel her way under the mosquito net in the mornings. She was always trying to do so; but she never could acquire the knack and shrieked imperiously to be let in and out.

It was September, 1941, and the Japanese menace was increasing. Mr. Duff Cooper arrived then in Singapore and made a smooth speech on the radio, picturing Japan mainly as a blot on the Far Eastern scene, but so surrounded by mighty powers that she was unlikely to bother anyone very much. . . .

Petrol rationing tightened a little. Food rationing, besides rice, which was already controlled, was under consideration. At Lumut Stuart formed a local committee of women from the European, Malay, Chinese and Indian communities to give him an idea of the various food needs of his district.

There was a great deal of talk in the papers about the wonderful jungle aerodromes and the impossibility of over-running Malaya. . . .

We could see less of our friends now that petrol rationing was more strict. The Steeles lived seven miles away and Vanessa and the others fourteen or fifteen. It was the wet season, and tennis was hopeless, so we played billiards at the tiny club, though sometimes old Apu, the Boy, smelt so abominably rank, we were forced outside. Occasionally Ptolemy followed us down there, explored the building and waited a trifle impatiently while we played: he was almost full-grown then, a fine young cat with all the lovable characteristics of a good Siamese.

At times the force of the Sumatras off the sea blew the billiard balls across the baize, and on one stifling evening, Apu had a brazier beneath the table to air it; the fumes and the blazing heat once more drove us out to walk restlessly up and down by the sea.

One night a young captain of the Gurkha Rifles arrived at the Club. He had come down with a handful of men on some mysterious military errand. The next day large white marks, evidently their handiwork, appeared on the rocks in the jungle above the house. The officer lent me one of his men for a short sitting.

The soldier arrived, shepherded by his captain, at eight o'clock punctually, both had the Frontier medal ribbon. I was delighted at the way the young officer like a proud mother fussed about his square, sturdy corporal—the man must have five-minute rests, and cigarettes, and he would be called for at ten-thirty. . . . So I had not long and I worked feverishly. The Gurkha was a tough little fellow, grand to draw with his stubborn face, tremendous cheek-bones, Mongol eyes and shaven head.

About this time I managed to persuade Bob to pose for me in L.D.C. uniform; he was reluctant when I said I wanted to draw him.

"Must I be hanged and quartered too?" he asked.

Among a row of last-war medal ribbons on his khaki shirt was the D.F.C. won in the Royal Flying Corps days, but he would not speak about it.

Those restless months raced by. I drew Samad and Sareh; I drew the cats, the house, the garden and the village. One evening I was nearly suffocated with the smells while sketching a Chinese back-yard full of wood piles and pink and mauve washing under stunted palms. To get the view I wanted I had to stand on the grass verge beside the open drain. When the odours became suddenly more potent than ever, I turned round to get a breath of fresher air and was amazed to see the whole road packed with humanity, quite a traffic block: most of the people had come up on silent bare feet and now hemmed me in. . . .

The explorations for coast-watching sites were still under way: out on the north headland, to Bukit Hantu (haunted hill) with its long wild grass—wind-swept like Van Gogh's—its tide-race, jagged rocks and ruined huts backed by dense jungle; down south, to an island covered in leggy, brown orchids; along the coast, near the Chinese temple and out on the farthest seaward points of Pangkor Island.

One of the best of these expeditions was to the northern tip of Pangkor where a former Sultan of Perak had built a house on an islet. Sheltering behind this islet was a lagoon where we landed and Stuart went off along the rough coast to explore.

Out on the rocks there was a strong refreshing wind blowing and the waves were wild. Across the wide estuary was Bukit Hantu with its lighthouse white and small on the green headland. There were slimy black beche-de-mer in the rock pools, and even a little seaweed which was not often to be seen.

When Stuart returned, soaked through with sweat and sea water, we lay on the sand at the edge of the lagoon and as we were having tea, fifteen long slim Malay boats appeared rapidly one after the other; there were three men in each boat standing up to row. They anchored directly opposite, a few yards from the shore and, as if at a signal, every man sat down and proceeded to change from sarong into old trousers, much to our amusement. Then they waited, presumably plucking up courage or more likely timing the exact running of the tide, before leaving the calm lagoon and passing out between the rocks into the broken sea beyond. Those boats looked too delicate to breast the waves of the open sea, but they rode them safely. When they had gone and were only dark cockle-shells tossing beyond the point, we took the dinghy and went over to the Sultan's island. We were greeted there by a rabble of friendly black and white cats and a smiling Malay couple, the caretakers in that lonely place. It was a curious little house, built on a perfect site, which looked north over the open sea to Penang with the blue hills rolling away to Taiping, and the wide mouth of the estuary unfolding. There was a tiny beach of sand below the terrace with tree-crowned rocks on either side. A pleasant, peaceful place, but the new Sultan never used it; he complained that it was too lonely: it was there that the former Sultan had been taken fatally ill and no Malay cares to live where a relative has died.

When we left, all the cats came scampering down the beach

with us. They had no fear of the water; they danced into the shallows, and as we rowed away, cavorted on the sand, capering about, jumping and chasing each other up the trees.

The north end had that day proved useless for coast-watching and finally a spot was chosen on the hill above Pangkor House which commanded a wide view of the Malacca Straits, north and south. It was a superb sunny day when that place was finally explored and selected. The sea was clear and glassy. I remember mangoes were in season and formed a large and succulent part of the supplies. One of Stuart's men, a young Indian, climbed a tall tree on which the look-out was to be built. He went up it with as much ease as a monkey; a strip of rope tied between his ankles giving him a grip. The forest was full of leeches and it was good to climb down from the headland and wade back through the warm sea to the Rest House.

That was a happy evening of perfect calm; a big planet was already bright in the still sky, although the sun had not yet set, so quickly did the night creep out of the east as the sun sank rapidly towards the glowing west.

When the coast-watching sites were prepared, a military gentleman from Singapore arranged to inspect them. The launch went down south to the mouth of the Perak River to meet him. It was eight hours at sea and for nothing, because he failed to appear, having gone up Cameron Highlands, it was said, for the week-end instead. . . .

In November the Japanese Diet was sitting and we waited. On the edge of the abyss there were moments of outstanding peace. I remember particularly waking one morning; it was cool and the sun was shining on the dark green leaves of a fruit tree above the kitchen roof, and the gibbons were singing in the forest. As I lay in bed, it was good to see the lambent freshness of the Malay morning through the softly swaying fine white mesh of the mosquito net. Smoke from the wood fire was pouring out of the kitchen chimney, very blue smoke against the shining leaves, and the more distant dark jungle trees, and here and there a cobalt-enamelled sky showed through. When I got up, the sun was slanting into the bathroom; the "shower" was cool, every drop golden with sunlight, sparkling with miniature rainbows. . . .

I happened to be in Singapore once again on November 29th when the Army was mobilized. Messages were flashed on the cinema screens. A week later in the Naval Base I stood on a hill with Bung and Marjorie and looked down at the ships which represented Malaya's security—the *Prince of Wales* and the *Repulse*. That was on Saturday, December the 6th, and the same night all Naval leave was cancelled. I was due to go home to Lumut the following day and was afraid I would be prevented, but Bung got me out of the Base and put me on the night-mail for the north. The train was full after Kuala Lumpur. People seemed quite confident; opposite me was a cheerful United States' newspaper-man going up to the frontier. Stuart met the train as usual at Ipoh and we drove back to Lumut to spend the last evening of bright lights and peace quietly in our own house. As usual Ah Chi had the sweet-scented flowers for me and the cats gave us a loud and cheerful welcome.

That night Pearl Harbour was shattered, Singapore bombed, and the Japs landed at Kota Bharu. On the Wednesday we heard a rumour that the *Prince of Wales* and the *Repulse* were sunk; this blow was confirmed the next day. News from Kota Bharu was extremely vague: no one really knew what was happening. In Sitiawan there was a local paratroop scare.

I worked on the brown-out arrangements: black-out was only ordered when the siren (a gong) sounded. The gloomy brown-out was stifling enough. Mat joined up as an Army lorry driver in Penang and Sareh went away to live with friends.

Kuki asked: "How can the British hold the Japs in Malaya with so few men, if the Chinese with their hundreds and thousands of men cannot beat them in China?"

On Friday the 12th, we heard unofficially, but from an "unimpeachable source" that we had lost Kelantan aerodrome and also about thirty 'planes on the ground at Kuantan. There seems to have been some mystery about Kuantan.

The next day the depression and sickening foreboding grew worse. Stuart executed a successful Food Control raid in Sitiawan and arrested a Chinese profiteer making 200 per cent profit on rice. After this long raid we both went to Vanessa's house. She had already packed and gone to Taiping to be near her husband when the Volunteers had been called up. She wanted us to look after her three cats and small kitten and some of her pictures and china; laden with these and sick at heart we returned drearily to Lumut.

Gangs of coolies were at work at Sitiawan to dig defences and erect barbed wire entanglements round the aerodrome: two days later they were told to destroy it. Chaos reigned, with orders and counter-orders following one after the other as the Japs rapidly advanced from the north. Rumours said that from the air they could be seen coming from Siam like ants, in a never-ending stream.

At the Bank, Stephen was working at top speed to duplicate all papers; and all the men were so busy that fortunately there was not much time to contemplate what was happening.

On Monday, December 15th, the weather was hotter than usual and the sky grey with oppressive clouds. Thinking we might have to billet refugees from the north, I started to pack a little of the silver to get it out of the way and to make less work for the servants. By sheer luck this one packing case was eventually sent down to Singapore. I packed this and cut out bandages all the morning during which we had our first alert as Ipoh was raided. In the evening an order came through to call the local craft in from the sea. The *Rimau* was sent out to warn all coastal shipping. We wondered if the Japs were going to choose the Dindings river for a landing, but no sooner had the order been executed than a second one came through cancelling it. . . . The *Rompin*, the Straits steamship, was already alongside; she had been in for days, but was being held as her next port of call was Penang.

A friend in Parit Buntar 'phoned to say he had sent his wife and child south and that the Penang women and children had already been evacuated; actually this had happened on December 13th; but it was not announced till much later.

That night we discussed what to do, if and when the Japs reached the Dindings. As a last resort there was always the jungle behind the house, a tin of bully beef and the office revolver. But we presumed I might have to be sent away one day like the women of Penang.

The following morning, December 16th, at 9.30 a.m. the order came. The women were to collect as quickly as possible at Bob's estate, not later than eleven o'clock, with two small suitcases each.

I could not really believe it had come to that so soon. Ah Chi tried to help me pack; she could not understand why I was taking so little. I told her I would be back for Christmas, that it was all a mistake, trying to persuade myself to believe what I said. She fussed around me anxiously. . . .

There was a pile of Christmas presents unopened in a cupboard; my palette shining against the studio wall; a half-finished portrait of Stuart on the easel; a willow-pattern plate on a bookcase; a model Swiss village Stuart had made for the Christmas table decoration; and in the hall Louisa curled up peacefully asleep on a green cushion. . . . Curious, the things you see when you leave your home for the last time, but that glimpse of Louisa hurt most.

One man told me later that what had hurt him was the sight of his first kill, a stuffed crocodile hanging on the wall. . . !

Ah Chi was in tears by then. I was still kidding myself and trying to make the servants believe that I would return soon. They stood on the verandah, a pathetic little group, as Stuart drove me away, out of the garden and down the hill. The mountains were as blue as ever, the sun sparkled on the water, it seemed odd that the village looked exactly as usual: and I refused to believe I was seeing it all for the last time.

XX

WAR COMES TO ALL MALAYA

THERE WERE TEN of us in four cars, including, of course, Joan and the other planters' wives. At Bob's estate we said good-bye to the men, not knowing what would happen to them or how far the Japs had infiltrated; and then we set off on the hundred and forty mile drive to Kuala Lumpur. I was with Deedee and Mrs. T——, in a small Austin.

In spite of all the unhappiness I could not help being amused at Mrs. T——, who, determined that if she had to meet the Japs, she would do it well-dressed, was wearing a white shark-skin frock, sheer silk stockings, white shoes and a smart white hat. Not so Deedee, who had been in Ipoh the day before and had been forced to take refuge under her car while the Jap 'planes machine-gunned the streets; she wore a serviceable linen frock and carried a battered old felt hat, in case we had to lie in the hot sun sheltering in a drain from machine-gun bullets.

However the journey was uneventful. Deedee drove fast and led the little convoy of cars.

On the arterial road south of Ipoh we joined the swelling stream of refugee cars coming from the north, all driven by women or Malay syces. The main street of every town was lined with silent Asiatics; their bewildered faces watched the ominous procession. I felt sick at the thought of what was coming to them and shall never forget those turning heads and frightened stares. However, our Military had ordered European women and children out of the way and there was nothing we could do except obey. But the idea that we were leaving the Asiatics alone in the lurch stuck very unpleasantly. I felt guilty, we seemed horribly conspicuous and the whole situation was unreal, but I was almost convinced the order was mistaken and we should yet be told to return. . . .

A few small convoys of Army lorries passed going north,

driven wildly all over the road. There were not many soldiers; some of the lorries appeared to be packed with barricades and others looked half empty. The one and only gun we saw on the entire journey was capsized in a deep ditch.

At Tanjong Malim the Rest House was packed with women and children from the north with their amahs. Some had been evacuated from Kedah with no more than a toothbrush. The place looked *en fête*; the light-coloured summer frocks and the crowds of children gave it an incredibly, incongruous atmosphere of a children's party. It was heartrending; but everyone was very calm, still keyed up and not yet overcome with the terrible weariness and reaction which set in later.

Chaos reigned in Kuala Lumpur. We had to find a billet for the night and went to the station where someone was reputed to be receiving evacuees—or were we refugees?

The station yard was crammed with civilian cars. A few muddy armoured vehicles were being unloaded off the train from the north; they looked depressingly small and battered. We had the luck to run into Mrs. Jones of the *Malay Mail* who warm-heartedly offered to put all three of us up for the night and was wonderfully good to us.

The following day we set out to drive to Jasin, near Malacca where Deedee had arranged to go, but after crossing the Selangor boundary we were stopped by harassed police officials at Seremban. An order had come through from the Governor that refugees were not to be allowed any further south. The overwrought and sweating officer thrust the chit under our noses for us to see for ourselves. It read something as follows: "The evacuation of southern Perak is entirely unauthorized and extremely dangerous. (We were from northern Perak.) Europeans must remain where they are and set an example to the Asiatic population, etc., etc."

My spirits rose immediately. Perhaps, after all, the *whole* order to evacuate, like the shipping order at Lumut on Monday, was a mistake and we could go back to our homes! Always over-optimistic, my hopes were soon dashed. We were told to go to the Seremban Club where local European women were arranging billeting.

It was depressing, especially as the woman to whose house we were allotted was overheard to say:

"What! Three of them, how ghastly, my dear!"

One of us knew her slightly. And she turned and sat down to talk with us:

"Such a bore—last week I had to put up a woman with two children from Kedah. She has gone now luckily . . . it upset everything so, you know . . . we couldn't enjoy our bridge in the mornings with those children playing round. . . ."

After some more of this we three exchanged meaning looks and soon Deedee escaped, button-holed a police officer and explained that we had a definite address to go to in Jasin. After some anxious moments he admitted that if so it would be in order for us to proceed and gave her a permit.

Mrs. T—— and I heaved sighs of relief and looked admiringly at Deedee who had handled the situation with her usual calm.

The grumbling, bridge-playing lady was landed then with a large family of very plump Portuguese Eurasians. . . .

After this the paddy lands of Malacca were a welcome sight, of fresh tender green with here and there beautifully woven Malay houses and pretty little bullock wagons. A very lovely district and I wished I had the heart to enjoy it.

An old friend of Bob's, a planter named Sandy, put us up with noble hospitality in his enormous bungalow.

December 18th: The news was a shock as the Japs had reached the Krian river and were infiltrating fast down the Province Wellesley coast. The unspoken fear for us three women was that the pontoon bridge, the Blanja Bridge that cut our own district off from the main road, would be destroyed. We wondered what was happening back there. That afternoon a tremendous thunderstorm relieved the tenseness of the air and lifted a little of the physical pressure at least from our aching heads.

The next morning a call came through from one of the Sitiawan planters' wives; she had heard the men had also received their evacuation order and had crossed the bridge at four that morning. All day we sat around waiting for news. In the evening Stuart 'phoned from Kuala Lumpur Customs. On the previous day, after the men of the district had already been warned by 'phone that they must soon leave, probably during the night, two soldiers had appeared from Ipoh and informed

Stuart that the Lumut jetty, the Post Office and Customs office and godown were to be blown up at once. Fortunately he had the Government papers prepared and everything was in order. The Military gave him ten minutes to clear his staff. The Straits boat was still lying alongside. She had a Penang-born, native crew. When the jetty was blown up she would have to leave the river and it was doubtful if her crew could be trusted to take her south under the circumstances, when obviously they must be longing to get back to their families in Penang. Stuart decided to take her south himself to ensure that she reached Port Swettenham safely and did not fall into enemy hands. It was a very bad moment for him when he had to make this decision; but he was sincerely congratulated by his chief in Kuala Lumpur on having brought her to port. He rushed up to the house, asked the servants if they would like to go with him; but they chose to stay and live with relations in the village. He gave them all the money he had and said good-bye. This time they were all in tears. They said they would pack up our belongings and try to look after the house and the cats as long as they could. He could scarcely speak of it except to tell me the bare details.

Back at the Customs, having seen previously that the rice stocks were distributed, he offered the entire staff the opportunity of going south with him on board the *Rompin*. Mostly they chose to stay; some wished to return to their families at Kuala Kangsar or Taiping. By this time the ten minutes were up and the Military waiting to carry out their demolition. The car was perforce abandoned, likewise everything else, including, of course, every line and stroke of my three years' work, not that that seemed to matter then. . . . There had not been time to destroy the cats. . . .

Punctually Stuart went on board the *Rompin* with two scantily packed little suitcases of clothes and some tinned food. And then with exasperating irony the ship's cook could not be found and ten more wasted minutes passed while he was unearthed in the village and hustled on board.

As the *Rompin* sailed down the estuary, the peaceful white houses of Lumut echoed to explosions.

December 20th: The Japs were driving down towards Ipoh, and Kuala Lumpur was raided.

At Jasin we waited for news. It rained and rained; every hour seemed like a hundred days; I was haunted by the sense of waste and loss; night after night in my dreams I returned to Lumut. Bob and Mr. T—— arrived in their cars at midday. Mr. and Mrs. T—— left shortly afterwards to get a job. Bob had managed to bring a little silver, some clothes of his wife's and even some of his Napoleon brandy. To see his smiling, cheerful face no one would believe he had just lost everything he possessed in the world, except what little he had in the car, his home of years and his Estate. He was full of stubborn confidence that we were going to hold the Japs, but I think in most people's hearts there was a sinking feeling, for they knew this could not be unless air reinforcements came in time. Surely "they" will send us Hurricanes soon from India, we told each other, and then we'll be able to show the Japs a thing or two. . . .

That evening we were taken to a Christmas party given by some local friends of Sandy's. It was dreadful: no one seemed to realize what was happening to the country. We advised them to start packing, but they only smiled; the Japs would never get right down there! In the south they scarcely seemed to be taking in what was going on up north. I remember there was a Christmas tree and everyone was very gay; it was a hell of an evening.

Meanwhile in Kuala Lumpur Stuart was working on Food Control, billeted with Derek. There were constant raids.

December 25th: It was a burning hot day. To take our minds off all that Christmas usually means Sandy took us to play golf before breakfast. It was a kind thought and helped considerably; the morning was golden and fresh; but the rest of the day was just one of those occasions that have to be lived through somehow; it seemed interminable.

We went to a lunch given for an Australian contingent in a nearby camp. The Army huts with their tin roofs were like ovens in the burning noon. We ate hot plum pudding and tried to be cheerful, while the sweat dripped off our faces, and our hearts were like lead.

That evening on the six o'clock news we heard of the fall of Hong Kong. Not even the quarts of champagne which Sandy lavished on us could do anything to lift the gloom. In the middle of dinner Stuart 'phoned from Kuala Lumpur. He was insistent that Deedee and I should go on to Singapore as soon as possible. Bob agreed and we spent the remainder of Christmas night 'phoning friends in Singapore in the hope of getting an address to go to, as the town was rapidly becoming overcrowded.

December 26th: As Deedee and I left Jasin, Malacca had its first alert and we encountered cars and lorries driven by Asiatics racing to get clear of the town before the raiders came over.

We took the coast road south, luckily for us, as the other road was machine-gunned during the day. The first address we went to in Singapore was a bungalow, where the headmistress of Cameron's School was living. It was already packed, with four beds in one room and two in the sitting-room. So we next tried Taffy, who was living at 13, Fort Canning Road. A cheerful sort of number we thought, especially as it was in an ideal target area—just below Fort Canning, the main Signals Station, and opposite the Cathay "skyscraper" building, home of the Malayan Broadcasting Company!

Here, although the house had only two real bedrooms and a kind of passage room, we received a kindly welcome. There were already two men from Penang besides Taffy ensconced there; the two other men who normally lived in it were with the Volunteers; every midday two more Government men regularly appeared for lunch. So all told ten people used the house and later the numbers swelled to about fourteen at times, with only two house boys and a cook to cope with us all. With so many people attached to the house it was occasionally rather confusing. One aftermoon at tea-time I found a stranger in the lounge, and thinking one of the men had asked him in I started acting hostess. To my surprise he turned out to be one of the two original owners of the house, while he, of course, did not know who on earth I was.

Lloyd, whom we had known for some years, had come from Penang on December 16th, when the entire European population of the Island, except two doctors who elected to stay behind, was evacuated by orders which seem to have had a mysterious origin. His wife had left with the women on December 13th and had already been sent on to Java. He told us of the raids in Penang and how, when the first formation of Jap 'planes came over, the Asiatics had run out and stood in the streets to wave. It had been grim. After that not unnaturally when the siren sounded the whole Asiatic population fled into the jungle. There was *not a single* anti-aircraft gun in the Island. There was no labour left to bury the dead, so the Europeans who had to keep order, fight fires, and carry on, had not time to do the job properly and attempted to burn the rapidly decomposing bodies as they lay in the hot streets. But, Lloyd said, it was a sickening business, as in most cases only the clothes would burn. . . .

Up to the night of the thirteenth, when the women and children were evacuated, some of the survivors of the *Prince of Wales* were keeping the ferry boats running across the Straits. On the sixteenth the rest of the Europeans left Penang in those two old flat-bottomed boats and set out to sea for Singapore. Somewhere off Pangkor at dawn they were stopped by a British patrol boat and taken on board her. She sank one of the ferry boats apparently with a single shot, but the other was left to wallow her way south and eventually reached Keppel Harbour in safety.

December 27th: I heard that Stuart was now driving Food lorries in the Kuala Lumpur area dispersing Government rice stocks. He was most anxious for me to put my name down on any sailing list, as his one idea was to get me out of the country. Although on the surface he never gave up hope that we might hold the onslaught, I think he knew, as most people did, what was going to happen. So I promised I would put my name down with the P. & O. people for a passage to South Africa. I felt more cheerful when I was told it was unlikely I should get one. There was no organized evacuation of women, but women with two or more children would naturally be given priority to leave if they so wished, as opportunity occurred.

I had no coat, so I next attempted to buy one in case I ever had to sail. There was only one to be had in all the town and that was several sizes too big, so eventually a little tailor made me one of sorts. Shopping was difficult as the women coming from the north, often with literally no belongings at all, had naturally bought up most things, and in the Selfridge of Singapore it was almost impossible to get attended.

We bought shoes and odds and ends to replenish our depleted wardrobes. We went to register our names and obtain identity cards, queuing up with the amazingly cosmopolitan population. We washed and ironed our clothes as, of course, we had no amahs now. We ran into several women we knew from up-country; their faces were pale and drawn; many had no news yet of their husbands. And we put our names down at the Man Power Bureau immediately, but in this crowded city it proved to be extremely difficult to get useful work to do. Singapore was packed; every car park was crammed to overflowing.

December 29th: The mosque at Kuala Lumpur was bombed, to the great indignation of the Moslems.

We spent the afternoon blacking out the house as far as possible and making an improvised shelter indoors; a trench was being dug outside. That night the raids started: there were three altogether within a few hours.

For several days now it had been impossible to get through by 'phone to Kuala Lumpur; one was informed the line was for Military purposes only, but on the 30th it was cleared again. Apparently—with incredibly little foresight—Kuala Lumpur Aerodrome, obviously a target, had been made over the line, which consequently had been cut by bombing. That night the Volunteers who were guarding the Aerodrome, seeing lights in the middle of the runway, called a challenge, received no reply and opened fire. Unfortunately someone had forgotten to inform them that a gang of P. & T. coolies had been sent to mend the line. The coolies scattered in fear and it was some little time before repairs were effected. . . .

After this there were raids every night. There was a full moon and on New Year's Eve it was exceptionally brilliant, the streets as bright as day. The New Year was ushered in with raids before and after midnight.

January 1, 1942: Stuart arrived unexpectedly in Singapore on forty-eight hours leave, having travelled down on the night mail. He had just been on a special mission with the Naval Intelligence. It was because of his knowledge of the coast of north Perak that he was asked to join the expedition. They had been as far north as Pangkor Island where they landed in Pasir Bogah bay. The first person they encountered was old Abdullah, the hire-car driver. He was amazed: his eyes grew big with incredulous surprise as he was confronted by *Tuan Custom* and a British bluejacket armed with tommy guns. They all marched across the Island to Pangkor village to investigate; it was a curious feeling for Stuart to be once more so tantalizingly near our home; there the Chinese were carrying on calmly and everything was as usual. On the previous day, they said, thirteen Japanese soldiers had ridden into Lumut on bicycles—there had been no incidents. Here on Pangkor, a Japanese patrol launch had landed one of its crew, a slightly wounded man. There was some little hesitation in the flow of information at this point and it was considered better not to press the matter.

The rest of the job completed, they re-embarked and headed south for Port Swettenham. The boat was spotted in the Straits by three Jap patrol 'planes and machine-gunned steadily for half-an-hour. Stuart, who had been sunbathing on deck, seized his tommy gun and began firing with the others at the 'planes. It was a hellish half-hour, but they came through safely to Port Swettenham, their casualties—one man killed and a bluejacket at Stuart's side mortally wounded. A fine man he was, with a fair curling beard; although terribly wounded in the groin, he never uttered a sound and was smiling as they carried him ashore.

Japanese forces were landed at Port Weld and at Lumut just at this time, presumably in order to facilitate the encirclement of Ipoh which fell about December 30th.

The short leave went all too quickly. We shopped, dined out and went to see our friends. Vanessa and Roberta were in town; Joan was somewhere in Johore; Jean had already left for Colombo; Bung we visited in the Naval Base and it was good to see his chunky, cheerful face again; but he was alone in a stripped bungalow as Marjorie and the children had already sailed to South Africa. He told us that on Christmas Day he had put a call through to Lumut, being anxious about us, but was surprised to get no answer, though he heard the 'phone ring in the empty house. This goes to show how extraordinarily little the population of Singapore or in fact any people fifty miles south of the "front" were informed of the situation. Events moved fast. There was no time for people to grasp the facts.

At the hospital, where we went for anti-typhoid injections, we met some Customs people from the east coast who had been days trekking through the jungle to safety and arrived with not so much as a toothbrush and their clothes in rags.

At that time there was almost a sense of exhilaration in being relieved of all one's possessions. We talked of the future and visualized a flat in post-war England furnished with soap-boxes and spoons and forks from Woolworth's. But it was impossible to speak of the cats.

For days Deedee and I tried to get war work to do; none was forthcoming from the Man Power Bureau. More than a week passed before she managed to get a transport job, driving blood donors to the hospital. I went to the Ministry of Information, the Signals, the First Aid and many other places.

January 6th: The women and children were evacuated from Kuala Lumpur, as the tragic Slim River engagement took place. Rumours of the air reinforcements, that everyone felt must be on the way, grew daily. Someone had seen a shipment! "500 Hurricanes in packing-cases had arrived . . .!" and so on. Actually no more than fifty odd arrived about the middle of January. Many, I believe, were destroyed on the ground. In Singapore we never saw more than six in the air; but even that sight raised our hopes; I remember getting out of the car to look and wave. They were an encouraging sight after the noisy stub-nosed Buffaloes which were rapidly being shot out of the skies, lacking speed and fire-power as they did.

Other kinds of rumours, too, were circulating: detrimental and deplorable ones, probably spread by fifth columnists, and horrifying ones of atrocities up-country; Christian Chinese girls found wearing crosses had been crucified by the Japanese. . . .

I still had no job, so I wangled one at a Customs Food Control Office, sorting out and typing lists of registered rice-dealers, not very useful, but it helped a little and passed the time. And I wrote short stories for broadcasting as the M.B.C. could not find anyone else to do so; but the sense of frustration in not having anything to do in such a crisis was appalling.

In Kuala Lumpur Stuart and Derek had been distributing the rice stocks to all outlying villages. In one place they were ahead of the Japs by an hour only. Food Control work was now finished there, so they began to use the lorry to evacuate some engineering equipment from the town. And on January 7th they suddenly appeared in Singapore with a big lorry crammed with useful P.W.D. stuff which they took to headquarters. The lorry was parked at 13, Fort Canning Road, camouflaged with an Army net they had picked up on the journey. The next day they returned to Kuala Lumpur to fetch another load of valuable equipment which would otherwise have been abandoned. Our front "line" was already then at Tanjong Malim.

On January 9th Kuala Lumpur was evacuated and it was set alight the next day.

Stuart and Derek reappeared with another load of stores on that Saturday morning, having driven all night. Their faces were drawn and white. And Bob arrived too; he had been right up at Tanjong Malim on a job. That night at dinner he opened his last bottle of Napoleon brandy and we drank rather solemnly to Victory, which now seemed further away than ever.

The next day Stuart and Derek took the lorry north again, but they never made Kuala Lumpur. Seremban was already being evacuated when they reached it and they were turned back, but before doing so they broke into the locked and deserted P.W.D. store and loaded the lorry with more useful engineering equipment. Driving all night again, they arrived in Singapore soon after dawn on the Monday. That day the raiders came over in the morning and thereafter every morning as well as every night. Stuart continued for the time being with the Food Control Department in Singapore, and Derek and Taffy joined the R.N.V.R. and underwent a week's training.

So far the afternoons were raid-free. The men worked on the trench in the evenings, which were damp and gloomy. I never remember so much rain, a finer rain than usual; the afternoons were grey, but the nights were clear and bright, and the mornings generally sunny with towering clouds from which the unbroken formations of Jap 'planes appeared high over the city. The trench was a good one, well drained and lined with *atap* and duckboards. The trouble with most trenches in the city was that they were not drained and consequently filled with water. Had simple instructions been issued, it should have been comparatively easy to make usable trenches in many areas. In the crowded area near the markets and food shops there were no public shelters at all and it was not until *February 11th* with incredible tardiness that it was decided to build some.

But the First-Aid Posts were well staffed. I tried to get a job with them, but when I had to confess my name was on a sailing list they turned me down. The same thing occurred at the Naval Control Office, though there I did actually land a job in the end. Although I had no wish to leave Singapore I was bound to tell the Naval Officer, who interviewed me very early one morning, that my name was down to sail but that there did not appear much likelihood of getting a passage. My statement was received with scorn:

"Who ever heard of the population running away? The women of London did not desert their posts, did they?"

I felt very small and useless; but exactly a week after that the entire personnel of the Naval Base itself was evacuated to Colombo.

While I was having my interview the first siren of that day blared forth. I left the offices and joined Stuart who was waiting for me in a borrowed car. I acted as spotter as usual while he ran me back to the house. One formation of twenty-five or twenty-seven bombers was already crossing over the city and as we neared Fort Canning I saw another formation of the same size approaching head-on from a different angle. The borrowed car was slow to accelerate, but we just reached the trench and jumped in as the Jap leader pressed the button and the whole formation let go their load. I never felt more glad of my tin hat than at that moment as we crouched at the bottom of the trench making ourselves as small as possible, while the bombs fell neatly along Orchard Road, two hundred yards away. That was just one of many raids of its kind, but I'll not forget the sight of those two perfect formations calmly crossing overhead in the serene blue sky.

There was a First-Aid Post in an old Chinese Temple near the house and I was told I could go there unofficially to help as the casualties came in after bad raids. Here at last was something I could do; but the place swarmed with M.A.S. girls who positively fell over each other to get at the casualties.

I was struck with the stoicism of the Chinese who never uttered a sound when their wounds were probed and dressed.

Then at last I discovered that the Anzac Club Canteen was

really short of helpers. I worked there every day for six hours, cooking eggs and bacon and hot pies for the Australian troops who crowded in tired, sweat-stained and filthy. They watched us hungrily while we worked; the heat in that kitchen was terrific. Sometimes there were only three of us, and one memorable stifling afternoon we three fried and served six hundred eggs in four hours.

Saturday, January 24th: The mythical Muar-Endau line had failed to hold and the Japs were at Batu Pahat. We had almost given up listening to the news, but for the head-lines, as it was invariably two days behind what was actually happening. Men down from the north kept us better informed.

Lloyd's brother arrived having walked sixty miles through the jungle from Batu Pahat; his arms were covered with sores set up by the poisonous scratches of thorny plants. As a Volunteer with a knowledge of the country he had been drafted to an Australian battalion on a Commando job. The Australians could not distinguish between Malay and Japanese when they heard voices in the jungle. It seemed extraordinary that the Volunteers, many of whom had intimate knowledge of both Indians and Malays and of the country, had not been employed to assist the troops at an earlier stage in the campaign.

The raids grew worse every day.[1] Heavy black smoke from the burning oil tanks in the Naval Base drifted across the Island. In the town it was the closely packed Chinese communities that suffered most. Beach Road, in the direction of the civil airport, was a terrible shambles. Bodies were still lying there under the gimcrack rubble of the Chinese houses and had been lying there for a week. The warm, noxious-sweet stench of decay was appalling; but, as in Penang, there was no labour available. The coolies became more and more reluctant.

January 27th: The great Jap convoy in the Macassar Straits was bearing down towards Java. Singapore would then be almost encircled. It was during the previous week that the few Hurricanes had appeared over the city, but I never saw a Jap formation broken up. Often they came, as I have described, in two waves from different directions. By this time it had dawned on most people that these Hurricanes were a mere handful

[1] Little has been heard of the work of the Asiatics in the A.R.P. and Civil Defence services, but I believe it was excellent.

only and that, unless those miraculous, much-talked-of, much-needed air reinforcements arrived soon, Singapore would be in a very bad way indeed. But we were fully prepared to endure a siege and had hopes of the Island becoming as heroic in its defence as Malta: "We shall be a second Malta," we assured one another.

A Volunteer came to the house that evening: "What, you're still here! Don't forget what happened at Hong Kong," he said to me ominously. I felt wretched for I had no desire to leave.

January 29th: There was little news; but the Japs were coming through Johore rapidly.

It was a quiet morning at the Canteen, only one raid and only a few men to serve. There was a rumour the Naval Base was being evacuated, which was true. In the afternoon I went to the hospital for blood donation. The Chinese transport official who drove me there expounded gaily on the differences in British and Chinese temperaments.

"We Chinese," he said, "are fatalists. I have no shelter for my household, but you English are always expending energy; you rush around busily building shelters and getting hot and bothered. In normal life, too, your one idea is to have exercise for relaxation; our idea is to lie back quietly and grow fat and old in peace."

I was entertained by his philosophy though I could not agree with it at that time—especially as regards air-raid precautions! The hospital was crowded to overflowing with blood donors. There were Europeans and Eurasians, Chinese and Indians of all types. The nurse told me that six illiterate Chinese seamen had come ashore from a junk and offered their services.

There were several raids that night. The moon was nearly full again. About midnight a friend rang up to say a ship was sailing and I had better go at once to the P. & O. Office; I was not informed officially at all. Sir Shenton Thomas apparently adhered to his policy of no evacuation to the last.

Stuart and I left the sleeping house and went out into the brilliant moonlight and to the P. & O., much against my will. The office had been evacuated from the waterfront to a house on the outskirts, off the Bukit Timah Road, in a big garden.

Rarely had Malaya looked so beautiful. In the cold white light there were dense, black shadows and silvered leaves.

There was a dark queue of men and women standing in the inky shadow of the porch; every ten minutes the door opened and a tired voice said monotonously:

"Colombo on the right. U.K. on the left."

This was the first intimation of a possibility of going right home to England, but when it came to the point my heart failed me; we had always intended to stick together after all. . . . Slipping out through the pantry at the back of the house, we caught sight of a ship's officer sleeping exhausted in a chair with his feet up on the refrigerator.

But the next morning Stuart persuaded me to change my mind and I thought perhaps after all he had a better chance with me out of the way. So we returned to the Shipping Office. The same four sweating, dead-tired men were at work there and I received a "ticket" to sail on, of all ironies, the *Empress of Japan* and was told briefly to be on board at 3 p.m. prepared to sleep on a mattress on deck, bringing my own sheets, blankets, cutlery and mug for drinking water, with one trunk and two suitcases, no more. Driving back towards Fort Canning we were very quiet, but I asked Stuart how long he thought it would be now before the Japs arrived in Singapore.

"About twelve days I should think," was his answer.

He was not far wrong; the town was surrendered exactly sixteen days later.

There were three raids over the town that morning. I washed and ironed Stuart's clothes, packed my own, "borrowed" a trunk and transferred to it what silver I had so fortuitously packed in Lumut, and was ready in good time.

Stuart obtained leave to see me off and was out calmly arranging about money, buying sheets, towels and cutlery and even eau-de-Cologne, soap, cigarettes, books, talc powder, and medicines. He returned at noon having thought of everything I could possibly need—in spite of the growing chaos of the town, the distraught men and women and the frequent disturbance of the raids.

Vanessa came to say good-bye; she too was unable then to make up her mind whether to leave with the Naval staffs (she was working in a Control Office) or to stay behind. She eventually stayed—one of the very few women to do so. Deedee decided to go on the next boat—if there was one.

The dock area was packed with cars. There was a raid, but fortunately no bombs were dropped in that area. The harbour had been damaged, so everyone and all their luggage had to be shipped laboriously in a tug across the Empire Dock.

Stuart got me and my luggage on board punctually, found a mattress for me—the last one—and we said good-bye. He did not wait but went ashore directly to get back to work. He planned to join the R.N.V.R. as soon as possible, if he could be released from Food Control.

I ran up the great staircases and reached the dirty promenade deck, in time to see him far below threading his way swiftly through the dense crowd on the quayside.

After a dazed half-hour I had the immense luck to run into Joan Steele. How good it was to meet her in that crowd of quiet, tragic-eyed women wandering about among the swift dreadful partings.

Still we did not sail. All night more and more women and children crowded on board. It was intensely hot and airless, shut in down below on the blacked-out troop deck, with the baleful glare of the emergency lights and a foul stench from a troops' filthy latrine. Files of Indian soldiers tramped heavily by carrying mattresses on their backs. Their great boots clanged incessantly close to my head and their shadows loomed distortedly on the bulkhead, marching endlessly past like hump-backed trolls.

All that night, although we did not know it till two days later, our troops were evacuating Johore and retiring to the Island of Singapore. The Argylls and Sutherlands were the last to cross the causeway in the light of the full moon, led by the pipers of the Gordon Highlanders.

Saturday, January 31st: We woke to find we still had not sailed. As volunteers had been asked to serve the meals, Joan and I helped with the breakfast which consisted of cans of sticky tea, porridge unadorned and pails of hash. There were about two thousand four hundred women on board and two hundred children. The meals were served in two shifts, four decks below. The *Empress* had very recently brought three thousand Indian troops into Singapore and during the last two days of bombing a good many of the Hong Kong Chinese crew had deserted, so, as there was a dearth of stewards, we took their place. This ship had evacuated the English women from Hong Kong the previous year and the crew had not a high opinion of the British. Also they were scared: it was very unpleasant.

The ship put out and lay off among the oil islands during that morning. There were many alerts; the kapok lifebelts were as warm as two fur coats, greasy and only too reminiscent of the Indian troops who had worn them last.

At eleven-thirty we helped serve the lunches. Then there was a boat drill, after which Joan and I retired exhausted to the boat deck. Smoke rolled off the Island from numerous fires. Several launches and tugs came alongside; one brought survivors of the destroyer *Thanet*, which had been sunk off the east coast. A rumour then spread rapidly through the ship that the Governor had ordered a general evacuation of all civilians from Singapore; and presently we followed the *Duchess of Bedford*, also filled with refugees and crippled by bombing, slowly back into Keppel Harbour. Hopes rose: we were going back to pick up the others! But no, the quays were empty; only a few soldiers at the entrance waved a farewell and I heard a small boy cry ecstatically to his mother:

"Look Mummy! That's father, I'm *sure* that's father!"

She could not answer him.

Keppel harbour was empty of big shipping; but I caught sight of the little old ferry from Penang. Slowly we steamed through, out past the boom, and headed for Batavia by the way of "Bomb Alley"—the Bangka Straits.

Slowly the masts of Fort Canning and the white block of the Cathay building drew in line, swung together and fell away to the west. Soon there was little left of Singapore but a strip of low-lying shadowy land, with the tall Cathay now rapidly dwindling in the distance.

At that moment it became all-important to hold to the idea that life *still* had something, more than mere survival, to offer —one day in the future. . . .

We went below to serve the evening meal.

THE ULU
CHARCOAL KILNS
THE ULU
TO IPOH
BUKIT HANTU
THE SULTAN'S ISLAND
"OVER THE RIVER"
DINDINGS RIVER
LUMUT
MANGROVE
TELOK MURON
CHURCH
OLD SITIAWAN
AERODROME
SITIAWAN
KAMPONG KOH
TURTLE BAY
DUTCH FORT
JUNGLE
THE BAY
PASIR BOGAH BAY
LEKIR
ORCHID ISLAND
SKETCH MAP OF LUMUT AND THE ISLANDS
scale: one inch to 3½ miles
NIPIS
SEMBILAN ISLANDS
RUMBIA
LALANG
BULOH
WHITE ROCK
PERAK RIVER
KATHARINE SIM